Secret Cinema and the immersive experience industry

Manchester University Press

Secret Cinema and the immersive experience industry

Sarah Atkinson and Helen W. Kennedy

MANCHESTER UNIVERSITY PRESS

Copyright © Sarah Atkinson and Helen W. Kennedy 2022

The right of Sarah Atkinson and Helen W. Kennedy to be identified as the authors of this work has been asserted by them in accordance with the Copyright, Designs and Patents Act 1988.

Published by Manchester University Press
Oxford Road, Manchester M13 9PL
www.manchesteruniversitypress.co.uk

British Library Cataloguing-in-Publication Data
A catalogue record for this book is available from the British Library

ISBN 978 1 5261 4017 3 hardback
ISBN 978 1 5261 8237 1 paperback

First published 2022

The publisher has no responsibility for the persistence or accuracy of URLs for any external or third-party internet websites referred to in this book, and does not guarantee that any content on such websites is, or will remain, accurate or appropriate.

Typeset
by New Best-set Typesetters Ltd

For Professor Martin Barker
1946–2022

Contents

List of figures	*page* viii
Preface	xii
Acknowledgements	xiv
1 Secret Cinema and the immersive experience industry	1
2 Secret Cinema as sandbox	22
3 Secret Cinema as format	61
4 Secret Cinema as immersive activism	95
5 Secret Cinema as industry	134
6 Secret Cinema as experience community	172
7 Secret Cinema, 2020–2021: pivoting, pipelines and poaching	205
Appendix 1: Secret Cinema productions	230
Appendix 2: Secret Cinema post-experience promotional videos	248
Filmography	254
Bibliography	257
Index	266

Figures

1.1 Immersive experience industry ecosystem model 2019. Author's own. Graphic design by Bullet Creative. — 5
2.1 'Welcome to the world of Future Cinema'. Graphic design by Alex Brittain. — 23
2.2 Costumed audience members at Secret Cinema's *Alien* production. Image courtesy of Gavin and Jason Fox. — 34
2.3 A branded screen installation at *Secret Cinema's Alien* production sponsored by Windows Phone. Image courtesy of Gavin and Jason Fox. — 35
2.4 Menu for the *Bugsy Malone* experience. Image courtesy of Gavin and Jason Fox. — 36
2.5 A *Bugsy Malone* mirror moment. Image courtesy of Gavin and Jason Fox. — 37
2.6 Secret Cinema audience member being subjected to a 'Voight-Kampff' test. Image courtesy of Gavin and Jason Fox. — 38
2.7 An interactive installation at Secret Cinema's *Lawrence of Arabia* experience sponsored by Windows Phone. Source: Secret Cinema, 'Secret Cinema presents *Lawrence of Arabia*', 28 September 2010. YouTube video, 3:50, available at www.youtube.com/watch?v=uB3YnVX3bFU (accessed 13 December 2021). — 40
2.8 Examples of pre-narrative flash mobs. All sources: www.facebook.com/pg/SecretCinema/posts/; (top left) posted 7 February 2011; (top right) posted 5 February 2011; (bottom left) posted 24 May 2012; (bottom right) posted 24 May 2012. — 51
2.9 Future Cinema: *Prometheus*. Image courtesy of Gavin and Jason Fox. — 53
3.1 Timeline of the audience's experiential journey in the Secret Cinema format. Author's own. Graphic Design by Bullet Creative. — 62

3.2	Secret Cinema presents … *Brazil*. Image courtesy of Gavin and Jason Fox.	66
3.3	Examples of Secret Cinema audience ID cards. Images courtesy of Gavin and Jason Fox.	71
3.4	Examples of Secret Cinema's in-world newspapers. Images courtesy of Gavin and Jason Fox.	73
3.5	Thematised maps guiding audience members to the Secret Cinema site. Images courtesy of Gavin and Jason Fox.	73
3.6	Phased ticket release strategy for *Back to the Future*. Source: https://secretcinema.org/tickets (accessed 10 June 2014).	79
3.7	*Secret Cinema's* Doc Brown pictured during a promotional flash mob. Source: Twitter, https://twitter.com/TheMovieBrats/status/487648804485996544, 11 July 2014.	82
3.8	Mirror moments from *Who Framed Roger Rabbit?* and *Back to the Future*'s post-experience promotional videos. Sources: Future, 'Who Framed Roger Rabbit	Secret Cinema', 16 February 2014, YouTube video, 1:14, available at www.youtube.com/watch?v=9ekMl3V1ff0 (accessed 13 December 2021) and Secret Cinema Presents, 'Secret Cinema presents *Back to the Future*', 18 November 2014, Vimeo video, 3:15, available at https://vimeo.com/112151676 (accessed 13 December 2021).	87
3.9	*The Back to the Future* post-experience promotional video. Source: Secret Cinema Presents, 'Secret Cinema presents *Back to the Future*', 18 November 2014, Vimeo video, 3:15, available at https://vimeo.com/112151676 (accessed 13 December 2021).	90
4.1	The 4 May 2015 flash mob for Secret Cinema presents … *Star Wars: The Empire Strikes Back*. Sources: https://twitter.com/WithYouRebelX/status/595279945271799808, posted on 4 May 2015; https://twitter.com/WithYouRebelX/status/595543801457938432, posted on 5 May 2015.	99
4.2	Secret Cinema bespoke costume kits for *28 Days Later* and *Casino Royale*. Sources: top left: https://nsh-england.org.uk (accessed 12 February 2016); top right: author's own; bottom left: author's own; bottom right: https://shop.universal-exports.london (accessed 8 June 2019).	109
4.3	The evolution of dancing mirror moments. Sources: 'Secret Cinema – *Wings of Desire*', 26 March 2010,	

YouTube video, 2:13, available at www.youtube.com/watch?v=XDN0YitShiE; Support Future Shorts, 'Future Cinema presents *Saturday Night Fever*', 5 September 2013, YouTube video, 2:56, available at www.youtube.com/watch?v=Qgql23rh5Ys&t=25s; Secret Cinema Presents, 'Secret Cinema presents *Dirty Dancing*', 24 July 2016, Vimeo video, 1:41, available at https://vimeo.com/176063142; Secret Cinema Presents, 'Secret Cinema presents Baz Luhrmann's *Moulin Rouge!* – trailer', 20 December 2017, Vimeo video, 3:08, available at https://vimeo.com/248180966 (all accessed 13 December 2021). 117

4.4 In-world corporate logos and branding created for fictional organisations in pre-narrative experiences. Sources: screen grab from Secret Cinema's Facebook page (10 June 2010); screen grab from www.bravenewventures.org (12 June 2012); screen grab from https://usdocs.co/ (3 March 2016); screen grab from https://twitter.com/NSHEngland (2 February 2016); screen grab from www.rebelxbase.co (8 August 2015). 120

4.5 Secret Cinema presents … *Blade Runner* production designs for in-world food outlets. Production designs and image courtesy of Tim McQuillen-Wright. 123

4.6 Embedded branding in Secret Cinema presents … *Blade Runner*. Screen grab from www.liveutopia.today (accessed 29 August 2021). 124

4.7 Secret Cinema presents … *Blade Runner* production designs showing Asahi branding embedded into the set design. Production designs and image courtesy of Tim McQuillen-Wright. 125

4.8 *Romeo + Juliet* post-experience promotional video. Sources: Secret Cinema, 'Secret Cinema presents William Shakespeare's *Romeo + Juliet*', 9 December 2019, Vimeo video, 0:34, available at https://vimeo.com/378328807 and *Romeo + Juliet* (1996, dir: Baz Luhrmann). 128

5.1 The immersive experience production model. Author's own. Graphic design by Bullet Creative. 137

5.2 Secret Cinema departments involved in a Secret Cinema production and the different roles that can exist within them. Authors' own compilation. 138

5.3 Secret Cinema presents … *Stranger Things* production designs. Production designs and image courtesy of Tim McQuillen-Wright. 154

5.4 A sample page from the show caller's book. Book design
    and image courtesy of Lorna Adamson. 160
6.1 Audience members capture images of costumes and
    preparations, to share on social media. Bottom left
    – author's own, all other images courtesy of Darren
    Carnall. 178
6.2 *Casino Royale* identities and costuming. Screen grabs
    from https://shop.universal-exports.london (accessed 8
    June 2019). 180
6.3 Secret Cinema audience members as tourists. Images
    courtesy of Darren Carnall; bottom left image courtesy of
    Victoria Cohen Slaymaker. 182
6.4 Positive People of Secret Cinema (PPSC) group night at
    Casino Royale, 2019. Image courtesy of Darren Carnall. 194
6.5 PPSC badges designed and created by Darren Carnall.
    Image courtesy of Darren Carnall. 196
6.6 James Bond influencers. Screen grab from Calvin Dyson,
    'Secret Cinema *Casino Royale* experience and review', 17
    July 2019, YouTube video, 13:39, available at www.
    youtube.com/watch?v=YSKqXiCZjAM&t=3s (accessed 13
    December 2021). 198
7.1 The immersive experience industry ecosystem model
    2021. Author's image. Graphic design by Bullet Creative. 213
7.2 Immersive performance continuum. Author's own.
    Graphic design by Bullet Creative. 220

Preface

Viewed through the lens of December 2021, from the perspective of a reader who has lived through a global pandemic, our cover image looks unremarkable. This is a world where masked faces are commonplace and hospital signage and PPE-wearing hospital workers feature regularly in news reports. For readers in the UK, there are also the immediately recognisable colours and branding of the NHS. But this image does not originate in the blighted decade of the 2020s. Rather, it was taken in April 2016, when the idea of a global pandemic and of mass vaccination programmes were the very stuff of fiction – and of *play* – in apocalyptic movies and video games.

Look closer at the image and you might discern the wording of the signs: 'Rage treatment' and 'Do not enter if showing symptoms of rage virus'. Looking through this revised lens, the picture takes on a whole new set of meanings. You might think of this semiotically rich image as a simulated premediation.

Pictured in the image are ourselves, Sarah on the left and Helen on the right, *costumed* in hospital scrubs, standing outside an abandoned printing press that has been *set-dressed* to look like a hospital, in Harmsworth Quays, London, UK. We are ready to enter Secret Cinema's *28 Days Later* – about to be *vaccinated* and chased around a warehouse by howling, snarling performers playing rage-infected zombies, compelled to run at breakneck speed by a cacophonic soundtrack and strobe lighting in the company of hundreds of other audience members …

And this was all in the name of entertainment … or in our case, research. Our experience, and that of other audience members that evening, became the subject of a book chapter written by Helen.[1]

We began the journey of writing this book in 2014, having become fascinated by the increasing popularity and commercial significance of Secret Cinema events,[2] and the rise in ludic and immersive experiences more generally. These experiences could not be made sense of by one discipline alone, nor through a singular methodological design, and our shared interest in these phenomena presented an opportunity to bring together our expertise in cinema and games. We began in 2014 with an in-depth study of the *Back to the Future* experience,³ and have continued to map, document and study the journey of Secret Cinema's growth, reach and influence ever since as part of our wider live cinema project.⁴

Where we had previously looked at isolated productions, here we advance a holistic study that is the result of seven years of research, which maps the highs and lows of an organisation at the centre of an industry in formation. The sector is once again under considerable threat from a new variant of the coronavirus, and the impositions of another set of restrictions which are likely to pose a considerable challenge.

As we write this preface in December 2021, we are once again wearing face-coverings in public spaces, preparing to queue outside vaccination centres – but this time for real.

Notes

1. Helen W. Kennedy, 'Funfear Attractions: the playful affects of carefully managed terror in immersive *28 Days Later* live experiences', in *Live cinema: cultures, economies, aesthetics*, ed. Sarah Atkinson and H.W. Kennedy (New York: Bloomsbury, 2017), 167–84.
2. Sarah Atkinson, *Beyond the screen: Emerging cinema and engaging audiences* (New York: Bloomsbury, 2014).
3. Sarah Atkinson and H.W. Kennedy (2015a), 'Tell no one: cinema as game-space – audience participation, performance and play', G|A|M|E: *The Italian Journal of Game Studies* (2015) 5; Sarah Atkinson and H.W. Kennedy (2015b), '"Where we're going, we don't need an effective online audience engagement strategy": the case of the Secret Cinema viral backlash', *Frames Cinema Journal* (2015), 1–24.
4. See www.livecinemanetwork.org (accessed 13 December 2021) and Sarah Atkinson and H.W. Kennedy, *Live cinema: walking the tightrope between stage and screen*, short film, 16:30, 2019.

Acknowledgements

This book would not have been possible without the support of a lot of wonderful, talented and creative individuals and we are very grateful to them all. Firstly, we would like to thank Natalie Wreyford, our researcher and friend, who undertook and coded thirteen of our interviews for us. Her insights and enthusiasm further inspired and motivated us to progress with the project, to seek out and give voice to the incredible individuals creating the immersive experiences at the heart of this book. We also owe a special thanks to our keen-eyed and thoughtful readers, Jane Arthurs, Seth Giddings, Paul Grainge, Richard Hornsey, Paul McDonald, Roberta Pearson and Sherryl Wilson – we are so grateful for their time and their support. We would like to thank the Department of Culture, Media & Creative Industries, Faculty of Arts & Humanities at King's College London for the funding contributions that facilitated some of this work, and for their ongoing support of the live cinema project. We would also like to thank the Department of Cultural, Media and Visual Studies, Faculty of Arts, University of Nottingham, for funding ongoing live cinema conferences and events. We are also grateful to the King's Undergraduate Research Fellowship Scheme (2016 and 2020) and to two enthusiastic and hard-working researchers for their input on the project: Emma St. Lawrence and Alexis Lawrence.

To those whose contributions have been so central to the work of this book, a huge debt of gratitude to you all: Lorna Adamson, Max Alexander, Debs Armstrong, Gorm Ashurst, Andy Barnes, Gemma Bates, Charlotte Bence, Tom Beynon, Lee Brotherhood, Frankie Bunce, Sophie Cairns, Darren Carnall, Jane Carnall, Vix Cohen, Terry Cook, Samantha Collins, Daniel Dingsdale, Charlie Dixon, Amy Doran, Maxine Doyle, Ken Ferguson, Gavin Fox, Victoria Gagliano, Ian William Galloway, Dan Gammon, Simon Gordon, Eddy Hackett, Mika Handley, Harry Harrold, Daniel Hemsley, Brian Hook, Hamish Jenkinson, Sophie Kendrick, Susan Kulkarni, William Ma, Thomas Maller, Charlotte March, Alex Marian, Duncan McClean, Tim McQuillen-Wright, Michelle Messmer, Thom Mitchell, Garrett Moore, Claire Moulton, Philippa Mutch, Charlotte Newton John, Colin Nightingale, Daniel Nolan,

Emmet O'Donnell, Helen Scarlett O'Neill, Francesco Pastori, Sheena Patel, Tina Rahman, Justin Raulli, David Rosenberg, Harry Ross, Helen Smith, Luke Swaffield, Kath Tee, Ollie Tiong, Nina Tolstoy, Brodie Turner, Melinda Lee Ward and Tim Q. Wilson. We would also like to extend our thanks to all of our contributors who wished to remain anonymous and who we cannot name here but who have provided such rich detail of their experiences and their expertise.

1

Secret Cinema and the immersive experience industry

> There was always this overambitious quality to it. It was always about making it bigger.
>
> *Secret Cinema creative director*
>
> I don't even know if there's a method to his madness. There's a market *for* his madness is probably a better way of putting it.
>
> *Secret Cinema collaborator, on the founder of Secret Cinema*

If measured by turnover, box office returns and audience size, in 2019 Secret Cinema (SC) was the leading organisation operating within the immersive experience sector in the UK. During that year, their turnover was £15 million; they generated £8 million in box office takings and engaged a greater number of participants than any other experience with more than 120,000 people attending their production of *Casino Royale* and a further 110,000 attending their *Stranger Things* experience. As such, SC have been a major contributor to UK gross domestic product and are a key provider of employment and creative development within the sector with more than 400 employees working on each production. In 2019, SC also established a number of high-profile partnerships signalling the company's growth and recognition on a global scale. First, they exported their *Casino Royale* experience for a three-month run in Shanghai, before collaborating with Netflix to stage a *Stranger Things* experience in the UK during November 2019, a partnership that continued with a socially distanced 'drive into' experience launched in October 2020 in Los Angeles. SC also signed a landmark deal with Disney in 2020 to design experiences around both existing and new intellectual property. SC have played a critical role in demonstrating both the economic and cultural value of live and immersive cinema and, as we shall demonstrate in this book, over the course of their fifteen-year evolution they have shaped a formula for their experiences which is now both profitable and replicable by other emergent organisations.[1] These factors make SC an organisation of considerable national significance for the UK as well as clearly indicating their global reach and influence. This is an organisation which has evolved novel aesthetic practices, as well as providing an interdisciplinary creative 'cauldron' for the development and advancement of new forms of expertise which, despite their economic and cultural significance, have until now been unrecorded and unexamined.

This book seeks to accomplish two goals: firstly, to present a never-before-written detailed case study and critical interrogation of SC; secondly, to use the case study as a lens through which to understand the wider immersive experience industry. Our in-depth research into SC has enabled us to access creatives and practitioners who – by virtue of the ecosystem underpinning the sector (see figure 1.1) – all contribute to other experiences and organisations both nationally and internationally.

SC do not exist within a vacuum; as an organisation they are situated within the immersive entertainment sector that, in 2019, was considered to be one of the fastest growing sectors globally (see Immerse UK report 2019 and US reports from 2019 and 2020).[2] SC have grown alongside, and belong among, the increasing number of companies who define themselves as operating within the immersive economy. Formally established in 2007, by 2020 SC had 75 productions in its portfolio (see Appendix 1),[3] attracting more than 600,000 audience members between 2015 and 2020 alone. By tracing the history of all of SC's productions from 2006 to 2021, we present how the 'SC' format has been refined through an iterative and experimental process, drawing on numerous creative practices, industry relations and artistic influences. We identify when the different aesthetic elements of the formula emerge throughout the fifteen years of productions and how they evolve over time to establish what is now a settled and *commercial* format.

The experience economy

The immersive sector should be understood as central to the wider experience economy – this is a way of understanding shifts in consumer behaviour and commodity marketing first introduced by economists B. Joseph Pine and James Gilmore in an article in the *Harvard Business Review* in 1998.[4] In this article they state:

> Experiences have always been at the heart of the entertainment business – a fact that Walt Disney and the company he founded have creatively exploited. But today the concept of selling an entertainment experience is taking root in businesses *far removed* from theaters and amusement parks.

We have recently evolved an account of this sector which builds upon Trine Bille and Mark Lorenzen's 2008 demarcation of the experience economy,[5] in which they have defined three groups of experience industries, distinguishing between creativity in the domain of production and experiences in the domain of consumption:

- Creative experience industries that take the production of experiences as their primary goal, where creativity is essential to production – for example, theatre, music, visual arts, literature, film and computer games.
- Experience industries with the production of experiences as their primary goal, where creativity is not essential but may very well be present – for example, museums, libraries, cultural heritage sites, restaurants and spectator sports.
- Creative industries where creativity is essential, but the production of experiences is not a primary goal, and rather than producing directly for the consumer market, they instead provide business-to-business services built into or around mixed products – for example, design, architecture and advertising.[6]

Immersive experiences may straddle all three of these groupings at the levels both of production and of consumption. The immersive sector in the UK still has not been *fully* mapped and understood, although sector reports do capture aspects of its activity. Immerse UK, the cross-sector network for immersive technologies, reports annually on the state of the field. Its 2019 report surveyed more than 200 organisations, with a particular focus on the immersive technologies of Virtual Reality (VR) and Augmented Reality (AR).[7] Only a small handful of these would easily map on to the specific sector that we are identifying in this volume. The more cultural forms, such as SC and others, have not yet been fully represented in these UK-based immersive sector reports, which have tended so far to focus on capturing the rapid growth of immersive *technology* applications across diverse industries and do include some entertainment (notably VR and gaming), but also engineering, medicine, manufacturing, etc. The growth and influence of immersive experiences such as SC in cinema and Coney, Shunt, Les Enfants Terribles and Punchdrunk in theatre, do not feature in these broader sectoral reports. However, sector reports published by industry leaders and advocates in the USA in both 2019 and 2020 are more inclusive of arts, theatre and film-based immersive experiences.[8] In these reports we also see the evidence of the global reach, influence and reputation of UK-based organisations, which are positioned as key leaders in this aspect of the broader experience economy. For example, the US 2020 report turns to the UK to identify the leading players in this space as SC, Punchdrunk and *Immersive Gatsby*, citing their box office success and global expansions.[9] While showcasing the increased economic and cultural potential of these experiences the report also points to the continued need for greater clarity around the nature of the offer being made by organisations in this sector. Our book makes a significant contribution to generating this clarity through an extensive, in-depth engagement with SC – which offers complex, hybrid experiences situated at the intersection of a number of histories and trajectories shown in our immersive experience industry ecosystem model (Figure 1.1). This model illustrates both the state of the field 'experience economy' in the UK in 2019 and SC's centrality within it. The year 2019 was a pinnacle for immersive experiences in the UK, with a significant expansion and proliferation of the sector across multiple high-profile attractions and collaborations. These included *The War of the Worlds Immersive Experience* which opened in May and *The Wolf of Wall Street Immersive Experience* in September. Also, 2019 was the year in which the Guild of Misrule's immersive version of *The Great Gatsby* – now renamed *Immersive Gatsby* – achieved considerable critical acclaim and established itself as the longest-running immersive theatre show in the UK at that time.[10]

Punchdrunk also embarked on its first major television project, *The Third Day*, which was a co-production with Sky Studios and HBO. Team-based, live-action puzzle games such as Escape Rooms (where you are 'locked in' to a specific location and have to work together to solve a series of clues to escape) also exploded over 2018–2019 with more than a thousand empty retail and warehouse units in cities across the UK being converted to house these intense, immersive, team-based 'games'.[11] The live-action version of popular 1990s television series *The Crystal Maze* was also launched in London in March 2019.[12]

Controversial interactive theatre innovators You Me Bum Bum Train also had a new show planned for 2019, but this was postponed and has not been rescheduled due to COVID-19. That year also saw an explosion of immersive dining opportunities, where a meal is designed around a character, a book, a film or a specific thematic. These can range from a tray of canapes designed to accompany or augment a particular film if eaten at specific moments in the story, such as provided by Edible Cinema,[13] to a multi-room experience where participants are fed or presented with plates of elaborately designed food as part of an intense theatrical experience, such as those designed by sector leaders Gingerline. These may or may not require participants/diners to dress up in thematically appropriate attire. This period also saw a further proliferation of themed cocktail bars marketed as immersive, from intimate speakeasys, to Alcatraz-styled 'prisons'. In 2019, 'immersive' was everywhere and at this point became a highly overused and often misrepresentative term. This was a point of contention in the industry, where there was an oversaturation by companies claiming that they offered immersive experiences along with an absence of standards or agreed quality framework. This led to poor practices and to both audiences and workers being misled and, in some cases, put at risk.[14]

... and the immersive experience industry

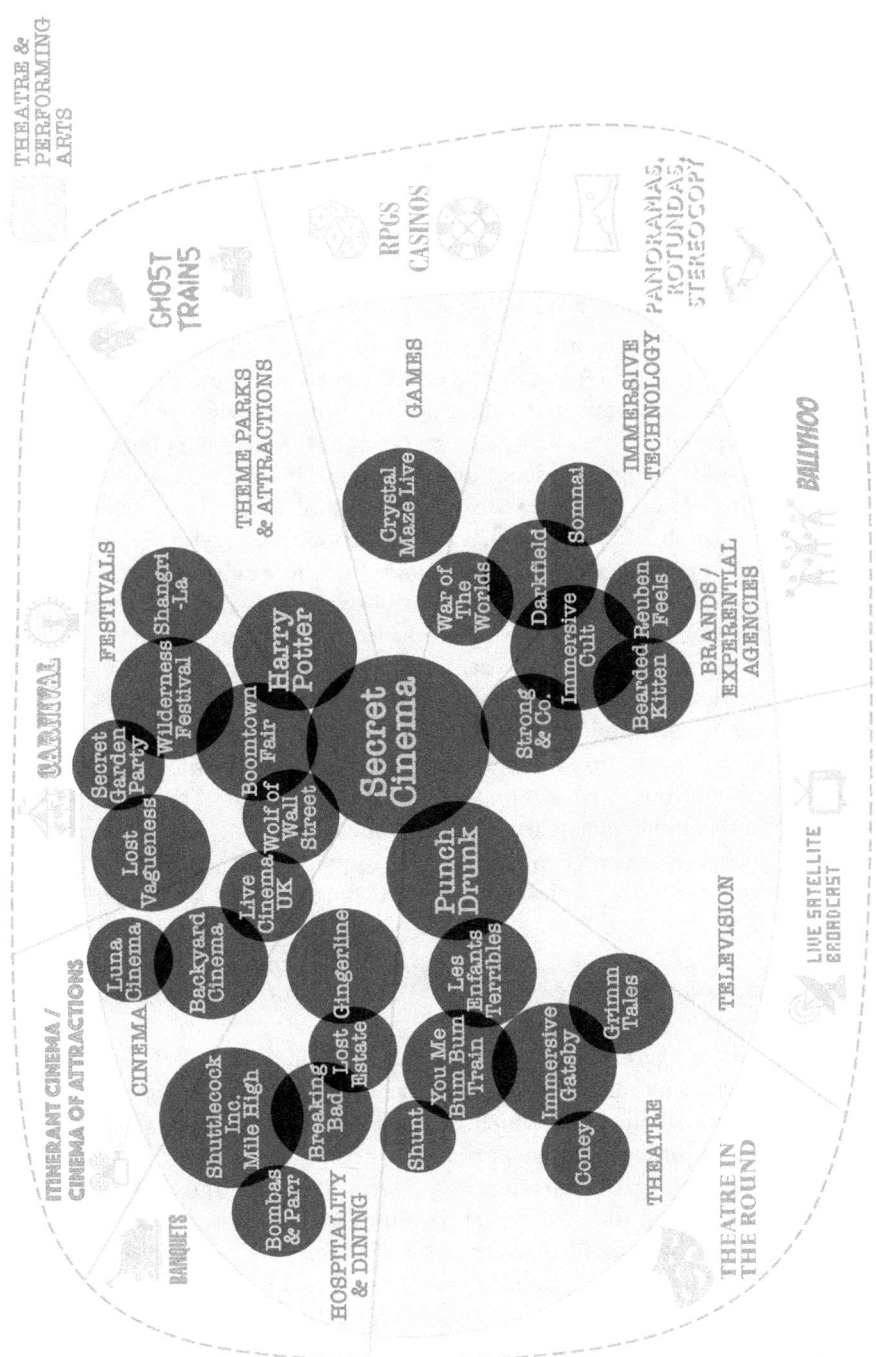

1.1 Immersive experience industry ecosystem model 2019. A model of the cultural and industrial ecosystem which supported the creation of immersive experiences in 2019.

In this industry context and in the absence of a clear, written consensus, we use the term 'immersive experiences' to refer to events that are all-encompassing, that place the participant or audience within a specific, narrativised milieu and that incorporate elements of theatre and performance. Experiences within this model maintain an 'in-world' coherence and fictional register throughout. In practice this means that, in the *Immersive Gatsby* experience for instance, we are situated within the world of the novel *The Great Gatsby* through historically specific set-dressing and performers in appropriate costume, whose interactions are shaped by and contribute to a spatialised narrative that remains faithful to the book or film. The term 'experiential' has come to be used in the advertising and marketing industries, particularly by agencies who specialise in brand activations – and can be most usefully applied to distinguish smaller-scale, one-off experiences from the full-scale immersion of *Gatsby* and SC. 'Experiential' events may merge the real world (i.e. addressing attendees 'out-of-character') with the experiential element and are often used in experience-led brand activations, where a one-off live event is created to launch a brand, product or service. There are numerous experiential agencies in advertising, but there is a definite crossover between immersive and experiential with organisations and individuals working across both, sharing practices and a common language.[15]

Despite the terminological imprecision, it was clear that, in 2019, the immersive/experiential sectors were growing significantly, attracting a keen interest from audiences and investors alike. At the centre of this extraordinary expansion was SC; and during this period we see a marked step change in the sophistication of their production values, the elaboration of the audience experience and the public-facing articulation of the events. The year 2019 was the one in which 'immersive' proliferated and in many ways dominated the experience economy, with SC clearly marked as *the* ascendant organisation.

The immersive experience industry – histories and trajectories

As our immersive experience industry ecosystem model shows, the period 2000–2019 evidences a rapid evolution of immersive organisations, experiences and formats in the UK most of which are hybrid forms crossing over nine key areas: cinema, festivals, theme parks and attractions, games, immersive technologies, brands/experiential agencies, television, theatre and performing arts, and the hospitality and dining sectors. Our model is designed to reveal the intersection of the historical trajectories of these nine areas, combined with the sectoral hybridity currently shaping the evolution of this sector. We use this model as the basis from which to trace the influential moments and industrial practices that have shaped the emergence of our case study example *and* are shaping the clear establishment of an immersive 'sector'. We have highlighted 2019 as a key year in which there was a sudden proliferation of forms and practices that fit within this model but, more importantly, this was the year in which the cluster of innovative immersive practices coalesced into a definable and describable sector.

Cinema and simulational technologies

As the model shows, each of the nine areas has its own historical trajectory and antecedents, which are also marked by key points of cross-over and convergence – all the way back to the earliest stages of their evolution. The first is the early history of cinema in the late nineteenth and early twentieth centuries, with the first film exhibitions taking place as part of programmes of theatrical or spectacular entertainment,[16] or as part of itinerant (or early models of 'pop-up') circus and fairground attractions. As cultural historian Vanessa Toulmin describes:

> Moving Pictures first appeared on the fairground at the King's Lynn Mart on 15th February 1897 introduced by Randall Williams. Williams, 'the King of Showmen', adapted his Ghost show at the end of December 1896 in order to introduce the latest novelty into his presentation at the World's Fair Exhibition in Islington. Within a few months showpeople across the country were exhibiting moving pictures to the fairgoing public.[17]

Toulmin has tracked the important interconnections between fairs, travelling shows and early cinema, arguing that 'the moving picture industry was shaped in its initial years by the traveling showmen'.[18] These early connections between fairground and film were the precursors to present-day film-themed rides and contemporary cinema attractions such as 4DX. This early 'cinema of attractions' also contained elements of 'ballyhoo' that can be traced back to early marketing practices for films in the 1920s, where on-street happenings and stunts were performed to generate press interest and public intrigue.[19] The same principles now apply to the approaches taken by immersive brand and 'experiential' agencies which are reshaping the marketing and promotions industry through live events and brand activations. Early 'screen' technologies which were often displayed in these spaces – such as the rotunda, the stereoscope and panoramas – transported early 'experiencers' to distant or imaginary lands and find their contemporary manifestation in the technologies of VR and AR. These are increasingly embedded in immersive experiences along with advances in immersive sound technologies, projection mapping and lighting design. The now established industrial model of immersive simulated environments developed by SC, brought to life through *embodied* participation, also reaches all the way back to the very earliest moments of cinema's becoming and has its own trajectory through to contemporary, participatory, cinema exhibition practices and cinephiliac pleasures.[20] In 'More than the movies: a history of somatic visual culture through Hale's Tours, IMAX, and motion simulation rides'[21] Lauren Rabinovitz further underscores the interconnections between early cinema pleasures, practices and technologies, and contemporary exhibition environments in movie theatres and fairground attractions:

> Cinema was arguably the single most important new communication technology at the outset of the twentieth century and the best one for prefiguring the digital technologies that promise virtual worlds and simulated realities.[22]

Immersive theatre, participation and sensual aesthetics

The history and evolution of immersive theatre is also a key point of convergence in this sector, from the theatre-in-the-round developments of the 1940s and 1950s, via promenade theatre and street theatre to the early immersive theatre productions and experimental, participatory art of the late 1990s and early 2000s. Shunt (founded in 1998) were a key UK-based organisation which influenced the immersive aesthetics that dominate today. Josephine Machon's important research on the design, performance and participant aesthetics of immersive theatre positions these works as arising from 'a fusion of installation art and physical and visual theatres of the 1980s' that 'owes its sensual aesthetic primarily to a mix of ingredients involving landscape, architecture, scenography, sound and direct, human contact'.[23] This fusion is what underpins the 'physical, sensual and participatory' experiences of troupes such as Punchdrunk and Les Enfants Terribles – two of the most widely recognised innovators in the immersive theatre sector – that have achieved significant audiences and critical acclaim for their productions. There is established scholarship on the immersive theatre sector more generally and Punchdrunk in particular.[24] We seek to both contribute to and extend this work through our consideration of how these immersive theatre practices have evolved and developed within SC and broader, commercialised areas of the ecosystem.

Festivals, the carnivalesque and alternate realities

Music festivals, already a fusion of a number of distinct cultural practices and histories, are an important precursor to the evolution of SC and other immersive organisations. One key influence, cited by many, is Lost Vagueness (LV) – an audience attraction that opened to attendees in 1998 in one of the outer fields of Glastonbury's (then annual) music festival. The anarchic attraction was founded by Roy Gurvitz, a member of the new age traveller community, who had attended the festival on the periphery since the late 1980s. It started out as a casino, a dark cabaret and a neo-burlesque venue in a field, later expanding to a ballroom with attendees encouraged to dress in ball gowns and evening wear, and latterly included a roller disco, silver service restaurant, American diner and a makeshift Chapel of Love, 'in which Kate (Moss) and Pete (Docherty) were rumoured to have married'.[25] All attractions were characterised by eccentricity and flamboyance, coupled with drink- and drug-fuelled late-night excess. The resounding influence of LV has been widely noted in the festival cultures and immersive entertainment experiences that have followed. A feature documentary about LV and its maverick founder reported that 'Roy and his gang created an entire culture that's around us today in cabaret, performance art and music'.[26] Debs Armstrong, LV producer from 2002 to 2005, said 'it was the breaking down audience/performer boundaries that had so much influence on SC, Shunt and Punchdrunk, and everything else that's out there now'.[27] When Gurvitz resigned from the festival in 2008, Armstrong was asked to programme the three fields of 'the new late night entertainment area' which replaced LV.[28] Armstrong went on to be the founder and creative director of the renamed Shangri-La (2008–2015), an area that curated and celebrated alternative artistic practices and underground culture, which has been described as 'a film set the size of a town and one of Glastonbury Festival's best loved areas'. From her LinkedIn page Armstrong claims that 'it was the first experiential to articulate key notions such as the importance of storytelling and audience/performer boundary dissolution'. This was through the use of fictional story themes which became the connective tissue with which to bind and unify the experience design of the area. Armstrong explains that '[b]oth events [LV and Shangri-La] have been described as "legendary" and "game-changing" in the media, inspiring a host of younger Producers creating mass participation experientials such as Boomtown and SC'. Boomtown (also known as Boomtown Fair) was founded by Christopher Rutherford and Lak Mitchell in 2009 and has since been held annually at a site near Winchester, Hampshire. This independent five-day music festival has been described as an immersive theatrical production composed of sets, live performers and alternate reality games (ARGs). The diverse line-up of bands, DJs and speakers perform on numerous stages within several fictional 'districts' that have their own unique theming, venues and streets.

Playable spaces and aesthetic experiences

Our ecosystem model also shows the other sectors that are converging here – contemporary immersive dining, for instance, can be traced back to banquets and medieval-themed meals in historic settings such as battle re-enactments and heritage sites. This converges with developments within the hospitality sector more widely to include themed restaurants, themed cocktail bars and the like. Escape rooms can be traced back through multiple histories such as role-playing games, murder mystery weekends and ARGs. In an article tracing the origins of the 3D narrative environments within massive, multi-player, online, role-playing games such as World of Warcraft Celia Pearce underlines the important aesthetic entanglements between early theme parks and open navigable worlds in these emergent and highly popular online spaces.[29]

In the current immersive forms included in our model, the aesthetics incorporate facets of the theme park with the now evolved and easy-to-recognise mechanics of the digital game. An example included here is the London-based, live-action *Crystal Maze Live* which is branded as an *attraction* and combines the game-based elements of the escape room with immersive theatre. This early fairground, theme park and 'attractions' trajectory begins in the UK with early ghost train experiences (the earliest ghost train adapted an American ride called the Pretzel and dates from the 1930s)[30] and ghoulish attractions such as the Chamber of Horrors at Madam Tussauds (established in 1835). The trend for these attractions continues through the London Dungeons (opened in 1974), more recent examples such as the Warner Bros Harry Potter walk-through exhibition (2012) and the revival of 'scare attractions' including zombie runs.[31]

Our research has demonstrated that, over the past fifteen to twenty years, there has been a significant transition of these contemporary immersive practices from marginal, artisanal or even experimental productions to an alignment with the key characteristics of an established cultural *industry*. The central organisations discussed here and our lead case study of SC have steadily shifted to a more professionalised and corporatised business model through which to fund, recruit to and market their creative outputs. This has not been without its challenges and controversies and significant lessons have been learned throughout this process by SC, allied organisations and sector professionals – many of which we will uncover and interrogate within this book.

Our research reveals that, since the design and performance expertise of immersive theatre is in *every* example of the forms and formats we identify within our model, it represents a considerable sphere of influence. The reason that SC – an immersive *cinema* form – is our central case study is that, as it has evolved into a stable format, it has drawn on *every one* of the nine forms captured in our model. Crucially, all these practices converge in the SC productions of 2019. The interviews that we have conducted as part of our research reveal complex interconnections between these forms at the levels of the creative talent, the development of new techniques and of advancing innovations in immersive technologies. A significant number of our interviewees have worked (and continue to work) across these sectors. As they have developed and honed their format, SC have also played a role in the establishment and recognition of this new sector within the cultural economy, as well as providing a fertile, creative, playful and experimental sandbox through which experiential and design aesthetics could be imagined and perfected.

Approach and method

We have been researching and compiling materials for this book since 2014, closely mapping the development, growth and expansion of the immersive experience sector in the UK and the centrality of SC. As our model illustrates, SC productions are a hybridised and complex form. In response, our research and analysis of these productions have required the development of new conceptual vocabularies, new combinatory, methodological practices and the incorporation of a range of theoretical frameworks. These include media studies (in our analysis of audiences, press reporting and paratexts), film studies (in our consideration of both texts and festivals), game studies (in order to understand play and game mechanics and distinct game aesthetics), media industry studies (in order to pay attention to working practices, economies, etc.), critical event management studies and cultural and sub-cultural studies (drawing from fan studies).

The underpinning research for this book was conducted through comprehensive searches of the publicly available Future Shorts, Future Cinema (FC) and SC video archives on their YouTube, Vimeo and MySpace channels as well as time-based searches of the secretcinema.org website using the 'Wayback Machine'. SC's Flickr, Facebook and Twitter accounts were also used as sources, as well as the fictional 'microsites' that are now routinely created for each SC production. We have also drawn from numerous press interviews published across various media outlets and have conducted our own in-depth interviews with fifty-two creative practitioners and industry professionals.[32] Thirty-eight of these are either past or present employees of SC, or contracted freelancers on SC productions, who collectively represent a period of engagement with SC between 2008 and 2020. Like the film industry, and other areas of the creative industries, the immersive experience industry is a project-based sector in which numerous small organisations and freelancers are hired to temporarily come together to work on one production, which, as much previous research into the media industries has shown, brings with it significant challenges, precarity and inequalities. We seek to draw these out and interrogate them within the context of this specific sector. We have drawn our interviewee contributors from the creative, technical, operational and management areas, ensuring a representative sample from all departments. Their expertise covers producing, web design, pre-narrative engagement, performance design, performance direction, acting, video design, sound design, sound composing, lighting design, special effects, stage management, operations and merchandising. Our other fourteen interviewees include people who work in the wider immersive sector in the UK, including representatives from the *Dr Who: Time Fracture* immersive experience (hereafter DWTF), *Monopoly Lifesized* and *Immersive Gatsby*, among others. As we have indicated, SC productions fuse the specialist input and expertise of professionals from across different disciplinary domains – from the film industry, the theatre sector and the live/events industries. As we shall illuminate, this emerging sector is both constituted and shaped by unique collaborative formations between creatives in film production and exhibition, theatre performers and professionals, brand developers, experience designers, live event/festival infrastructure specialists, construction, technology providers, caterers, security and site-management professionals. As all our interviewees bring with them expertise of working on numerous other projects and in other organisations in the immersive sector, they provide vital insight into the expansion, development and creative practices that dominate this sector.

Our research into the participant experience that emerges through these productions has incorporated a diverse range of practices, including audience surveys, interviews, the curation of distinct researcher groups to engage, participate and debrief on their experiences, and engagement with social media content, including participant-produced 'how to' videos providing insights to how to achieve the best SC experience. We have also attended and participated in eleven SC productions ourselves.

In addition, we have taken a sample 'post-experience promotional video' from sixty-four of their sixty-six identified productions (listed in Appendix 2). Always released one or two months after the experience, these short videos (1–3 minutes long) are routinely published on the 'Previous Worlds' page of the SC website (and the back catalogue of all other videos can be found scattered across the various social media channels that we have mentioned SC using above).[33] These videos are a key staple in SC's marketing and promotion campaign – they capture and communicate the excitement, energy and dynamism of the productions in a highly mediated and visualised way. They work to promote future events by showcasing excited audience responses to the earlier experiences, and the high production values of the later experiences. We have used these videos to identify the different elements of the production, recurring approaches and any changes in practice. As well as being useful documentary sources, they are unique and highly inter-referential paratexts and, as such, a key site for analysis. Their content, approach, style, aesthetics, language and structure have evolved over time and reveal a particular formula which is characterised by hyper-simulation of the SC events (which are themselves a form of simulation). These are complex and multilayered texts, challenging to distinguish visually from their central, film-based reference point since they have now been stylised to look like and replicate the original film. Those featured on the SC website at the time of writing are characterised by high production values and a polished house style, conforming to the aesthetic norms of a film trailer. We include observations of these videos throughout the book as we discuss the various productions in temporal order. In so doing, we are able to trace the process of the shift from marginal or subcultural practices to recognisable and replicable industrial processes through the lens of an organisation. We have structured the book under five central chapter headings: SC as sandbox; SC as format; SC as immersive activism; SC as industry; and SC as experience community.

Chapter outlines

In Chapter 2: Secret Cinema as sandbox, we trace the history of SC through its first six years of practice and fifty productions from 2006 to 2013. We describe a highly experimental and exploratory period in which different approaches, working practices and collaborations are tested, which build on the key historical antecedents of itinerant cinema, festival and the fairground. We start to see how a particular format emerges as a result of an iterative and experimental process which draws from the nine sector spaces identified in our immersive experience industry ecosystem model. The representation of the organisation in this period is inchoate and incoherent – with multiple brand 'visions' (i.e. Future Cinema, Secret Cinema, Secret Screenings and The Other Cinema), artistic identities, social, cultural and even political initiatives. The chapter presents a genealogy of key transitional periods, which we argue are defined by a number of binary tensions. These polarities exist in a cyclical continuum and are subject to constant negotiation and renegotiation. Within each of these periods we identify how the productions undergo a transition – when and how the aesthetic elements of the formula emerge – whereby some elements are taken forwards as a key part of the now-established format, and others fall away; but almost always the tensions remain ever-present. We have identified these periods as: Festivals to Financing (2006–2009) where we see the introduction of corporate sponsorship; Ephemerality to Replicability (2009–2010) where there is a move away from one-off screenings; Movements to Markets (2011) where narratives of resistance and disruption are introduced through the creation of parallel, online, fictional worlds to augment engagement with the event, but which also act as key marketing and promotional tools; and Spatialisation to Stratification (2012–2013) where the combined use of institutionalised spaces and narratives exert control over the audience, while delivering highly stratified experiences bound up in class-based ideologies – which is richly epitomised by the penultimate SC production of this period, *The Shawshank Redemption*.

Chapter 3 focusses on the continued evolution of the SC format over the next five-year period, 2013–2018, across thirteen productions spanning four self-defined subformats: 'Tell No One', 'SC Presents … ', 'SC X Presents …' and 'SC X Tell No One'. The evolution of both the productions and the organisation are shaped by two further tensions which we identify as Participation to Passivity, and Covert and Clandestine to Commercial and Commodified. Key influential productions in the period include *Brazil*, *The Grand Budapest Hotel* and *Back to the Future*. Through an examination of these productions, we show how the format has evolved to much larger scale in terms of both audience numbers and repeatability over an extended period. We lay out a set of experience design principles and their associated experiential aesthetics as they are encountered by the audiences, covering pre-ticket promotion and pre-narrative experience and engagement – including an in-depth look into the in-world microsites, social media accounts, flash mobs and pop-ups; the different places, sites and spaces of the productions; and the pre-screening show and the screening itself. Bearing a close resemblance to both the established ARG and Pervasive Games-format conventions, we show how the SC experience design maximises opportunities for promotion and marketing; how the productions *simulate liveness* at all stages; and how the format has evolved so that audiences can be both passive and/or participatory. These characteristics are epitomised by the largest production of this period – *Back to the Future* – which marked SC's most significant turning point in its evolution so far where the impact of the shift from the organisation's clandestine roots to a more commercialised operation led to significant challenges, disruptions and discomfort for both the producers and audiences alike.

Chapter 4: SC as immersive activism captures a further turning point in the evolution of the organisation and its productions for two key, inter-related reasons. Firstly the move into large, semi-permanent warehouse spaces led to a considerable increase in the range of specialists and professionals who were required to design and manage the scale of these productions. Secondly, SC founder Fabien Riggall's increasing volubility in public and press accounts made apparent a particular discursive formation of *intended* audience subjectivities – as fellow *activists*, for instance. Riggall's public appearances and interviews also provided a narrative of these experiences as responding to and/or intervening in real-world socio-political issues of their moment of production. These two factors were instrumental in shaping the very real elaboration and evolution of the professional requirements and expectations of the format on the one hand and an attempt to shape the public corporate identity or 'brand' through which to communicate the value of these practices on the other. Through the analysis of press interviews, public appearances and conference presentations made by Riggall, we draw out the many tensions that existed in the organisation's communication of this corporate identity. These tensions are particularly acute in Riggall's multiple articulations of his own identity as *both* a cultural entrepreneur *and* an activist. His frequent public articulation of a defence of artistic freedom and his fierce opposition to formulaic cultural experiences is set against the backdrop of a specific period between 2015 and 2018 during which it is precisely a repeatable and commodifiable *formula* that is now being perfected through a series of successful and increasingly elaborate experiences. We examine this public discourse of an emergent 'brand activism' alongside the way in which brands have become increasingly embedded 'in-world'. We examine these contradictory forces in relation to wider macro-debates around the relationships between culture and industry, experience as commodity, social justice and the needs of the market.

In Chapter 5: Secret Cinema as industry we examine the two landmark productions of 2019, *Casino Royale* and *Stranger Things*, through the lens of the experts and professionals who developed, designed and delivered them. SC's productions involve the temporary coming together of a collaborative *troupe* of industrially recognised talented professionals that combine a complex range of practices: from film (studios, distributors, exhibitors, technologists, sound designers, action vehicles and the producers and creatives behind the original film texts); from theatre (performers, directors, stage managers, set designers, costume designers, video and lighting designers); from event and live (expertise from festivals, live sporting and music events such as infrastructure, crowd management, site management and logistics); from the theme park sector (narrative spatialisation, thematic interactions and immersive technologies); and from the service industries (catering, hospitality, food, drinks and outdoor 'festival' service provision). We draw from the thirty-eight in-depth interviews with SC collaborators who provide extensive insight into their working practices, logistical processes and creative techniques including experience design and spatialised game design. We present an 'immersive experience production model' which shows the division of labour and the various intersector collaborations that are unique to this type of immersive production. We also reveal the dynamic emergence of increasingly specialised divisions of labour practices and crafts, focussing on the particular strategies and challenges that building immersive experiences around established intellectual property brings. We reveal new, sector-specific, terminology and the unique roles that have emerged that span the performative and the logistical – such as front of house and global performance director. We show how these multidisciplinary collaborations are collectively pushing the boundaries of creative, technical and logistical problem-solving within highly hybridised spaces where the engagement with thousands of audience members is central – to innovate a model of experience design which simultaneously unites the apparently contradictory principles of massification and individualisation.

In Chapter 6: SC as experience community we turn our attention to the central facet of the experience – the audience. Over the seven-year period of researching these events, we have adopted a range of strategies to capture and render visible the ephemerality of these experiences. We have studied the audience in numerous ways – through questionnaires, interviews, focus groups and by establishing researcher groups to attend together and debrief on their distinctive *journeys* through the SC worlds; and through our own, embedded, experiential observations achieved through direct participation and by inhabiting different 'experiencing' subjectivities. We track the changing nature of this audience, from an early-adopter hipster elite, via a broader and more mainstream fan community through to the emergence of a group of super-fans. We identify the playful and performative nature of the audience participation within these events, establishing an aesthetics of engagement including elements of 'cosplay' and social media identity display. We consider the ways in which audiences form 'experience' and 'experiencing' communities around their participation in SC events. We also trace the emergence of a community of elite fans of SC who have dubbed themselves the Positive People of Secret Cinema (PPSC) – a group formed from a shared love of the SC experiences – who have evolved their own mores, values, rules, tastes and shared cultural practices. We conclude this chapter with a consideration of how the complex audience participation can be understood as forms of labour that contribute to the commercialisation and industrialisation of SC as an organisation.

In the concluding chapter, we recontextualise SC within the wider immersive industry of 2021 – reaffirming and extending the immersive experience industry ecosystem model introduced above. We present a near future of rich, overlapping experiences and collaborations within the immersive experience industry. We also show how the specific 'format' evolved by SC becomes established as replicable and is taken forwards by other organisations, which are increasingly significant across the immersive experience sector more generally, both in the UK and beyond.

An important note: SC and secrecy

It is important to note that not all of the eighty-one productions that we introduce in this book were released under the 'SC' branding.[34] The earliest events that we have identified were presented under the original organisation – Future Shorts Ltd, incorporated on 12 March 2004 – which was founded by Fabien Riggall, a cinephile and producer of short films who studied at the New York Film Academy. Events then went on to be presented under the banner Future Cinema, an organisation later incorporated by Riggall on 20 December 2006. As we will discuss in detail, the first 'official' SC-branded production was in 2007, and the brand operated alongside the FC titles until 2014 at which point all productions were launched under the SC 'label'. FC ceased to be used or referred to after this point, and on 30 July 2015 the company changed its registered name from Future Shorts LTD to 'Secret Group Limited', which remains its operating title at the time of writing (while FC has been a subsidiary company retaining dormant status since 2007).[35] The eighty-one productions are all listed in Appendix 1 identifying the 'brand' under which they were presented, along with key factual details including exact dates, locations, ticket prices, audience sizes and box office data.

The history we present in this book has been carefully pieced together by assembling and examining the many scattered materials described above to bring together a holistic, comprehensive and coherent picture of SC as an organisation as well as an industrial and creative process. We should be clear that, about the following, we cannot be entirely certain that this is the 'complete' history *and* that the assembled history presented here has not been officially verified or endorsed by SC.

In March 2020, prior to the COVID-19 pandemic, there was limited access to information and data to engage in the level of depth and detail that we have since achieved in this book; at that point only one SC credit listing existed, for the *Romeo + Juliet* production in 2018. However, in 2020 SC received public support from Arts Council England as part of the pandemic cultural recovery programme of funding,[36] and have notably become far more open about their practices, publishing further credit listings, reports and minutes from public planning meetings, and providing far more detailed insight and information through press interviews and through a high-profile crowdfunding campaign in 2021.[37] In an interview with the authors in December 2021, Max Alexander, CEO of SC, underscored the shift to a much more transparent and inclusive model of audience engagement, evidenced here in his description of how he would like the 'Secret' element of the SC brand to evolve:

> In as much as *secret* means *exclusive* – I hate it. In as much as *secret* means mysterious and something that deserves to be kept mysterious – I love it, and everyone is welcome.[38]

This new level of transparency, along with the interviews that we have conducted, has allowed us to gain a richer insight into both the specifics of the productions and the characteristics of this emerging industry. We have captured an organisation and a sector that is in transition from marginal and subcultural roots to a commodifiable and commercial form, now with recognisable professional roles and practices, which has contributed to the establishment of an immersive experience industry of national importance and global reach.

Notes

1. Including Underground Cinema (www.undergroundcinema.com.au – accessed 13 December 2021), an organisation in Australia running secret, live, immersive cinema experiences in undisclosed locations in Melbourne and Sydney. Launched in 2009, they teamed up with Frontier Touring in March 2019 for a major production of *Dirty Dancing* (www.frontiertouring.com/dirtydancing – accessed 13 December 2021) which appears to be operating at the same scale and level of detail as recent Secret Cinema events.
2. Immerse UK and Digital Catapult, *The immersive economy in the UK report 2019: the growth of the virtual, augmented and mixed reality technologies ecosystem* (London: Immerse UK/Digital Catapult, 2019), available at www.immerseuk.org/wp-content/uploads/2019/11/The-Immersive-Economy-in-the-UK-Report-2019.pdf (accessed 13 December 2021); Ricky Brigante, *Interactive, intimate, experiential: the impact of immersive design*, ed. Noah Nelson, with additional contributions by Kathryn Yu and Rachel Stoll (San Francisco: Immersive Design Summit, 2019); Ricky Brigante and Sarah A.S. Elger, *New adventures: the strength of immersive entertainment. 2020 immersive entertainment industry annual report*, ed. Noah Nelson (Los Angeles: HERE Institute, 2020).
3. This book includes reference to each of these productions from June 2006 up until 2021. The majority of these events were held in locations in London UK, with a handful of exceptions. These are almost all based on feature film titles, with one immersive event based around a music album – Laura Marling's *Once I Was an Eagle* (in 2013) – and another based on a television series – Netflix's *Stranger Things* (in 2019–2020). Some of the films have received multiple treatments, including *Ghostbusters* (twice), *Dirty Dancing* (twice with a third run planned in 2022, having been postponed both in 2020 and 2021 due to the coronavirus

pandemic), *Blade Runner* (twice), *Bugsy Malone* (three times), *Alien* (twice) and *La Haine* (three times). The rest of the films range from back-catalogue cult and indie classics to new-release preview screenings.
4 B. Joseph Pine and James Gilmore, 'Welcome to the experience economy', *Harvard Business Review* (1998) July–August, 98–105.
5 Trine Bille and Mark Lorenzen, *Den Danske plevelsesøkonomi: afgrænsning, økonomisk betydning og vækstmuligheder* (Copenhagen: Forlaget Samfundslitteratur, 2008).
6 Developed from Sarah Atkinson and Helen. W. Kennedy, 'The immersive cinema experience economy: the UK film industry's third sector', in *The Routledge companion to media industries,* ed. Paul McDonald (London: Routledge, 2022), 392–403.
7 Immerse UK and Digital Catapult, *The immersive economy*.
8 [2019]: Brigante, *Interactive, intimate, experiential*. [2020]: Brigante and Elger, *New adventures*.
9 Brigante and Elger, *New adventures*, 12.
10 The production first featured in the Vault Festival in 2017, and has played in Dublin, Brussels and Seoul, with plans for several other international productions.
11 In 2018, there were 1,139 rooms spread across 288 companies with 415 distinct venues in the UK, offering 852 distinct scenarios, according to Ken Ferguson, 'Analysis of the UK market 2018', The logic escapes me: London-based blog on escape rooms, 13 August 2018, available at https://thelogicescapesme.com/opinion/analysis-of-the-uk-market-2018/#comment-883 (accessed 13 December 2021). In 2019, this had grown to a total of 2,403 rooms (in correspondence with Ken Ferguson, 20 September 2021). This included the launch of a live version of *The Crystal Maze*, at the site of the old Trocadero arcade in London.
12 *The Crystal Maze* was piloted in 1989 and based on the French series *Fort Boyard*. The successful UK series ran from 1990 to 1995.
13 See Sarah Atkinson, 'Hangmen rehanged – fusing event cinema, live cinema and sensory cinema in the evolution of site and screen responsive theatre', in *Live cinema: cultures, economies, aesthetics,* ed. Sarah Atkinson and H.W. Kennedy (New York: Bloomsbury, 2017), 243–64.
14 A purpose-built site opened in April 2019. Space 18 was a 25,000-square-foot spot in New Oxford Street devoted entirely to immersive and experimental theatre. The first production to be hosted was an immersive survival experience called 'Variant 31' and, according to Equity, serious health and safety concerns were raised about the suitability of the venue after several workers and performers employed for the event reported breathing and lung problems, due to the inhalation of dust at the venue. The organisation reportedly went bankrupt and the venue subsequently closed down. Another 'purpose-built' site in the Borough in London, called 'The Buzz', was due to host an immersive *Thunderbirds* experience but ran into problems : Lucy Brooks, 'Postponed: *Thunderbirds: beyond the horizon*, The Buzz at Mercato Metropolitano', *Culture Whisper*, 27 September 2018, available at www.culturewhisper.com/r/theatre/

thunderbirds_beyond_the_horizon_the_buzz_at_mercato_metropolitano/11514 (accessed 13 December 2021). At the time of writing, this has yet to be realised.
15 In previous work we have used the term 'experiential' in relation to specific cinema practices to demarcate '… the growing trend toward the creation of a cinema that escapes beyond the boundaries of the auditorium whereby film-screenings are augmented by synchronous live performance, site-specific locations, technological intervention, social media engagement, and all manner of simultaneous interactive moments including singing, dancing, eating, drinking and smelling – what we are describing as the broader field of *experiential cinema*'. See Sarah Atkinson and Helen W. Kennedy, 'Introduction – Inside-the-scenes: the rise of experiential cinema', *Participations: Journal of Audience and Reception Studies* (2016) 13(1), 139–40. In this book we address the use of the term 'experiential' in promotional, marketing and broader industry discourse.
16 Tom Gunning, 'The cinema of attraction[s]: early film, its spectator and the avant-garde', *The Animation Studies Reader* (1986), 17–27.
17 Vanessa Toulmin's extensive Fairground and Circus Archive project contains a wealth of evidence of this history and the intersection between carnival, theatrical and cinematic practices exhibited: National Fairground and Circus Archive, The University of Sheffield, available at www.sheffield.ac.uk/nfca/researchandarticles/bioscopeshows (accessed 13 December 2021).
18 Vanessa Toulmin, 'Telling the tale. The story of the fairground bioscope shows and the showmen who operated them', *Film History* (1994) 6(2), 236.
19 Atkinson, *Beyond the screen*, 18–19.
20 'Whilst recognizing that these experiences are not radically new (some belong in a continuum of peripheral marketing around film screenings that have existed since early cinema) we do now see these previously marginal experiences (i.e. *The Rocky Horror Picture Show*, 1975) beginning to find access to a much wider public, alongside a significant rise in organisations dedicated to the design and delivery of augmented cinematic *main* events.' From Atkinson and Kennedy, 'Introduction – Inside-the-scenes', 140.
21 Lauren Rabinovitz, 'More than the movies: a history of somatic visual culture through Hale's Tours, IMAX, and motion simulation rides', in *Memory bytes: history, technology, and digital culture*, ed. Lauren Rabinovitz and Abraham Geil (Durham, NC: Duke University Press, 2004), 99–125.
22 Rabinovitz, 'More than the movies', 100.
23 Josephine Machon, *Immersive theatres: intimacy and immediacy in contemporary performance* (London: Macmillan, 2013), xv.
24 [Generally]: Including Machon, *Immersive theatres* and Adam Alston, *Beyond immersive theatre* (London: Palgrave Macmillan, 2016). [Specifically]: Josephine Machon, Stephen Dobbie, *The Punchdrunk encyclopaedia* (London: Routledge, 2018) and Carina. E. Westling, *Immersion and participation in Punchdrunk's theatrical worlds* (New York: Bloomsbury, 2020).
25 Cole Moreton, 'The future of Britain's best gig: the lost spirit of Glastonbury', *The Independent*, 3 February 2008, available at www.independent.co.uk/arts-entertainment/music/features/the-future-of-britain-s-best-gig-the-lost-spirit-of-glastonbury-777547.html (accessed 13 December 2021).

26 Narrator, *Lost in Vagueness* (film) 2017, dir. Sofia Olins.
27 Narrator, *Lost in Vagueness*.
28 *New Musical Express*, 'Lost Vagueness organiser leaves Glastonbury Festival: popular field set for revamp in 2008', 4 February 2008, available at www.nme.com/news/music/glastonbury-239-1331769 (accessed 10 May 2022).
29 Celia Pearce, 'Narrative environments', *Space Time Play* (2007), 200–205.
30 Joel Zika, 'Dark rides and the evolution of immersive media', *Journal of Themed Experience and Attractions Studies* (2018) 1(1), 54–60.
31 Emma Austin, 'Zombie culture: dissent, celebration and the carnivalesque in social spaces', in *The zombie renaissance in popular culture*, ed. Laura Hubner, Marcus Leaning and Paul Manning (London: Palgrave Macmillan, 2015), 174–90.
32 As an approved element of our ethics process, all interviewees were given three options: to be named, to be partially identified (i.e. by their job role) or to remain anonymous. You will see these choices reflected in the endnotes which accompany any direct quotation.
33 At the time of writing (21 July 2021) the following videos were available via www.secretcinema.org/previous-worlds (accessed 13 December 2021): *Stranger Things, Casino Royale, Romeo +Juliet, A Secret Live Experience*, Baz Luhrmann's *Moulin Rouge!, 28 Days Later, Star Wars: The Empire Strikes Back, The Grand Budapest Hotel, Miller's Crossing, Casablanca, The Shawshank Redemption, The Battle of Algiers* and *Alien*, with the words 'and many, many more' written beneath the video listings.
34 This is an approximation calculated from information gathered from online sources. This figure has not been verified by the organisation. In many press accounts, SC will often state that there has been 'over 50 productions', e.g. Max Alexander in a crowdfunding video 2021: Secret Cinema, *Secret Cinema – highlights reel of Secret's history and our future plans*, Crowdcube, 24 May 2021, video, 5:11, available at www.crowdcube.com/companies/secret-cinema/pitches/qD0gEq (accessed 13 December 2021).
35 According to the annual financial reports posted to Secret Group Limited, Companies House, UK, available at https://find-and-update.companyinformation.service.gov.uk/company/05071764 (accessed 13 December 2021).
36 Arts Council England, 'Cultural Recovery Fund: data', 19 November 2021, available at www.artscouncil.org.uk/publication/culture-recovery-fund-data (accessed 13 December 2021).
37 K.J. Yossman, 'As Secret Cinema launches crowdfunding initiative, is its business model working?' *Variety*, 7 June 2021, available at https://variety.com/2021/tv/news/secret-cinema-crowdfunding-business-model-1234987811/ (accessed 13 December 2021).
38 Max Alexander, interviewed by author, 6 December 2021.

2

Secret Cinema as sandbox

In this chapter, we trace the history of Secret Cinema through its first seven years. We present a highly experimental and exploratory period which is born of the historical antecedents of itinerant cinema, fairground and festival. During this prolific period, SC initiate and engage in numerous strands of film screening activity and events, seemingly building their own entire secret empire, which is captured in figure 2.1 below.

The founder Fabien Riggall explained the differences between *some* of the strands of activity:

> There's Future Shorts which is the short film festival and we also do stuff with bands. There's also Future Cinema where we create events, and this latest thing we do called Secret Cinema, basically it's a bit like the old days when you used to go to raves, you used to get a phone call and meet at this petrol station, you all pile up and go to the country in the middle of Surrey and there's an event. It's the same idea but taking film – people don't know what they're going to see or where they're going to see it until the day. And they get an email that says meet at this place, bring your top hat ...[1]

In Riggall's description here we see articulated some interesting tensions, e.g. between a sub-cultural practice (a rave) and the possession of an upper-class piece of formal attire (*your* top hat). These tensions will be drawn out more fully in Chapter 4 but, for now, we concentrate on the explosion of activity that occurs within this period across multiple strands, locations and events and the clear line of influence that stems from music and rave culture. There were (at least) fifty productions during this period: eighteen under the banner of Secret Cinema (SC), twenty-seven under Future Cinema (FC), three 'Secret Screenings' and two 'The Other Cinema' events. This chapter presents these within a genealogy of key transitional periods which we argue are defined by a number of binary tensions which we have identified as:

- Festivals to financing (2006–2009), where we see the introduction of corporate sponsorship

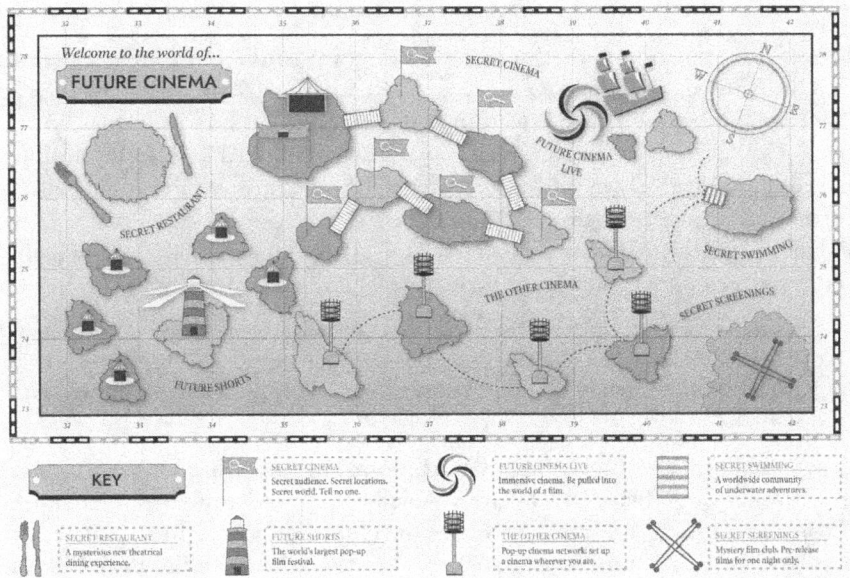

2.1 'Welcome to the world of Future Cinema'. A map created for Future Cinema in 2012 which shows a proliferation of sub-brands and experiences. At this point, Secret Cinema define themselves as a sub-brand under Future Cinema.

- Ephemerality to replicability (2009–2010), where there is a move away from one-off screenings
- Movements to markets (2011), where narratives of resistance and disruption are introduced through the creation of parallel, online, fictional worlds to augment engagement with the event, but which also act as key marketing and promotional tools; and
- Spatialisation to stratification (2012–2013), where the combined use of institutionalised spaces and narratives exerts control over the audience, while delivering highly stratified experiences bound up in class-based ideologies.

Festivals to financing (2006–2009)

This early period was characterised by the influence of music festival culture and aesthetics. The festivalisation of film screenings occurred explicitly with festivals used as screening sites (at the Glastonbury, Latitude and Wilderness festivals) and the aesthetics of the events themselves were visibly influenced by the dark cabaret and neo-burlesque roots of Glastonbury's Lost Vagueness.

Pre-Secret Cinema

Press accounts and SC themselves always point to the immersive screening of Gus Van Sant's *Paranoid Park* in December 2007 as the birth of SC.[2] That was indeed when the headline 'SC presents ...' was used for the first time. However, prior to this, there were earlier themed screenings and art-based events which evidenced elements of the now well-established SC format under the banners of Future Shorts (FS) and FC. There was a 'Pilton Palace' FS Electric Theatre installed at Glastonbury in 2005 – a marquee within which short films were screened. Then, Riggall reportedly:

> ... launched FC in 2005 as 'live cinema'; 1,000 people attended a screening of *Dreams Money Can Buy*, an experimental film from 1947. Riggall put on gypsy and flamenco bands; audio-visual group The Light Surgeons created an installation.[3]

A screening of *The Big Lebowski* at Bloomsbury bowling lanes took place in February 2006 before an FC tour which centralised a themed screening of *Nosferatu* (1922), launched at the seOne club, London in June 2006,[4] with further dates at Ashton Court mansion, Bristol and at the Edinburgh Festival. The post-experience promotional video for the seOne screening revealed that there were 'over one hundred performers, twenty installation artists and ten live bands', including various cabaret and burlesque performances. These early events reveal SC's origins and influences in festival culture, following the style of Glastonbury's Lost Vagueness. Riggall acknowledged:

> ... what I found about Glastonbury was this wonderful sense of mystery, of uncovering and discovering all of these secret fields, and finding yourself in a place, like Lost Vagueness with Roy Gurvitz. That scene really started off a lot of the immersive culture that we have today.[5]

In 2006–2007, a number of other events were held within heritage sites and exhibition environments under the FC banner. These were not centred on a feature film and are therefore not included in Appendix 1, but they are worthy of note here as their aesthetic influences and deployment of experimental art installation practices continued as a creative through-line into future experiences. These include the FC 'Dive In' at Tooting Bec Lido in July 2006, where short films were projected onto an inflatable screen augmented by swimmers in eccentric vintage costumes performing pool-side dance routines. 'Dream of Elephants' at Battersea Arts Centre (BAC) in September 2006 included a set of experimental, avant garde art installations and performances.[6] A Dresden Dolls performance at the Roundhouse in London in November 2006 was hosted by FC – this musical duo are lead proponents of the dark cabaret movement of the noughties, which fuses the aesthetics of German Weimar-era cabarets, burlesque and vaudeville with the goth and punk music scene. There was another gallery-based event at the Tate Britain in April 2007 – 'Late at Tate' – where short films were screened. These four early events were characterised and influenced by dark cabaret and neo-burlesque themes, practices and aesthetics, while also drawing from experimental art installation practices. These two lines of creative expression persisted in later experiences – the description of Dream of Elephants particularly resonates with approaches to multi-room experience design: the BAC was reportedly transformed '… into a dreamscape [...] with each room taking on an experience'.[7]

An FC Village was created for an outdoor festival in July 2006 in Greenwich Park, London in partnership with 'Studio Artois Live': FS claimed it to be the 'UK's first outdoor film festival' and it reportedly featured 'a cult or classic film, with all elements brought to life'.[8] Visual documentation shows costumed performers playing characters from the featured screenings of *Kill Bill: Vol. I* (2003) and *Ferris Bueller's Day Off* (1986). Music entertainment was provided by DJ Yoda (a renowned live cinema practitioner who has collaborated with many other live cinema producers since that time) and Guilty Pleasures – a 1980s tribute band. Although this was not branded as an SC event (and it was hosted by Stella Artois who had also delivered similar live cinema events at the time),[9] the post-experience promotional video clearly shows some key SC experiential aesthetic elements – the fusion of live music, film and carnival.

In November 2006 there was an FC event based around the science fiction film *The Matrix* (1999) at Mansion House, in Dublin, Ireland. Once again, Stella Artois were the headline sponsors. This event signalled a notable shift from the previous outdoor focus of the festival and open-air screenings; instead, an indoor site was adapted and 'dressed' to reflect both the thematics and narrative spaces of the film. Insight is available through an account provided by the event's artistic director, Margaret Krawecka, who describes the event as 'thematic performance installations [which] included a machine that transmitted audience members' brain activity on screen (in the form of short films!) as well as a pod-like "oculus" allowing shorts to be viewed in a more intimate setting, one person at a time'.[10] The event featured the famous video remixer Johnny Wilson – known as Eclectic Method[11] – a solo video remixer renowned for musical remixes of feature film content. Although some augmentations to the screening are clearly evidenced, the participatory elements that later became a key feature of SC are not fully delineated, although the available images show audience members embedded in the spaces of performance and installation – including footage of audience members attached to the 'brain-scanning' machines.[12]

A further live cinema event is then documented in November 2007 – *Metropolis* (1927) at Fabric nightclub, London. *Metropolis* is a film which has been subject to a number of live cinema treatments over the years by a number of different artists,[13] and it exemplifies the cinephiliac motivations of both the founder and his collaborators. In the post-experience promotional video, the ident featured the FC logo with the tag line 'The Cinematic Event Company'.[14] The augmentations evidenced include elements of VJing with live music and in-character costumed dancers and cabaret acts. The end credits reveal that these included 'Voodoo Vaudeville', a Lost Vagueness regular.

It is in these early examples of both outdoor and indoor events that the SC experiential format started to take shape. We can see in the *Metropolis* credit listing that the skillsets of the creative contributors are not too dissimilar from those employed in producing the 2018–2019 SC events.[15]

Secret Cinema

The formal launch of the SC brand took place on 16 December 2007 with a one-off preview screening of *Paranoid Park* (2007) at Shipwright Yard, a disused part of London Bridge.[16] This event inaugurated the 'official' birth of the long-standing and familiar format that we see continue until 2014 – a thematically appropriate location dressed and designed to reflect the *mise-en-scène* of the film, *and* (importantly) to establish the 'Secret' aesthetic and the 'Tell No One' branding. The title of the film was withheld from the audience until the start of the screening. This was in contrast to FC events, where the film title was always known to the audience beforehand. The screening was augmented through: performances by skateboarders and graffiti artists, and open fires, mirroring some of the film's key locations – an infamous skate park and a railway line. *Paranoid Park* had its theatrical release in the UK on 26 December 2007, so this can also be considered the first example of SC's 'event-led' distribution. The event also inaugurated the SC logo which featured at the start and end of the post-experience video.[17] In a press interview, Riggall laid out the ambitions of the organisation at its outset:

> It's not going to be just pre-releases. It's really going to be a mixture of strong pre-releases, thought-provoking animation and old, classic films. It is about showing films in a different environment as cinema-going has become so *formulaic* in my view.[18] (our emphasis)

Note the use of 'formulaic' here to describe cinema-going; in this promotional discourse Riggall positioned these events *against* what he identified as a problem in cinema-going practice that his endeavours would *fix*. We also see here this reference to an experience design strategy that includes intentionally thought-provoking material. This ambition to create experiences that invite critical engagement was repeated in a number of contexts. This positioning was in opposition to mainstream viewing practices and was continually repeated in Riggall's articulation of the events and SC's organisational values, but these values ultimately collided with the process of commodification and commercialisation that we see taking place for SC later on.

The second SC event was *Funny Face* (1957), at the Royal Academy of the Arts in London for one night in February 2008. The film stars Fred Astaire as fashion photographer Dick Avery, and Audrey Hepburn as Jo Stockton – his unlikely model with a 'funny face'. They both travel to Paris to launch a new brand at a fashion show – the location and staging of the SC event reflected this fashion show *mise-en-scène* along with costumed performers. As Riggall described:

> We've got a dance sequence performed by a really great dance organisation called Chameleon Collective. It's a dance inspired from the film, so it's taken from the idea of the film and we've created a five-minute sequence. It's a little bit like what you'd get before the features, the idea of giving a little vignette, a little performance ... We had a short film tonight ... and it was re-scored live, so we had a pianist play live to it.[19]

Common strategies that became consistently used in the post-experience video were established with *Funny Face*:[20] for example, the original graphic title from the source film is overlaid onto the SC video. The film's original title track or music from the soundtrack is used, as was always the case subsequently. As we shall see, the post-experience videos were consistently shaped and framed by the original text.

The third SC, *If ...* (1968), was screened in May 2008 at Dulwich College in London, an independent boarding school for boys. Whereas with *Paranoid Park* we can assume that the film determined the selection and dressing of the location, this is the first event where we have direct testimony that the *location came first* and the film was chosen to suit the potential of the site.[21] The setting was particularly appropriate (and required minimal adaptation) for an event based around the cult countercultural film which features a revolt within a boy's public boarding school.[22] The post-experience promotional video shows audiences holding instructional documents and participating in a moment of collective singing under instruction at the start of the screening; the song is unknown, but the context suggests it may well have been a hymn or school anthem.[23]

Music festivals: 2008–2012

The FC strand of activity included the use of established music festival venues with films selected which contain musical elements. The first of these was an augmented, live, re-scored screening of *Eraserhead* (1977) at the

2008 Latitude festival. *Eraserhead* is set in a desolate industrial landscape featuring vivid experimental imagery and a soundscape deemed appropriate for re-scoring. British indie rock band The Guillemots performed a new and improvised live 'score' accompanied by dancers from the Chameleon Collective.[24] Live re-scoring has continued to flourish across the live cinema sector,[25] but did not go on to form a significant element in the evolving formula at the heart of SC.

At the Latitude festival in 2009, there was an augmented screening of the comedy *Black Cat, White Cat* (1998) incorporating live music and a costumed procession set against the carnivalesque backdrop of the festival. The promotional materials describe this happening as 'The wedding of the festival featuring legendary 14-piece Gypsy orchestra Taraf de Haidouks'. This mirrored the film score itself which includes the music of director Emir Kusturica's own travelling gypsy band.

The Blues Brothers (1980) was screened at the Latitude festival in 2010. The promotional flyer describes this as an 'all singing, all dancing, live experience' featuring 'Kitty, Daisy and Lewis' (a rhythm'n'blues band), and an American police action vehicle drove around the festival site to promote the event. The narrative of the film describes a musical reunion tour that ends in a dramatic 'comeback' performance, which was the centrepiece of its staging here.

The last recorded association with a music festival was the Wilderness festival 'takeover' in August 2012. *Bugsy Malone* and *La Haine* were screened under the 'FC' banner with thematic augmented performances and re-enactments. The *La Haine* event included graffiti artists, BMXers and a live soundtrack by the Asian Dub Foundation (ADF). The festival also included 'secret swimming' – participants could enjoy a nude swim in the lake. These events represented the festival roots of SC and also highlight a persistent tension between the eccentric expression and chaos of festivals and the more formulaic promotional events associated with corporate brand partnerships.

Previews, premieres and branding

On 27 August 2008, an FC preview screening of the soon-to-be-released film *RockNRolla* (2008) was the second instance of 'event-led' distribution where a brand-new release would be previewed within the timeframe of its promotional campaign (as was the case with *Paranoid Park*). This British film is set in London's gangster underworld, and the seOne club venue was designed with a matching seedy, macho atmosphere that included the presence of scantily clad women. Actors engaged with audience members outside the venue, while action vehicles like those seen in the film drove past.[26] The post-experience promotional video shows director Guy Ritchie on stage introducing the screening,[27] suggesting that this was a more traditional and formal promotional 'launch' style of event which broke the fourth wall between the audience and the fictional staging. The sense of being fully embedded in the coherent world of the film was temporarily suspended by an engagement with a discourse about the film's production. This is an element of the experience which was not taken forward in later SC screenings, although the documentaries featured in the 'Secret Screenings' branch of activity that will be introduced shortly did also feature talks and introductions much more in keeping with the overall aesthetic of a promotional pre-release event.

A new major brand sponsor was evidenced in the next SC event, which was based around a screening of the Marx Brothers film *A Night at the Opera* (1935) in October 2008. It was presented 'In association with Nokia connecting people', which sees a notable transition from associations with music festivals and alcoholic brand sponsorships to corporate financing, and a distinct 'scaling up' of the production values and quality of the event. *A Night at the Opera* was held at the Hackney Empire where SC performers staged re-enactments to entertain the queues of people outside. It is the first instance of ticket price stratification occurring and, importantly, aligning prices to 'in-world' identities. At this event, Plebeians were priced at £10 and Partisans at £13.50. These identities were drawn from the class-based thematics of *A Night at the Opera*. This is also the first evidenced instance of the participatory elements of the event including explicit costume instructions, which become a prototypical and enduring staple of the SC events that followed. In this case, this is an example of the message received by ticket-holders:

> Lords and Ladies, Dukes and Duchesses, Partisans and Plebeians and the Claypool Foundation of Arts. Dress should be majestic and wondrous for this shall be an evening of wild, wild romance, honey song, long journeys, laughter and dance. Lords[,] fetch your top hats. Ladies[,] your most treasured frocks. Plebeians[,] caps and leather shoes if you can.[28]

The core participatory element of audience costume is now firmly established. The sponsorship partnership with Nokia continued in the four events that follow. This marked a significant turning point in the relationship between these immersive experiences and brand identity. Here Nokia's involvement was fairly standard – there was a promotional advert for the Nokia Capsule in the opening credits for the screening. This relationship with Nokia potentially disrupted the original sub-cultural ethos of the organisation as Nokia presented a different brand association dynamic to previous sponsors Stella Artois. Here the brand alignment worked very effectively for Nokia as an opportunity to relate their product identity with the sub-cultural vibrancy of these innovative forms of entertainment. The relationship with brands evolved significantly as the SC format developed, to include much more nuanced, narratively aligned branding – as we shall see in Chapter 4.

The first of two events centred around a screening of *Ghostbusters* (1984) took place in November 2008 – a two-sited simultaneous screening held at both the Royal Horticultural Hall in London and the Brighton Corn Exchange.[29] The identity of the film was withheld but instructions regarding costumes and props formed a key part of the participant communication. All of the guests who registered online received a cryptic email asking them to meet at a pre-arranged location. 'Bring a torch – it might be dark,' the email says. 'Dress code: 1980s loud and proud.' The film is based on the interactions between three eccentric scientists from New York, who set up the 'Ghostbusters' to save the city from imminent paranormal destruction. The augmentation outside the London venue included a New York taxi and police officers 'performing' and, importantly, *controlling* the audiences. The identity of the film was finally revealed as performers dressed up as the Ghostbusters arrived in their notorious car. Inside the venue, augmentation included a live-on-screen show that preceded the screening.

An SC screening of *Anvil! The Story of Anvil* (2008) took place in February 2009 at the Shepherd's Bush Empire. This was the official British premiere of the film, which tells the story of a Canadian heavy metal band who released a highly influential album in 1982 (that was said to inspire the likes of Anthrax and Metallica), before subsequently falling into obscurity. Ticket holders were instructed to arrive at the screening dressed up as rockers and metal heads. After the screening, the band 'metal on metal' played before Scott Ian from Anthrax (who also appears as an interviewee in the film) took to the stage. The marriage of music, performance and cinema at the heart of SC events was once again instantiated.

A further FC exclusive preview event was held in March 2009 for *Watchmen* (2009) – a dystopian superhero-genre film set in an alternate 1985.[30] This was the third event to be hosted at the seOne Club and, as with *RockNRolla*, the road outside the venue was used as a performance space for vehicles, including a tank. There was a far more elaborate, performative staging of events around the film including a dramatic protest sequence and the arrival of a blue-skinned Dr Manhattan. This was the third in the 'event-led' distribution strand, and the staging and set-dressing conventions appear to have advanced significantly, undoubtedly enabled by sponsorship support from 'Smirnoff Original Nights' and Nokia. Inside the venue (which again was an exceptionally seedy, hyper-masculine environment with semi-nude women performers present), there was a re-creation of the film's 'Gunga' diner, a dance floor and live band. The screening was introduced by Dave Gibbons, the illustrator of the *Watchmen* graphic novel, again breaking the fourth wall between the fictional text and the event. This once again had the feeling of a standard (but highly augmented) 'promotional' event. Gibbons captured the essence of the event on the post-experience video,[31] where he stated 'it's like walking into some amazing, fragmented restructuring of the whole movie that I've been seeing; it's fantastic, it adds so much to the experience'.

Secret Screenings, 2009–2012

In May 2009, a new sub-brand emerged: 'Secret Screenings'. The first of the three titles to be released under this banner was an exclusive preview of *Sounds Like Teen Spirit?* (2008), a British documentary centred on the junior version of the annual Eurovision Song Contest, which was simultaneously screened in venues in London, Brighton and Edinburgh with the film's director speaking in person in London. Secret Screenings were described as 'a new monthly film club ... bringing back mystery films to the UK for one night only ... to bring back a sense of community, discovery and collective experience to cinema, giving audiences access to incredible unseen films combined with one of a kind unforgettable experiences'.[32]

The second title in this strand was a premiere screening of *Searching for Sugar Man* (2012) in July 2012 at the Troxy (the significance of this particular venue in SC's evolution will be explained in 'From ephemerality to replicability' below). This is a documentary film which traces the efforts of two South African music fans to uncover the mysterious disappearance of early 1970s American musician Sixto Rodriguez. The Troxy was dressed to look like a small record fair leading into a South African stadium. Audiences were unaware of the film's identity but given the dress code 'Motown ... Springbok ... 90s arena ... Newport Folk Festival 1975 ... Vinyl Junkie ... Jo-burg beachwear' and asked to 'bring one secret record or Mix Tape to give to a stranger'. After the screening, the subject of the documentary, Rodriguez, took to the stage (the screen lifted to reveal his presence) for a surprise full set. The night concluded with a talk from director Malik Bendjelloul.

The third and final Secret Screening was held in August 2012 – a pre-release preview of *The Imposter* (2012) at Conway Hall, London. The film tells the story of Frederic Bourdin, a con artist who seemingly tricked a Texas family into believing he was a relative who had disappeared years earlier. The film includes interviews with Bourdin and members of the missing boy's family, as well as archive television news footage and re-enacted dramatic sequences. Before the screening, audience members were emailed a court summons and received prison-related links and hints. The screening venue was transformed into a courtroom with actors playing barristers, court clerks and police officers and the audience serving as jury (separated into 'truth' and 'fiction', decided by casting a vote earlier in the event). After the screening, there was a Q&A with director Bart Layton, and private investigator Charlie Parker who features in the film. All three of the Secret Screenings were documentaries, making this an interesting application of the SC format as it added a fiction/fact cross-over in the augmentation of the screening. One of the distinctive features of these Secret Screenings was that they all featured the live guest appearance of someone associated with the film; this was a short-lived 'branch' of activity within the SC slate.

Carnivals, funfairs and phones

In June 2009, an SC screening of *The Harder They Come* (1972), the first Jamaican feature film, made famous by its reggae soundtrack, took place at the Coronet cinema at Elephant and Castle in London. The host welcomed the guests to 'the Rialto Theatre, Kingston, Jamaica'. There was singing, dancing and themed food outside in a carnival-/festival-like atmosphere, with pre- and post-screening band performances. In the same month there was an 'FC Presents' premiere of *All Tomorrow's Parties* (2009) at the Edinburgh Picturehouse. Dancing girls and donkeys entertained the queue outside, a traditional ice cream stand was provided and the band Mogwai gave a live performance.[33]

In September 2009 *The Warriors* (1979), sponsored by Absolut Vodka, was set in a park with a funfair in London Fields. This was the first event to mention a charity in its promotional materials: the video states that it was made in association with Fairbridge, an organisation supporting inner city youth. The film's narrative centres around the street gangs in New York city. When charismatic gang leader Cyrus (Roger Hill) is killed, the gang known as the Warriors are falsely accused and forced to fight their way home while every other gang is hunting them down. This was the first SC title where there is an explicit narrative that includes factions or oppositional groupings. It also indicated a continued predominance of films with masculine themes that were further extrapolated into the elements of experience design.[34] These thematic elements lent themselves to the evolving SC format, a propensity for separating participants into distinct gangs or groups. Within this evolving experiential device we shall see how the establishment of these 'neo-tribes' and/or 'experience communities' operated in distinct ways to structure the participation and involvement in the experience in later productions.[35] The post-experience promotional video was the first to mix in clips from the original film and is a hybrid between factual and fictional storytelling techniques – vox pops of audience reactions are included.[36] The video also shows a re-enactment from the SC pre-show in which Cyrus addressed the crowds before he was shot; this was followed by the corresponding clip from the film.

What followed was a highly significant event – the first screening since *Paranoid Park* to return to the use of a disused and repurposed indoor venue. This was a one-off screening of *Alien* (1979) in October 2009, in a disused warehouse in Shoreditch, London. All intervening screenings had been held in established music, theatre or cinema auditorium venues, or else in outdoor festival locales. The screening also initiated a new and sustained partnership with Windows Phone, which extended across all SC productions in 2010, signalling a further step up in production values and marking the completion of the ongoing shift that characterised this period – from festivals to financing. One of SC's creative producers explained the motivation for this brand alliance, stating it is 'the first major partner with SC because [Windows Phone] saw the innovation'.[37]

The science fiction classic starring Sigourney Weaver is set aboard the *Nostromo* spaceship and SC event participants were required to dress in *Nostromo*-branded white overalls (see Figure 2.2). The approaches taken in the management of audience behaviour and movement through the venue signified the continued emergence of a controlling aesthetic, where crowd control is an embedded aspect of the experience while also being an increasing requirement as venues and participant numbers expanded. In the post-experience promotional video audience members can be seen being bellowed at through megaphones and pushed through 'check points' and various different spaces.[38] There was a notable increase in staging and set design for this experience with vehicles, special effects, stage lighting and dry ice present. 'Tweeting' was actively encouraged as part of the experience, as evidenced by a prominently displayed screen. This appears to be the first visual evidence of the embedding of a brand into the narrative of the experience (see Figure 2.3), and a shift away from the much more conventional use of graphic idents at the start of the film. Interestingly, images of the tweet board reveal that, at this stage at least, the 'audience chatter' was neither in-character nor wholly positive. It featured 'out-of-world' and 'out-of-character' comments from the audience about the poor audio quality of the film.

The key elements of the established SC formula which emerged in this 'festivals to financing' period were embedded branding, audience flow control, grouping and gang allocation, and audience costuming.

From ephemerality to replicability (2009–2010)

This next period was shaped by repeated screenings that extended from one-off, one-night events, and the start of a long-standing relationship between SC and one particular venue – the Troxy in Stepney, London, at which SC have hosted at least fourteen events. The Troxy is a Grade II-listed art deco

2.2 Costumed audience members at Secret Cinema's *Alien* production. Audiences become increasingly embedded in the narrative world.

music venue, originally built as a cinema in 1933 and converted to a live events space in 2006, with an audience capacity of 3,100. It was in this venue across two nights in November 2009 that *Bugsy Malone* (1976) was screened. The film is a musical spoof of old gangster movies, with a cast consisting entirely of children who brandish toy guns that fire whipped cream instead of machine guns and bullets. As audience members queued to enter, 1920s vehicles drove about them outside, before they were guided through an entrance hidden in a book-shelf. Again, a wall of live tweets was displayed, entitled 'Locomotion by Windows Phone'. We see curated and themed food becoming a feature (see Figure 2.4) and also the first evidence of the live augmentation and copying of on-screen action, which in this case included the live performance of a song simultaneously with the film (see Figure 2.5). These have come to be referred to as 'mirror moments' by SC and went on to be a characteristic and unique staple of their experience design and brand. These 'mirror moments' can be understood as a cinephilic practice which extends *audience* behaviours such as quote-along, sing-along and act-along, as inaugurated in the *The Rocky Horror Picture Show* (1975) tradition.[39]

2.3 A branded screen installation at Secret Cinema's *Alien* production sponsored by Windows Phone. This indicates active, encouraged use of mobile phones and social media (the use of mobile phones was later banned at all Secret Cinema events).

The *Bugsy Malone* post-experience promotional video was the first not to include audience-reaction vox pops,[40] and the narrative sequencing aligned more coherently with the original story of the film. Up to this point, all videos had been presented in a documentary/talking heads format, focussed on the audiences' journey and experience as opposed to the story and plot of the film. The 'showcase' element in this genre was the secrecy of the event and the novelty of the locations. Audiences were first asked to guess the identity of the film that they were about to see. For example, outside the *If …* event, audience responses included 'St Trinians', *Dead Poets Society* and 'Harry Potter'. For *Anvil* (a lesser-known new release), the audiences, all dressed as rockers, guessed *Spinal Tap*. Audiences were then asked to say what film they would like to see and in what location; responses included 'Indiana Jones at London Zoo' and 'Dr Strangelove in a nuclear bunker outside Rotherham'. At the end of each video, reaction shots were shown of audiences giving their immediate and emotional responses to the film. In many cases the interviewing, in-world 'reporter' was seen on screen

2.4 Menu for the *Bugsy Malone* experience. Food is specifically curated to fit the themes of the film by Bompas & Parr – who have gone on to become leading providers of hospitality in the experiential dining sector.

asking the questions with a mic flag denoting their (fictional) news channel. The showcase element of the post-experience promotional video for *Bugsy Malone* shifted from the celebration of secrecy which was foregrounded in previous videos, to displaying the visual and aesthetic qualities of the event and their textual and *textural* proximity to the original film texts.

The next SC event was *Wings of Desire* (1987), screened at the Pavilion, London across two nights in February 2010. Megaphones were used here (and in many subsequent experiences) to guide and marshal the audience. There were circus performances on stage including knife throwers and trapeze artists, which related to the themes of the film, in which one protagonist, Damiel (played by Bruno Ganz), falls in love with lonely trapeze artist Marion (Solveig Dommartin). In this experience we see the combination of the burlesque and the carnivalesque re-appear. The screening included the choreographed mirroring of on-screen action, with an aerial trapeze artist following the actions of an on-screen counterpart.

At the next SC production, *Blade Runner* (1982), another location was repurposed, this time a 23-acre site in Canary Wharf, London, to create an

2.5 A *Bugsy Malone* mirror moment. One of the first instances of simultaneous on-stage action augmenting the scenes on screen. Here we see the finale, 'You give a little love', being performed on stage as it is watched on the screen.

expanded internal and external world of Scott's cyberpunk vision of the future. Running for five nights in June 2010, this production exemplified the approach taken during the 'ephemerality to replicability' period, and also inaugurated some further key features of the SC format. These include pre-attendance preparatory instructions and pre-screening narrative engagement. Preparatory 'in-world' instructions were given to ticket holders via the SC Facebook page:

> Utopia Skyways welcomes A6006 Travellers to the final day of flights. Over 6000 adventurous travellers have now flown Utopia for the chance to begin again ... Please keep your goggles on and bring local currency. Please report back if you see anything unusual in your travels. Good Luck ...

Attendees were picked up by coaches at the railway station – and we start to see a recurring experience-design feature, a designed journey through the site and the spatialisation of the narrative, along with an increase in the use of techniques to marshal the participants along this journey. The spatialised narrative elements that related to the film now included an increased number of performed 'scenarios' and 'enactments'. These shifted significantly from spectacle-based adaptations of the film narrative or film environment to opportunities for direct participant engagement. These were not always

2.6 Secret Cinema audience member being subjected to a 'Voight-Kampff' test as part of the pre-screening engagement for *Blade Runner*, based on sequences from the film.

available to all but were now a distinct element of the experience design. Figure 2.6 above shows a participant being taken through the 'Voight-Kampff' test that features as a key element in the film (a test that separates 'real' from 'replicant' humans).

Despite the overarching shift to repeatability and replicability that defined this period, one-off events still continued to be staged. In January there was a charity screening of *Precious* (2009) at the Rio Cinema, Dalston in aid of Fairbridge. The screening featured performances from music artists Speech Debelle, Bridgette Amofah and Stephanie Thomas. *Blow Up* (1966) was screened in New York in June – the first evidence we have of SC activity in the USA. This cult film, which centres upon the story of a London-based mod photographer who discovers he may have inadvertently captured a murder on film, was screened within a photographic studio, Shangri La Studios, Brooklyn. This appears to have been a combined promotional event for Cheap Jack's Vintage Clothing, NYC. In July, there was an FC screening of *Blue Velvet* (1986) at the Troxy,[41] as a tribute to the life and work of Dennis Hopper.

More elaborate and detailed reproduction of the sets of the films continued to evolve to support increasingly complex narrative spatialisation and opportunities for participation within these spaces. *Lawrence of Arabia* (1962) was screened for three nights in September 2010 at the Alexandra Palace – a sporting and event venue in London with a capacity of more than 10,000. The film's narrative centres on British Lieutenant T.E. Lawrence (played by Peter O'Toole) as he rebels against the orders of his superior officer and strikes out on a perilous camel journey across the Arabian desert to attack a Turkish port. Live animals formed part of the elaborate SC set-dressing with horses and a camel present. Audience members were shouted at by soldiers as they entered the venue and instructed to complete 'camel corps' recruitment forms. Sepia-tinted images appeared on social media showing costumed audience members posing with their recruitment documentation, which invoked theme park tourist opportunities simulating a transportation to a different and more exotic place. The presence of military or militaristic personnel became a key device in this and later screenings, as mechanisms through which to choreograph audience movements throughout the space. These have been aligned and reinforced through a preference for films with themes of conflict and warring or competing factions, as we saw earlier in the *Warriors* example. A Windows Phone telephone exchange was installed as a key focal point for participants to log and register their attendance using hashtags in an embedded narrative strategy. The set design of the phone switchboard was designed to blend in to the *mise-en-scène* (see Figure 2.7).

There was also a pre-film, first-look, teaser trailer for the Windows Phone 7 which appears to have been directly inspired by the SC screening of *Laurence of Arabia*. The trailer was shown exclusively to this SC audience and included the strap line The Revolution is Coming. It combines a hybrid East-meets-West soundscape with a jarring clash between an arid, timeless, pre-modern topography and a digital consumer product – the phone was seen slowly emerging through the heat shimmer of a desert landscape.[42]

Chicago Daily Courier newspapers were printed and distributed to the audience as part of the experience. There was themed food on offer, and belly dancers, pipers and music. A significant re-enactment of scenes from the film preceded the screening before audience members settled on picnic blankets and cushions in the expansive viewing space.

Thematics of control and coercion continued to resonate within the narrative of the next film – *One Flew Over the Cuckoo's Nest* (1975) – an event held in November 2010. The film's protagonist Randle Patrick McMurphy (Jack Nicholson) finds himself under the abusive care of Nurse Ratched (Louise Fletcher) in a psychiatric ward represented as featuring

2.7 An interactive installation at Secret Cinema's *Lawrence of Arabia* experience sponsored by Windows Phone. The wooden cabinet set-design situates the digital installation in the film's historic space.

highly problematic practices and treatments. Audience members were instructed to meet at Ladbroke Grove Tube Station before being guided to Princess Louise Hospital, Kensington in London. They were given white robes to wear while queueing outside the set-dressed 'Oregon State Hospital'. Pre-assigned characteristics, personas, costume and preparatory instructions started to become the norm within SC experience design. Ticket holders were sent emails with prompts and a link to 'learn a song' which took them to the lyrics of Simon and Garfunkel's 'Sound of Silence'. Participants who followed this instruction were invited to perform this song as a key element of the performance at the event itself. This initiated the 'participant as performer' device which became an increasingly crucial element within the overall SC experience design. The inclusion of this opportunity for participant performance reinforced the value of compliance with the preparatory instructions – they achieve the frisson of an additional experiential pleasure. Here also, these 'singing' participants became extras in the performance community, part of and embedded within the experience. Embedded brand engagement continued – the entrance featured a screen entitled the 'Patient's Log Book', sponsored by Windows Phone as 'Benefactors of Oregon State Hospital', which collated and projected audience tweets.

This is the first screening which we have identified that included a highly elaborate multi-space staging. A lead performance designer for SC described the specific complexities of multi-sited production design and the extensive team required to design and populate the space:

> When we came to recce the Princess Louise Hospital, we walked around it and there were so many individual rooms. There's no way that this would work or would even be interesting to have 20 hospital rooms the same …
>
> We had what we called the dream ward, which is where we brought in the first installation artist or students who were going through this more performance art and design installation practice to work with people. For example, [we worked] with mental health professionals to explore different symptoms or stories or historical things in different areas. Each room would tell a story or add to your understanding of the piece and its time.
>
> We had another ward that was dedicated to science. We worked with Guerrilla Science, who are an art/science crossover company and they helped us to be in touch with artists and scientists who were looking at the impact of the film in terms of mental healthcare. We would have different wards and different characters and different doctors representing the different approaches at the time and also approaches now. It was all within a theatrical context.[43]

Alien (1979) was screened for the second time in December 2010 as 'FC launches in Berlin', at an old transformer building. It appears that the same format was rolled out as had previously been seen in the UK: all participants were given white overalls and shouted at by the performers through megaphones 'to obey the commands of your commanding officers'. The participants evidenced a different response in this location:

> Suddenly we were with an audience who had never done this before. It was incredible the difference because they would stand back in the way of performers. They'd be like, 'Is this a performer? Is this not a performer?' They would be trying to give space to everything or taking pictures.[44]

These reflections on this experience of executing the format in Berlin shows the extent to which the experience design had become accepted as normal by audiences in the UK. This reflects the extent to which SC and other pioneers in this field were building a committed 'repeat' audience who were by now very familiar with the norms and demands of these experiences – which is a key characteristic of this period, shaped by the binary tension of ephemerality to replicability. During this phase, the following elements of the formula were introduced: the pre-narrative experience; the curation of food; mirror moments; audience transportation; newspaper creation; the tourist picture opportunity; further control of audience movement; and the audience participating as performers while embedded branding and audience costuming – established in the previous period – became even more prominent.

From movements to markets (2011)

This next period was characterised by the further expansion of the filmic text by drawing the audiences into narratives of resistance and disruption through the creation of parallel, online, fictional worlds that were associated with the main themes of the film. Additional, flash mob-style happenings began to occur in the lead-up to the main SC event.[45] These promotional events were seemingly impromptu staged performances in public spaces involving in-character performers from the narrative world of the film. The flash mob is a hyper-temporary format that is designed to disrupt, confuse and intrigue the audience, as well as to market the experience and to generate ticket sales. The flash mob was originally a countercultural practice but has become increasingly commodified and has featured as a key promotional strategy within a number of brand activations.[46] The year 2011 was a particular turning point in the more widespread and commercial use of the flash mob aesthetic.[47]

These strategies were keenly illustrated by the first SC showing of this period – *The Red Shoes* (1948), which included staged physical events and a dedicated, fictionalised microsite (www.unknownculturemovement.org). Participants were encouraged to visit a dedicated Facebook site which then became a place of fervent speculation about what the film would be, thereby extending awareness of the event to new potential audience members. The first gathering of the 'Unknown Culture Movement' was held in February 2011 in Covent Garden, London. A group of 'in-the-know' audience members – ticket holders who had been invited to participate via the 'in-world' communications on Facebook – staged a public protest. They carried with them 'freedom to create' banners, which relate to an extraneous connection to the film's central theme – a performer's conflict between their art and their personal life. The film's central protagonist is Vicky Page (Moira Shearer), an aspiring ballerina torn between her dedication to dance and her desire to love. Commenting on this theme, director Michael Powell stated that the film is 'about dying for art, that art is worth dying for'. Images then quickly appeared on social media (see Figure 2.8) illustrating the flash mob's function as a key marketing tool.

For the screening, the key locales in the film – Covent Garden and the Royal Opera House – were recreated in the Tobacco Docks, London, throughout the February 2011 run. The event included collaborations with the Cloud Dance Festival and Diciembre Dance Group, and elaborate set reconstructions, including the costume and make-up departments, Boris Lermontov's office, Vicky Page's dressing room and a set workshop filled with actors who put on improvised performances, while dancers performed on stages and from silks and trapezes. Audiences could take part in activities like trying on shoes in the Covent Garden piazza, joining a ballet class, auditioning a song, undergoing a 1940s makeover and black-and-white photoshoot and playing jump rope with actors. Reflecting on this particular production, an SC creative director commented on how:

> Secret Cinema grew entirely out of Facebook ... it was used as a constant call to arms, because it was very much the idea that by getting people to engage on social media or getting people to do something, they felt an attachment to it.[48]

The post-experience promotional video for *The Red Shoes* marked a stylistic turning point with a bolder mixing of sound from the original film and a voice-over of a speech.[49] The video was colour-graded (to match the film's colour reproduction) and stylistically edited, combining the experiential essence of the SC event with the original film's style. The final screen of the video stated 'Join Us – secretcinema.org' and for the first time established SC as a movement or resistance organisation to 'join'. The 'call to action' that appears on the final frame of SC videos has evolved over time, from 'Register ...' (in 2008) to 'Sign up at' (in 2009–2011). These were all calls to action, but required different kinds of action, reflecting the evolution of the diverse experiences on offer and an increasing rhetoric of immersiveness.

The social movement theme that was inaugurated here went on to become a key aspect of the audience participation and narrativisation in future experiences and a central facet of the pre-event narrative engagement. This formulation of belonging to a social movement evolved alongside the distinct faction identities provided in the earlier examples where participants were invited to align together as an entire community in opposition to an external threat or issue.

High-end cultural and media partnerships also became a feature within this period, in contrast to the previous underground social movement strategy and the aesthetics of protest, thus characterising the 'movements to markets' binary tension. This could be seen in the screening of *Diva* (1981) in February 2011 at the London Coliseum in partnership with English National Opera. The film is a cult classic based on a young postman, Jules (played by Frederic Andrei), who becomes entranced with the voice of American diva Cynthia Hawkins (Wilhelmenia Wiggins Fernandez). Scenes were acted out in the stairwell of the opera house, and in the royal box before an onstage operatic performance by Elizabeth Llewellyn in the role of Cynthia Hawkins. Before the event, audience members were encouraged to tweet using #julesestou and #ouestjules if they spotted the character of Jules on his red moped around London – again embedding social media promotional opportunities in the design of the experience.

Militarised control tactics continued as a key tenet of this period. Film texts that enable passive and compliant audience subjectivities continued to emerge. For SC's *The Battle of Algiers* (1966) in April and May 2011 at the Old Vic tunnels under Waterloo Station, London audiences were requested to wear late-1950s suits, shades and scarves and instructed to bring their assigned identity cards. As a journalist explained:

> ... we received e-mails a week or so before, addressed to 'citizens' from the 'state'. We were told to fill out our census paper and 'Remain strong. Remain united.' As the event drew closer, further clues about the film were drip-fed through cryptic quotes and links on Facebook and Twitter (such as, 'Are you ready citizens?') Organisers also linked to Radio Noir, an online radio station playing nostalgic 1950s tunes, created especially for this event.[50]

This is the first event that is reported to have included the creation of a fictional news channel, a feature that went on to be a regular pre-narrative staple of SC screenings.

On arrival in the tunnels where *The Battle of Algiers* would be shown, audience members were herded into queues to be 'inspected' by French soldiers. They were then allowed to roam re-creations of a mosque, a prison, an interrogation zone, an airline office, a coffee bar and a dance hall with live music, all populated with actors interacting with them and re-creating scenes exclusively in French.

The post-experience promotional video depicts an extensive pre-screen narrative engagement, the most extensive seen so far.[51] It culminated in the dramatic and elaborate detonation of a bomb. This is another key element which was starting to emerge and crystallise in the SC experience design: now, almost always, there was a big-spectacle showcase – a climactic moment at which all audience members were gathered together, in what has come to be referred to by immersive experience practitioners as the 'hero moment'. The hero moment precedes the screening and is immediately followed by the audience's movement towards the seated screening area. In this instance, everyone was guided to an underground room to watch the film. They were marshalled as a quiet, submissive and passive mass. A new imperative also emerged here – and that is to link and contextualise the screening to external socio-political events. As Riggall explained:

> We did *Battle of Algiers* because the Arab Spring was happening, we found the venue in the Old Vic Tunnels, and it felt very close to the Kazbah and to the mood and the feel of the claustrophobia of living in the Kazbah in Algeria.[52]

The video was the first to be made completely in the style of the original film, shot in black and white and explicitly drawing from the film's narrative sequencing, with its own self-contained narrative arc of a bomb being built, concealed, planted and detonated in the film and in the event's climactic (or hero) moment. There was a huge explosion, the lights went out, torches flashed, the audience panicked and a body was carried through. It is edited in the style of a film trailer, fast paced, with frequent cuts. It also included English subtitles, as the performers were speaking in French. It used the theme music by Ennio Morricone while mixing in audio from the original film. At an initial glance, it is difficult to distinguish this derivative text from its original reference – such is the fidelity to the stylistic conventions employed. This is clearly evidenced in an interview with Steve Savale, the guitarist from ADF, who referred to seeing the video as if it was the real film:[53] 'He showed me clips from the experience and I was blown away; I thought it was part of the film, I thought the re-creation was so incredible – the fact that this was just members of the audience!'

In tandem with key indoor aesthetics starting to emerge in SC events, new outdoor aesthetics also developed in FC-branded events. This can be seen in the screenings of *The Lost Boys* (1987) and *Top Gun* (1986), which were shown in partnership with California Tourism on two consecutive nights in September 2011 at the same external screening site in Canary Wharf, London.

For *Lost Boys*, the location underwent a complete transformation into a Californian beach and Santa Carla pier, using seventy-nine tonnes of sand. The film tells the story of two teenage brothers, Michael (played by Jason Patric) and Sam (Corey Haim), who move with their mother (Dianne Wiest) to a small Californian town and become entangled within the exploits of a gang of vampires. Riggall outlines the game-like structure:

> we created five different gangs – Frog Brothers, vampires, etc. and the audience joined each different gang and on Facebook recreated their profile picture to match who they were following. So the idea is that they started exploring the narrative of the film online and it really did create a big engagement, and from a marketing point of view, it helped us sell 8,000 tickets in three weeks.[54]

A clear link is made here between the pre-event narrative engagement and event promotion and its impact upon audience growth, with events expanding in scale and audience numbers. This is key to the 'movements to markets' moment.

Once inside the venue, participants could play beach sports, dance, take fairground rides and eat California-themed food and drinks. The spatialisation of the narrative also included a re-creation of Grandpa's Lodge featuring live taxidermy. There were horses for audiences to ride and SC worked with a boat company, so that audiences could sail and windsurf as part of the event. Enlisting the audience in a common cause continued as a trope and here served to further unite the audience in acts of collective participation. At the start of the screening the audience engaged in a 'sing-along' to the film's title track 'Cry Little Sister' with performers dressed up as characters from the film. This was a non-diegetic engagement, distinct from the way in which future screenings embedded the engagement within the film's narrative world. Here the sing-along was 'branded' by the 'Lucky Voice Home Karaoke presents ...' banner that appeared on the screen as this activity unfolded. Another newspaper was created and distributed at the event, and we see the presence of another Twitter wall, allowing the participants to see each other's immediate responses to the experience as it unfolded.

On the following night, at the same location, *Top Gun* (1986) was screened. The film follows fighter pilot Maverick (Tom Cruise) who joins the Top Gun Naval Fighter Weapons School, where he falls in love with his flight instructor Charlotte Blackwood (Kelly McGillis). Before the event, audience members could sign up to a squadron on Facebook and be assigned a new identity, then, dressed in US Air Force jumpsuits, be welcomed into the venue by a billboard which stated 'You are entering Fightertown USA. All Personnel are subject to a search – use of deadly force authorised.' Audience control techniques continued with everyone treated as if in a training camp like the one depicted in the film. Just before the screening an announcement 'congratulations – you are all top guns' provoked cheering and celebrations which led to another sing-along to 'You've lost that lovin' feeling'. After the film was screened, the words 'Join us' were projected in a militaristic font. One of the creative producers recounted their experience of this event:

> One of the great problems with Secret Cinema was always that because of funding, because of trying to make things work, they would always get to a point where suddenly the money just ran out. For *Top Gun* in Canary Wharf, they'd forgotten to order enough toilets for an audience of 5,000. They'd ordered 10 toilets and suddenly they only have 25 actors for 5,000 people because they've had to cut things. I was one of the actors and helping the director – he was like 'manage that queue' and you're suddenly like 'well, what do I do?' I was dressed like a Navy sailor and I was like OK we're going to do military exercises, press ups! and you're desperately trying to think of anything to do.[55]

This account reveals three key insights: the experimental and emergent nature of these productions; the origins of recurring experiential devices such as enforced exercise regimes to occupy and control audiences; and the exposure of performers who were left on the front line to deal with the impacts of organisational mismanagement (we will examine how performance practices and techniques have evolved over time in Chapter 5).

The increasingly formulaic nature of the SC experience was made manifest in these two consecutive screenings of different films, where the base location and some of the set dressing remained the same, as did the temporal structuring of activities and experiential aspects such as the pre-screening sing-along, while the narrative elements were re-purposed to fit the themes and story of the specific film, further leading towards a model of expansion and repeat screenings.

That year, 2011, concluded with a brand-based marketing event to launch Windows Phone 7.5. It included characters from *Ghostbusters* and a screening of the film in a fictionalised 'Hotel 7.5' location in Berlin in collaboration with a German agency.[56] This brand partnership further invoked the characteristic tension of this period between markets and movements – where audiences were hailed to 'join' the movement and drawn into behaviours of resistance and rebellion, whilst simultaneously being engaged in commercial exchanges via 'in-world' social media promotions.

In this period, we see the following aspects of the formula emerge: the explicit alignment of the events with political movements and causes; the introduction of the pre-screening hero moment; and the routine creation of in-world, fictional, news channels.

The Other Cinema – 2012

Brief Encounter (1945) launched The Other Cinema brand identity in February, 2012 at the Troxy. It was also screened in Edinburgh, Leeds, Birmingham and Norwich simultaneously. The Other Cinema event website encouraged participants to:

> set up your own cinema wherever you are [and to] be part of a global network of pop up cinemas and bring back a sense of community, passion and shared experience to cinema.[57]

This was the first of only two of the SC portfolio to be released under this branding and the format appears to be an immersion in the context of viewing cinema in this period, as opposed to immersion in the film's narrative world itself. *Brief Encounter* centres on Laura, a married woman with children, whose conventional life becomes increasingly complicated following a chance meeting at a railway station with a married stranger. Audience members were asked to dress in black tie and carry a flower for a lover or a stranger. They were welcomed onto a red carpet by actors and usherettes and led in a sing-along to 'Maybe It's Because I'm a Londoner'. Audience members could swing dance, interact with actors and explore re-creation of a 1940s club environment, and listen to a live band. Before the screening there was a talk by Margaret Barton, one of the film's stars. Like the Secret Screening format and the earlier FC preview events, The Other Cinema involved breaking the fourth wall between the fictional world of the film and its production context, and instead provided an enhanced and thematised cinema-going experience. In the post-experience video,[58] there is a playful interaction between the film's original dialogue and the screening event – Alec (played by Trevor Howard) is heard asking 'are you going to the pictures this afternoon?' to which Laura replies 'yes' and Alec rejoins with 'extraordinary, so am I'. This serves as a self-reflexive meta-commentary – the black and white video, edited to a jazz soundtrack, shows audiences arriving at the cinema and later enjoying a dance. It is the quality and value of the audience viewing experience that is clearly being showcased within this video.

The second Other Cinema event constituted a politically motivated set of simultaneous screenings of *La Haine* (1995) in response to the London riots of 2012. Screenings took place in the UK, Paris and other international locations in May 2012,[59] one at the Broadwater Farm Community Centre in Tottenham. The cult film, set in Paris, follows three young men in the French suburbs the day after a violent riot. In London, it was screened the night before the London mayoral election with the aim of reopening debate about the causes of the London riots; in Paris, the screening took place just before the second round of the French presidential election. This signalled a further tendency of the organisation to align film screenings with significant social or political happenings or issues of the moment. The London screening was accompanied by live scoring by ADF as well as showcases by local musicians (including journalist, poet and rapper Akala) and three young film makers from the estate. There was some live-action augmentation of the screening – including a cow roaming the estate, young artists sketching and live poetry. ADF have gone on to tour their live soundtrack version of this film extensively.

From spatialisation to stratification (2012–2013)

The evolution and sophistication of narrative spatialisation emerged strongly in this period – where the pre-screening experience was designed over an ever-expanding and increasingly complex replication of the film's location, story and plot. In the first example, the production was sited across a number of storeys within a building (for *The Third Man*) and, in the last example, the experience took place across a number of buildings and transit vehicles (*The*

Shawshank Redemption). These films both included explicitly institutional and militarised themes which were drawn upon in the experiential design where audience members were strictly organised and tightly controlled. These complex experience environments also led to an expansion of temporal engagement, so that the participants spent much longer in the space of the narrative prior to the actual screening. In the showing of *The Shawshank Redemption* some audience members could even spend the night in the venue.

Characterised by a tension between the spaces becoming more expansive, enabling participants to move freely within them, and increasing control of movement through the spaces due to the growth in audience size, this period also saw both the stratification of ticket pricing and the experience becoming more pronounced, as we shall see in some of the following examples.

From December 2011 to January 2012, *The Third Man* (1949) reimagined the film's location in post-war Vienna, Austria as a four-storey version in the Farmiloe Building, Farringdon, London.[60] This was the longest SC run up to this point. Once a ticket had been purchased, and close to the time of the event, the primary ticket holder was sent an 'in-world' message resembling a 1920s wireless communication with instructions where to sign up. As a ticket holder, they were then always addressed in a fictional register. All audience members were given new identities and instructed to bring toys, books and unwanted clothing for the hospital, to be traded in the fictionalised 'black market' (these were then donated to charity after the event). Aesthetics of coercion continued as performers dressed as soldiers outside the venue organised and directed the audiences. After being led by the soldiers through a 'clue-ridden journey through the back streets of the Barbican', audience members were taken to an 'International Zone' with a jazz club, a police station, a penicillin lab, a hotel and the Mozart Café, and allowed to explore and interact with actors playing characters based around the film. It also included the first 'Secret Restaurant', run by Michelin-starred restaurant St John, at which sittings could be booked for lunch during matinees and dinner in the evening events. After the pre-screening activity, everyone was seated in a darkened screening venue where live re-enactments accompanied the screening. The post-experience promotional video draws from the same screen language as the film itself.[61] It is presented in black and white and uses elements of Anton Karas' soundtrack – The Third Man Theme – and mixes in dialogue from the film referencing the Harry Lime shooting and setting up the narrative of the film. It also uses the inter-title shown at the beginning of the original film to establish the location of the action in Vienna. A key line of the dialogue – 'so long, Holly' – is used as the final image in the video and is augmented by a shot of these words spelled in neon on the outside of the screening venue.

Bugsy Malone (1976) was screened for the second time in March and April 2012, in another re-creation of Fat Sam's Grand Slam Speakeasy at the Troxy, where audience members again entered the venue through a fake book-case. This was the first FC event to be open to children. The event featured actors playing journalists and gangsters as well as the film's characters, and included 'the biggest splurge and custard pie fight ever staged'. The promotional activity in the lead-up to the event included a flash mob of impromptu on-street performances by some of the SC actors.[62]

A high-profile SC preview event for *Prometheus* (2012) in June 2012 notoriously made more at the box office than the film's official IMAX premiere. This is the first SC event reported to have broken a box office record. The film, part of the *Alien* story world, is based on a team of explorers discovering a clue to mankind's origins on Earth, which leads to the darkest parts of the universe. This was also the first example of SC's use of advanced 'world building' techniques to set up the pre-narrative context of the film across an expanded canvas of physical and digital spaces and times. A fictional organisation entitled 'Brave New Ventures' was established using Facebook and a number of in-world videos were produced. This mirrored the expansive, branded, 'Weyland' online universe that was created to market the original film.[63] Ticket holders were directed to complete a questionnaire to be assigned to a particular group which included data scientists, ore surveyors and field analysts.

The flash mobs became more structured in the *Prometheus* campaign and were promoted in advance on Facebook. These were staged over four different days in May 2012.[64] Branded as 'missions,' they included physical conditioning, night-time data retrieval, psychological training and preparation, quarantine briefing, bio-hacking and real-world biohazard containment.[65] Riggall recounted:

> We did this huge fitness programme in Euston Station, and people were very confused, they didn't understand what was going on, but for me that's the core about everything that we do, it's disruption, how can we disrupt people, how can people feel happy and come out of their mould and do something different.[66]

Attendees were drawn into physical exercise regimes at these events, which are a key staple of the SC experience as audiences are frequently required to engage in exercise and repetitive action or activity. These flash mob-style events were designed to create maximum spectacle, providing a compelling photo opportunity for passers-by and press in highly public central London locations, raising awareness and promoting the main event. SC flash mobs performed a solely promotional function – they were a play form that was now fully commodified and served the purpose of marketing and promotion

... *as sandbox* 51

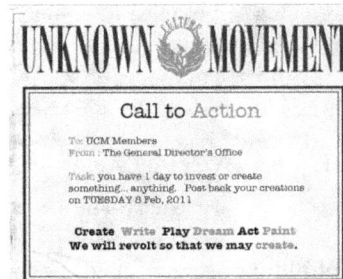

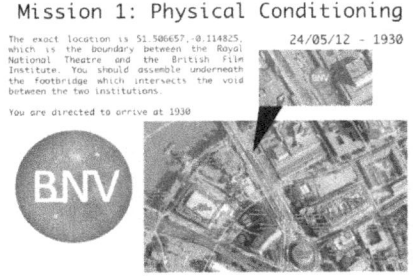

2.8 Examples of pre-narrative flash mobs. For *The Red Shoes* in 2011 in London's Covent Garden (above), *Prometheus* in 2012 on London's South Bank (below).

through narrativised spectacle across social media channels. As Jane McGonigal writes, even the early grass roots or countercultural flash mobs were part of the 'avant-garde of an emerging constellation of network practices that are both ludic, or game-like, and spectacular – that is, intended to generate an audience'.[67] SC's use of the flash mob aesthetic carried with it the hallmark of ARG techniques where participants are rewarded for their engagement in these exclusive, 'one-off', in-person activities.

The *Prometheus* 'main event' featured the re-creation of a spaceship in a 20,000-square-metre office complex on Hampstead Road in London, with some parts of the experience utilising outdoor spaces. Ticket holders were asked to arrive outside Euston Station in a blue boiler suit. After being led through a series of back roads and advancing through registration, an opportunity for currency exchange and decontamination, audience members were allowed to explore the multi-level 'spaceship' featuring 'R&R' and 'psychological behaviour' rooms, while actors performed select scenes from the film. After a simulated and dramatic 'attack', audience members were ushered into the 'escape pod' auditorium where a short clip of Ridley Scott playing 'Captain Scott' introduced the screening. This appears to have been the first production at which extensive additional video/moving image content was created to augment and populate the microsites and social media channels. This was another event sponsored by key partners Windows Phone; there was the same 'tweet wall' in the venue that had been present in previous experiences. The mobile phone interface was framed within the narrative world, so tweets were referred to as 'transmissions' in a further instance of embedded brand engagement.

The SC founder's previous insistence on upholding secrecy at all costs later waned in response to continued criticisms of the increasing price of tickets. Riggall became more willing to reveal some of the production secrets of previous experiences. Here he revealed:

> For *Prometheus* – sometimes I think about just the insanity of putting one of these productions on, and I don't think people realise, there's a lot of feedback sometimes where people say, 'I paid this amount of money for watching a film'. You don't get it – we took over a 400,000-square-foot building that was owned by a developer, we had to persuade the developer to give it to us for six months to turn it into a space-ship. Then we tried to convince Radiohead to give us the score of *Kid A* to become the soundscape ... we had a team of 350 people, we had to convince Twentieth-Century Fox to give us the film at the same time that they released it in cinemas. Then we built three 3D cinemas, and[,] with a cast of fifty, we created huge hydroponic indoor nurseries so we could bring plants to space, and it just goes on and on and on.[68]

These accounts of the process demonstrate the extent to which the experiences were increasingly drawing on an assemblage of talent to include musicians, sound designers, cinema technologists and, in this case, horticulturists (see Figure 2.9).

The post-experience promotional video,[69] in contrast to those previously produced, included just one clip from the *Prometheus* event itself – the in-world welcome by Ridley Scott. This is the only video to include a news report from one of the events – a London Tonight journalist is shown at a previous 2010 *Blade Runner* event. It used clips from the previous *Alien* events (in 2009 and 2010), intercut with quotes from newspapers, e.g. 'A spectacular way to keep your love of cinema alive – *The Telegraph*', boasting 'global press coverage', 'an unrivalled [social media] following of 2.7 million' as 'The Pioneers of Live Cinema. – *The Times*'. Here the increasing press and public interest was showcased, and SC built on their own *Zeitgeist* by adopting the 'live cinema experience' term to promote subsequent productions.

The outdoor aesthetics of fairground and spectacle returned with *Grease* (1978) in September 2012, a FC screening which included a re-creation of the Rydell High fair on Barnes Common, London. The cult 1970s musical

... *as sandbox* 53

2.9 Future Cinema: *Prometheus* – the most ambitious and extensive production to date. The images show the extensive and detailed set design, including extensive video design, as well as operational vehicles from the film itself.

classic, based on a group of 1950s high school friends, centres on the romance between wholesome exchange student Sandy (Olivia Newton-John) and leather-clad Danny (John Travolta). Audience members, instructed to dress as T Birds and Pink Ladies, were able to roam the space, which included an American-themed sports field, a working diner seating 300+, a fairground, a high school gym, a garage, Frenchie's house and a beauty parlour. Audience members could compete in the National Bandstand dance-off in the gym while actors recreated iconic scenes and mingled with them. The event attracted more than 10,000 attendees.

The final FC screening of this period was *Casablanca* (1942) in February and March 2013. It is filmed and set during the Second World War and focusses on American expatriate Rick (Humphrey Bogart) who must choose between his love for a woman (Ingrid Bergman) and helping her and her husband (Paul Henreid), a Czech resistance leader, escape from the Vichy-controlled city of Casablanca to continue the husband's fight against the Germans. The pre-narrative engagement involved the creation of the 'French Protectorate of Morocco'. The microsite allowed people who had bought tickets for the show to book their table at Rick's Café Américain, the best nightclub in Casablanca. Once they had booked their table, they were assigned one of six nationalities, along with a new name from that country. Audiences were encouraged to wear white suit jackets and 1940s attire (those not in costume were targeted by actors playing French Moroccan soldiers) and required to hold papers that could be checked at any point throughout the experience. The augmentation included detailed re-creations of locations from the film including the Blue Parrot Café and Rick's café. Participants could listen to live jazz by Benoit Villefon and his Orchestra, join dancers doing the Lindy Hop, sip cocktails or try their luck at the casino, activities interspersed with scene re-enactments. During the screening, audience members sat at low, cabaret-style tables around the stage with live performances augmenting the film. The post-experience promotional video is a blend of the original film stylistics with the liveness of the SC experience – it emulated the original film using black and white set design and theme music including 'As Time Goes By'. It started with a slow-motion chase outside and then included a voice-over (which we assume is from the event) welcoming everyone to Rick's café. The video blended shots of the event including mirror moments during the screening.

The final SC production of this period, *The Shawshank Redemption* (1994), was staged in an expansive re-creation of the Shawshank Prison in Cardinal Pole School, Hackney, London, between December 2012 and January 2013. It pushed forward key, creative, world-building techniques. For example, the idea of providing everyone with a specific name and an *individual* identity was established here – 12,500 names and profiles were generated through the fictional 'State of Oak Hampton' microsite.[70]

Upon arrival at the meeting point, audience members were addressed as male Americans (based on the identities that they had been assigned via the microsite) and transported by bus from a 'courtroom' in Bethnal Green Library to the 'prison'. Here they were treated like inmates, stripped of their own clothes, given a uniform and put in a cell with six other inmates. This production epitomisesd the militarised experience design where audience members are marshalled, depersonalised and intensely controlled. They were required to hold on to identity papers whilst being forced to engage in exercise routines and receive food dished out onto prison trays. They were invited and encouraged to trade with each other, to simulate a prison economy. Actors hurled insults and encouraged the inmates to take part in a planned escape and other interactive re-creations of iconic film scenes. Also, a clear connection was made to an external socio-political context built into the experience design:

> Participants wrote letters which were subsequently posted to inmates of UK prisons, and, on behalf of Amnesty International, to foreign embassies in Iran, Ethiopia, the Philippines and Turkey, petitioning for the release of journalists and activists.[71]

Audience members could take 'work placements' in brewing beer or cross-stitching; those with VIP tickets ate a three-course meal as the governor's guest (in another iteration of the 'secret restaurant') and stayed overnight in the cells to wake up to yoga and a canteen breakfast. The 'stratification' of audience experience was explicitly played out here with the inclusion of fine dining and differently priced VIP experiences, while 'standard' participants engaged with 'bar staff who were just walking around as prisoners, under-handedly selling shots'.[72] These embedded, 'in-world', narrative engagements provided thematic justifications for a stratified business model which replicated class-based ideologies. The 'spatialisation' of experience was shaped by the combined use of institutionalised spaces and narratives, which legitimised keeping the audience in order.

The Shawshank Redemption solidified numerous aspects of the emerging SC format: assigned personas; expanded use of space; the design of different audience journeys or what have come to be referred to by SC as 'tracks' through the experience; and ticket stratifications, with audiences willingly acceding to the utmost levels of control and management.

Conclusion

In this chapter, we have seen SC engage in an entire spectrum of activity which spanned different brand identities, artistic practices and social, cultural and even political initiatives. Latterly focussing on larger-scale events and venues, there was significant audience growth, and press awareness and interest increased.

The tensions that we have identified in this chapter (festivals to financing, ephemerality to replicability, movements to markets and spatialisation to stratification) persist in a cyclical continuum, subject to constant negotiation and renegotiation. They remain ever-present in the next period of SC's evolution, between 2013 and 2018 – which we will consider in Chapter 3 – where the different elements of the formula that emerged from this sandbox period were crystallised into a settled format.

Notes

1. Future Shorts, 'Fyfe Dangerfield, lead singer of Guillemots and creator of Secret Cinema Fabien Riggall talk about the Future Cinema live rescore event of David Lynch's *Eraserhead* back in 2007', 21 April 2020, YouTube video, 4:46, available at www.youtube.com/watch?v=JmA16lYt0ms (accessed 13 December 2021).
2. See page 34, this chapter for further detail.
3. As referenced in Tom Cheshire, 'The screen saver: Secret Cinema's mission to save the movies', *Wired*, 4 June 2013, available at www.wired.co.uk/article/the-screen-saver (accessed 13 December 2021).
4. seOne or SE1 was a nightclub in London that claimed to be the 'largest and most flexible' (see https://ra.co/clubs/733) (accessed 13 December 2021) in the city. The club was situated under the railway arches of London Bridge station and had a capacity of 3,000. It was demolished during the redevelopment of the station.
5. Fabien Riggall, 'Pioneering Secret Cinema's chief creative officer & founder Fabien Riggall', interview by Mishcon de Reya, *Jazz Shapers*, 15 May 2021, audio, 24:34, available at https://planetradio.co.uk/podcasts/jazz-shapers/listen/2044931/ (accessed 13 December 2021).
6. Held on 25 September 2006.
7. Taken from a description of the event provided here: All in London, 'Dream of Elephants', All in London, 1 September 2006, available at www.allinlondon.co.uk/whats-on/event-9433-dream-of-elephants (accessed 13 December 2021).
8. *The Times*, 'Win Tickets to UKs first outdoor film festival', *The Times*, 10 July 2006, available at www.thetimes.co.uk/article/win-tickets-to-uks-first-outdoor-film-festival-fmmrfjq50w3 (accessed 13 December 2021).
9. Tim Green, 'Stella Artois Film Festival, 22–23 July 2006 – Greenwich Park London', *Contact Music*, 17 July 2006, available at www.contactmusic.com/music/stellaartoisfilmfestivalx17x07x06 (accessed 13 December 2021). According to Green, this included '2005's *Donnie Darko* screening in Kensington Gardens with the National Symphony Orchestra, and *Pulp Fiction* with the Fun Lovin' Criminals in Manchester's Heaton Park, which entertained 20,000 film fans'.

10 Margaret Krawecka, 'Future Cinema events: *The Matrix* 2006', Space & Story (blog) 2006, available at www.spaceandstory.com/future-cinema (accessed 13 December 2021).
11 Eclectic Method were a three-piece act until 2011/12.
12 Krawecka, 'Future Cinema events', 2006.
13 Including, amongst others, Jeff Mills the dance music DJ, who toured with a newly composed soundtrack to the film in 2015, and Dmytro Morykit's *Metropolis* Live piano score performed at various international venues in 2018. See *Electronic Beats*, 'We saw Jeff Mills score the sci-fi classic *Metropolis*', *Electronic Beats*, 25 August 2017, available at www.electronicbeats.net/the-feed/saw-jeff-mills-score-sci-fi-classic-metropolis/ (accessed 13 December 2021) and Dmytro Morykit, '*Metropolis* live', Dmytro Morykit Composer, Pianist. 21 June 2021, available at http://dmytromorykit.co.uk/menu (accessed 13 December 2021).
14 Support Future Shorts, 'Future Cinema – *Metropolis* @ Fabric London', 28 November 2007, YouTube video, 2:01, available at www.youtube.com/watch?v=yPR_4unMohM (accessed 13 December 2021).
15 There is a credit listing appended to the *Metropolis* post-experience promotional video. This is the only time that a credit listing has been published on a SC video. The credits include: artistic direction and set conception; movement director; production manager; production coordinator; sound designer, sound engineer; lighting designer; technical manager; branding manager, marketing manager; projection manager; installation coordinator; visual designer, creative production designer; assistant stage manager; set designer, set carpenter; newspaper designer; costume designer, costume stylist, costume assistant; make up and hair.
16 There is a clear distinction in the industry between 'preview' screenings and film 'premieres', which we have retained in this genealogy.
17 Secret Cinema, 'New Secret Cinema launch video – *Paranoid Park*', 18 January 2008, YouTube video, 1:27, available at www.youtube.com/watch?v=1Ffzlm2LGG4 (accessed 13 December 2021).
18 In V. Selavy, 'Making cinema magical again: SC launch', *Electric Sheep Magazine*, 9 January 2008, available at www.electricsheepmagazine.co.uk/2008/01/09/making-cinema-magical-again-secret-cinema-launch/ (accessed 13 December 2021).
19 Secret Cinema, 'Secret Cinema on Sky Movies', 17 March 2008, YouTube video, 5:24, available at www.youtube.com/watch?v=QPaLhQAHGZ4&t=133s (accessed 13 December 2021).
20 Secret Cinema, 'Secret Cinema – *Funny Face*', 21 February 2008, YouTube video, 1:36, available at www.youtube.com/watch?v=uQts0qRPWuM (accessed 13 December 2021).
21 Helen Scarlett O'Neill, interviewed by Natalie Wreyford, 9 October 2020.
22 The original film was shot at director Anderson's old school, Cheltenham College.
23 Secret Cinema, 'Secret Cinema – *If …*', 18 June 2008, YouTube video, 1:44, available at www.youtube.com/watch?v=K3UXsVsYXAM&t=1s (accessed 13 December 2021).

24 Wendy Mitchell, 'Future Cinema plans *Eraserhead*/Guillemots event', *Screen Daily*, 10 July 2008, available at www.screendaily.com/future-cinema-plans-eraserhead/guillemots-event/4039812.article (accessed 13 December 2021).

25 See for instance Sarah Atkinson, 'Cinema remixed 4.0 – the rescoring, remixing and live performance of film soundtracks', in *The Routledge Handbook of Remix Studies and Digital Humanities*, ed. Eduardo Navas, Owen Gallagher and Xtine Burrough (London: Routledge), 443–55.

26 'Action vehicle' is the name given to vehicles that appear on screen.

27 Future, '*RockNRolla*, Future Cinema', 12 September 2008, YouTube video, 1:54, available at www.youtube.com/watch?v=xqhQG4QJBfo (accessed 13 December 2021).

28 This invitation was located in an attendee's blogpost: Ofilia, 'Secret Cinema presents *A Night at the Opera*', Ofilia's Fine Flicks (blog), 3 October 2008, available at https://ofilia.wordpress.com/tag/secret-cinema/ (accessed 13 December 2021).

29 Ed Potton, 'The true spirits of cinema are kept secret', *The Times*, 17 January 2009, available at www.thetimes.co.uk/article/the-true-spirits-of-cinema-are-kept-secret-9q0vrg3ltm6 (accessed 13 December 2021).

30 As indicated on the event's flyer, in the end title credits of the promotional film the *Watchmen* movie website address features alongside that of SC.

31 Future, '*Watchmen*, Future Cinema', 24 March 2009, YouTube video, 2:44, available at www.youtube.com/watch?v=I_v1HpTNG44 (accessed 13 December 2021).

32 Available at www.secretscreenings.com (accessed 13 December 2021).

33 Ally Brown, 'Future Cinema presents: *All Tomorrow's Parties* premiere', *The Skinny*, 29 June 2009, available at www.theskinny.co.uk/music/live-music/reviews/future-cinema-presents-all-tomorrows-parties-premiere (accessed 13 December 2021).

34 This ongoing preference for a rather narrow selection of more masculine films that feature strong narratives of competition or conflict could perhaps be attributed to the tastes of the male founder who, at this stage, is the key creative decision maker.

35 To be discussed in depth in Chapter 6, page 209.

36 Future, '*The Warriors*, Secret Cinema', 21 September 2009, YouTube video, 1:38, available at www.youtube.com/watch?v=GRQ2lKOtis4 (accessed 13 December 2021).

37 Garrett Moore, interviewed by author, 8 October 2021.

38 Secret Cinema, 'http://www.secretcinema.org/ presents *Alien*. October 2009. Somewhere in London', 11 November 2009, YouTube video, 1:39, available at www.youtube.com/watch?v=BJWtFtdQJDM (accessed 13 December 2021).

39 Bruce A. Austin, 'Portrait of a cult film audience: *The Rocky Horror Picture Show*', *Journal of Communication* (1981) 31(2), 43–54. Barbara Klinger, 'Re-enactment: fans performing movie scenes from the stage to YouTube', in *Ephemeral media: transitory screen culture from television to YouTube*, ed. Paul Grainge (New York: Bloomsbury Publishing, 2017), 195–213.

40 Secret Cinema, 'Secret Cinema presents *Bugsy Malone*', 17 December 2009, YouTube video, 2:28, available at www.youtube.com/watch?v=SOnswf7XaOE&t=15s (accessed 13 December 2021).
41 Ben Walters, 'Hopper mad: *Blue Velvet* screening prompts Lynchian tributes to Dennis', *The Guardian*, 4 August 2010, available at www.theguardian.com/film/filmblog/2010/aug/04/dennis-hopper-blue-velvet-screening (accessed 13 December 2021).
42 Shane O'Neill, 'First Windows Phone 7 ad: a revolution in the desert?', *CIO*, 7 September 2010, available at www.cio.com/article/2372522/first-windows-phone-7-ad–a-revolution-in-the-desert-.html (accessed 13 December 2021). The video can be viewed here: WPB7, 'Windows Phone 7 first ad | the revolution is coming', 27 September 2010, YouTube video, 1:01, available at www.youtube.com/watch?v=SrB2kDm-FoA (accessed 13 December 2021).
43 O'Neill, interviewed by Wreyford, 9 October 2020.
44 O'Neill, interviewed by Wreyford, 9 October 2020.
45 Flash mobs were the *Zeitgeist* of 2011 – as indicated by clear spike in a Google Trends search. The *Oxford English Dictionary* definition is: 'a large group of people who arrange (by mobile phone or email) to gather together in a public place at exactly the same time, spend a short time doing something there and then quickly all leave at the same time'.
46 Jane McGonigal, 'SuperGaming: ubiquitous play and performance for massively scaled community', *Modern Drama* (2005) 48(3), 471–91.
47 Paul Grainge, 'A song and dance: branded entertainment and mobile promotion', *International Journal of Cultural Studies* (2012) 15(2), 165–80.
48 Moore, interviewed by author, 8 October 2021.
49 Future, '*The Red Shoes*, Secret Cinema', 17 March 2011, YouTube video, 2:22, available at www.youtube.com/watch?v=d2CffTu0LH0 (accessed 13 December 2021).
50 Lucy Farmer, 'SC has fun in the dark, a creative concept that has people buying tickets to an undisclosed film in an undisclosed location', *1843 Magazine*, 11 May 2011, available at www.1843magazine.com/content/arts/lucy-farmer/fun-dark (accessed 13 December 2021).
51 Secret Cinema, 'Secret Cinema presents *The Battle of Algiers*', 11 May 2011, YouTube video, 3:32, available at www.youtube.com/watch?v=YRep76w-ads (accessed 13 December 2021).
52 Fabien Riggall, 'Beauty in the making (the senses)', It's Nice That, 29 July 2015, YouTube video, 24:39, available at www.youtube.com/watch?v=AsozWGEZXlI (accessed 13 December 2021).
53 Secret Cinema, 'On the road to Kabul part II – Asian Dub Foundation', Secret Cinema Presents, 4 September 2012, Vimeo video, 1:28, available at https://vimeo.com/48791234 (accessed 13 December 2021).
54 Riggall, 'Beauty in the making'.
55 Moore, interviewed by author, 8 October 2021.
56 Ollie Tiong, 'Windows Phone hotel 7.5 – *Ghostbusters*', Ollie Tiong (blog), 28 December 2011, available at http://blog.ollietiong.com/2011/ (accessed 13

December 2021) and Wildstyle Network, 'Windows Phone 7.5 hotel with Secret Cinema', 12 January 2012, Vimeo video, 3:46, available at https://vimeo.com/34950187 (accessed 13 December 2021).
57 Available at www.theothercinema.org (accessed 13 December 2021).
58 Secret Cinema Presents, 'The Other Cinema – *Brief Encounter*', 27 February 2013, Vimeo video, 1:13, available at https://vimeo.com/60670981 (accessed 13 December 2021).
59 There is a further screening of *La Haine* in Kabul, on 27 September 2012 with a live score by ADF and in partnership with Sound Central Music Festival, central Asia's alternative music festival.
60 There was also a one-off screening of the same film in Kabul on 8 December.
61 Secret Cinema, 'Secret Cinema presents – *The Third Man*', 24 January 2012, YouTube video, 3:18, available at www.youtube.com/watch?v=zz89LUWfHko (accessed 13 December 2021).
62 Rachel Bull, 'Picture gallery: *Bugsy Malone* flashmob', *Campaign*, 16 March 2012, available at www.campaignlive.co.uk/article/picture-gallery-bugsy-malone-flashmob/1122729 (accessed 13 December 2021).
63 See Atkinson, *Beyond the screen.*
64 Mayer Nissim, 'Secret Cinema teases special "expeditions" on new website: recruits are urged to attend for physical condition and training', *Digital Spy*, 23 May 2012, available at www.digitalspy.com/movies/a383140/secret-cinema-teases-special-expeditions-on-new-website/ (accessed 13 December 2021).
65 The schedule reads: May 24 – 7.30pm – Physical Conditioning; May 25 – 7.30pm – Night-time Data Retrieval; May 27 – 3pm – Psychological Training and Preparation; May 28 – 7.30pm – Quarantine Briefing, Bio-hacking and Real-World Biohazard Containment.
66 Fabien Riggall, 'TedxYouth@Bath 2012: Fabien Riggall secretyouth', Tedxyouthbath, 16 December 2012, YouTube video, 14:53, available at www.youtube.com/watch?v=Xyn65QXhZ-U (accessed 13 December 2021).
67 McGonigal, 'SuperGaming', 476.
68 Fabien Riggall, 'Fabien Riggall and Secret Cinema', interview by Etan Ilfeld, The Etan Ilfeld Podcast, 14 July 2021, audio, 49:11, available at https://anchor.fm/etan-ilfeld/episodes/Fabien-Riggall-and-Secret-Cinema-e14cit3 (accessed 13 December 2021).
69 Secret Cinema Presents, 'We live as we dream. Alone', 28 March 2012, Vimeo video, 1:35, available at https://vimeo.com/39343761 (accessed 13 December 2021).
70 This website and others that followed were created by Gavin and Jason Fox.
71 Confirmed here: Emma Bartholomew, 'Future Cinema offers out Hackney space used for Secret Cinema concept as a pop-up community centre', *Hackney Gazette*, 20 March 2013, available at www.hackneygazette.co.uk/news/future-cinema-offers-out-hackney-space-used-for-secret-cinema-3441438 (accessed 13 December 2021).
72 Sophie Kendrick, SC producer and pre-narrative manager, interviewed by Natalie Wreyford, 5 March 2021.

3

Secret Cinema as format

In this chapter we focus on the continued evolution of the SC format across thirteen productions over the five-year period between 2013 and 2018. The evolution of both the productions and the organisation were shaped by two further tensions which we identify as 'participation to passivity' and 'clandestine to commodified'. In the first, we see the format evolve so that audiences could be passive and/or participatory (or both) within these experiences, in part due to the inherent transition that audiences make when they move from active participation in the 'show' element to passive spectating when the screening begins. This was also due to the increasing 'layers' of the experience, which provided different opportunities for engagement. In the second, we show how the emergent SC experience design maximised opportunities for promotion, marketing and commercial exchange. We lay out a set of experience design principles and their associated experiential aesthetics as they are encountered by the audiences, including pre-ticket promotion; pre-narrative experience and engagement, including an in-depth look into the in-world microsites; social media accounts; flash mobs and pop-ups; the different places, sites and spaces of the productions; the pre-screening-show; and the screening itself.

The aesthetic and creative influence of festivals fell away in this period, but continued to resonate in two key facets: firstly, festival *infrastructure* and the expertise associated with this sector underpinned the two major, larger-scale, outdoor screenings of this period, and secondly, the productions increasingly *simulated liveness* at all stages. 'Simulated liveness' is a key experiential aesthetic that manifests in these events, and SC often referred to this as 'live cinema experiences' through the titling of their post-experience promotional videos between 2012 and 2014: first *Grease* in 2012, which was described as 'an all singing all dancing live cinema experience', followed by *The Shawshank Redemption, Casablanca, Ghostbusters* and *Who Framed Roger Rabbit?* which all shared this language in their videos. *Back to The Future* (BttF) was also described as a 'live cinema experience' on its promotional poster (see Figure 3.6). Liveness was

3.1 Timeline of the audience's experiential journey in the Secret Cinema format.

here capitalised upon, foregrounded and showcased, but 'live cinema' is an alignment which the organisation has latterly sought to avoid.[1] Simulated liveness most visibly emerged during the moments when additional action was layered alongside the mediated two-dimensional projection of the film on screen – what SC professionals themselves refer to as 'mirror moments'. These live, synchronised interactions and re-enactments significantly increased in some of the examples of this period with the inclusion of live performers, lighting, special effects and physical stunts including aerial performance, fight sequences and 'action vehicles'. This can be seen as SC's attempt to make the screening element as lively and as interactive as possible, since the transition into the screening can be an experientially jarring moment, when the audiences must shift from full, active participation to compliant and passive watching. The mirror moments became all the more spectacular in the first production considered in this chapter (*Brazil*) – both the spectacle and the artifice of its creation were simultaneously visible for all to see.[2]

Worldbuilding

The influence of gaming and theme parks were more keenly felt in how the events were designed and experienced. Bearing a close resemblance to both the established alternate reality game (ARG) and Pervasive Game format conventions, certain trends and tropes were central to this period: the world of the film was spread across different media, and new storylines, characters and content were developed. SC professionals often refer to this creative process as 'worldbuilding': their promotional literature refers to these experiences as 'worlds' and the films on their slate increasingly laid the fruitful ground for this immersive expansion.[3] We have identified five different worldbuilding techniques which emerged in this period and categorise them in the following ways:

- *trans-dimensional worldbuilding:* when elements of the film are replicated *across and beyond* either physical or digital form – e.g. the mimicking of characters that already exist in the film and the replication of locations seen in the film

- *intra-dimensional worldbuilding:* when there is a more detailed/deepened/extended creation *within* what exists already in the film; this can include extending or deepening very minor characters' narratives
- *multi-dimensional worldbuilding:* when *multiple* new threads and storylines are developed, either running in parallel or as a prequel to the main filmic narrative – new characters and perspectives are also introduced using this strategy
- *extra-dimensional worldbuilding:* when something additional or new is created *outside or beyond* the existing world but parallelling the themes of the film, e.g. the fictional news channels that were created for most events in this period
- *inter-dimensional worldbuilding:* in-world engagements that happen *between* audience members, for example through fictionalised communication channels on social media sites.

We will uncover numerous illustrative examples of these five techniques as they emerge in our consideration of the different events in this period.

From participation to passivity (2013–2014)

This first theme was shaped by two strands of experiential aesthetics: firstly, experimental and detailed worldbuilding – as exemplified by the *Brazil* and Laura Marling events – which both invited new forms of participation and play; and secondly, a 'standard', formulaic and repetitive use of film titles or venues where clear (and limited) participatory expectations were set – as exemplified by *Ghostbusters*, *Dirty Dancing* and the repeated use of the Troxy venue. Within these two strands, 'experimental' and 'standard', we see conflicting tensions between exclusivity and mass appeal, and between elitism and populism.

Brazil (1985) in May–June 2013 was the most visibly spectacular production to date and the one that truly epitomised the experimental strand with highly detailed worldbuilding, staged across thirteen floors of the BT Building in Croydon, London. The story of *Brazil* is set in a dystopian world in which there is a bureaucratic over-reliance on poorly maintained machines. An extended online world was created for audience members to engage with prior to the event. Upon purchase of a ticket, audiences were assigned 'employment identities' through a secret website 'goodorg.co.uk'. One of SC's pre-narrative producers explained the emerging dual imperative of these forms:

> The creative vision is about uniting everybody, giving them their costumes – that's what Fabien's vision was. But then there was also the business vision. We need all of our audience registered and we need to acquire their data so we can

grow our mailing lists ... We realised that there was only about a 30% uptake. So that's when my job became a little bit more important. We worked with a web designer who withheld [key] information so that audiences *had* to register on the website in order to get their character – it flipped to 100% uptake really quickly.[4]

Brazil marks a turning point in the increasing complexity of the pre-narrative microsite designed for participation during the month leading up to the show. It was also the first time that the 'pre-show' narrative was seeded in the online spaces; this became a key staple in later productions. In this case, how the audiences interacted with the system directly influenced their final show experience. The creators explained the complexity of the narrative experience:

> The moment any audience member bought a ticket, they became employees of G.O.O.D., a fictional company that mimics the bureaucratic and brutal themes of the film. Employees are given access to the company intranet after filling a deliberately lengthy appraisal form. Here they can keep abreast of all company developments, as well as access a G.O.O.D. subsidiary division called D.R.E.A.M.S., a research company that all employees have to record their dreams with. Employees are also tasked to form connections with their colleagues by collecting Social Identification Numbers from each other using the commenting system to increase their rank in the company. A few days before the show, each employee is informed that they have been transferred to a new department and given instructions of the proper dress code required for their new role. On the night of the show, employees are instructed to report to G.O.O.D. HQ ... and G.O.O.D. is revealed as the Government Office of Data, a play on the Ministry of Information from the film. Depending on your transfer, *there were 27 possible starting points to your journey through the show*, each with a different story and experience [our emphasis].[5]

This articulation was the first example of *multi-dimensional worldbuilding*, where *multiple* 'tracks' through the experience were created. The designers went on to describe how they installed and set up sixty separate computer consoles for the 'Department of Records', at which all 'employees' could log in. They were then given access to all manner of files, videos and games: 'just as in the film, you can hack the system to watch a selection of classic films or TV shows, as well as access high-level integration reports'.[6] Each rank of employee was given a different 'mission' to carry out within the building. Hidden away on the top floor was a secret console where employees could 'delete' themselves, freeing them from the system. If they tried to log back into the website after attending the show they would just see a rolling video of clouds, although a secret method to 'undelete' yourself was also provided. Here, the complex pre-narrative engagement crossed over into the 'main-event' experience and also continued post-event. A web designer also revealed an interesting insight into the experience design strategy as it related to the stratification of different experiences:

> If you had a really high number because you had done lots of interactions, you would have access to the corporate level. If you had a really low number because you didn't really bother with the website, you would have access to the slums and things like that. But both of those experiences were really good. In fact, I think the slums were more fun, as it turned out at the end. So whenever we do these systems, you don't want to make it so that you can't win or lose, it just changes your scenario.[7]

This signals a sophistication in the stratification of audience experience that first emerged in *The Shawshank Redemption*. In the earlier model the price of the ticket somewhat crudely determined distinctions between audience experiences available while simultaneously modelling any power structures that existed within the film text. In *The Shawshank Redemption*, for instance, the more expensive ticket holders were prison guards and those paying the least were prisoners. In *Brazil*, although these power structures were still axes of distinction within the world, the level of engagement equated to experiential differentiation. This also reflected the increasingly game-like nature of these experience, where time invested earns particular rewards and access to new areas. Although this effort leads to specific rewards, the creative team here emphasised that even those who did not do that preparatory work were still provided with a rich experience.

For the screening itself, the film was projected onto the external walls of the building culminating in a spectacular aerial 'hero moment' during the climactic scenes of the film.[8] The post-experience video showcases *Brazil*'s spectacular re-creation and its complex and detailed audience engagement whilst also emulating the narrative structuring of the original film.[9] Set to the film's title theme, 'Aquarela do Brasil' ('Watercolor of Brazil'),[10] the video starts with opening shots from the film intercut with an action vehicle's arrival at SC's Croydon venue, along with screen shots from the G.O.O.D microsite. There then follows a swiftly edited montage of shots that communicate the chaos and frenetic activity of the SC experience. The video concludes with the spectacular aerial staging – an aerialist performs the role of an angel and abseilers scale the internal sides of the building (see Figure 3.2). In this period, SC started to attract more mainstream press reporting, although not always for the right reasons – in this case it was due to last-minute cancellations as a result of a late objection from the council to SC's licence application.[11]

The union between music and film which began the SC journey and brand was drawn from further in the following, unique staging – SC presents Laura Marling at the Grand Eagle Hotel in east London, Summer 1927. This

3.2 Secret Cinema presents ... *Brazil*. The most expanded narrative canvas to date – staged across a complex series of websites and multiple storeys of an office block, it culminates in a spectacular visual finale

event took place at the Cardinal Pole School in east London, the location previously used for *The Shawshank Redemption* production. The event was branded as the beginning of 'Secret Music' and described by Riggall as a key new initiative through which the organisation would 'turn albums in to buildings' in a further innovation in spatialised experience design. It is important to note that this was a distinctive experience – entirely unique in its staging of a music album as opposed to a film and a format that was never repeated. Each room was thematised to represent a different track from the album, and audiences were able to explore these before Marling's performance. The experience ran across several dates in June 2013. Three hundred people attended each night, and were greeted by the hotel's manager 'Thomas Undine' and his uniformed staff and shown to their 'rooms' within a property complete with its own croquet lawn and chapel. Audiences had been instructed to bring unwanted books, a gift for a stranger and flowers for 'Mistress Josephine'. They were also expected to wear black-tie formal attire. This was the first event at which mobile phones were reportedly confiscated at the door. The venue also included a restaurant operated by Moro at which guests were served roast quail. This particular event was clearly designed to be intimate and exclusive – not something which could scale up or down in the same way as the core SC format that was emerging in this period. This was the only event of this kind that we have uncovered and appears to be another branch of activity that did not flourish.[12]

The *Brazil* and Laura Marling events exemplify the highly 'participatory' end of the spectrum that characterised this period of practice where audiences would navigate complex, multi-dimensional and multi-roomed venues and story spaces. Furthermore, they exemplify the rub between the higher-end elements of these experiences – such as expensive dining opportunities – and the lower-end, more popular or mass-appeal experiences, which were on the 'passive' side of the scale. The 'standard' experiences which follow were characterised by highly prescriptive instructions issued to audiences. We use these to show key elements of the SC format emerging: pre-ticket promotion and pre-narrative experience and engagement.

The first of these was *Saturday Night Fever* (1977) in June and July 2013. The film tells the story of Tony Manero (John Travolta) and his friends who frequent a local disco, the '2001: Odyssey Club', which was recreated in the Troxy. The pre-narrative experience at 2001odyssey.org enabled participants to be issued with ID cards and assigned to one of five New York gangs of the 1970s, along with costume instructions which included disco clothing, wild prints and platform heels. These could be purchased at the first 'pop-up' shop we have identified, which was held in collaboration with Beyond Retro in London on 6 June 2013. As we have already acknowledged, gangs and groups became a key thematic in the way that audiences were organised throughout the experience, and the particular character and costume designations they were given. These game-like elements became more and more crucial as the experiences matured and evolved and led to accessing different narrative tracks, experiences and treatments at the event. Once at the event itself, billed as 'The Live Immersive Disco Experience', audience members could dance and mingle with actors before the screening, participate in dance competitions and were awarded prizes for best dressing, best hair-do and best flares. During the screening, iconic scenes were re-enacted on the dance floor below the screen followed by an after-party with Horse Meat Disco.[13]

The second example was *Dirty Dancing* (1987), which ran over two nights in August and September 2013. *Dirty Dancing* has been used twice more by SC, their most frequent use of a title, clear evidence of the success of this formula and its replicability. In the film, set in the summer of 1963 in a sleepy resort in the Catskills, Baby (Jennifer Grey) holidays with her parents and falls in love with the resort's dance instructor, Johnny (Patrick Swayze). Billed as a Future Cinema (FC) event and staged at the Hackney Downs, London, the organisers created an expansive, festival-like experience in a park where 1960s-inspired costumed audiences, assigned alternate identities and carrying suitcases, beach balls and watermelons, explored a re-creation of the film's Kellerman's Resort. They took part in activities such as archery, life drawing and hula-hooping, and interacted with actors. During the screening, audiences sat on blankets and pillows while elements of the film were re-created on a stage below the screen, including live dance performances, with audiences encouraged to stand up and dance during and after the film.

Repetition continued with a second screening of the *Ghostbusters* (1984) experience in October–December 2013 at the Troxy, attracting more than 14,000 attendees. Five years on from the previous screening of *Ghostbusters*, this event serves to show the maturation and development of the experience, and the advancement and intensification of simultaneous augmentations of the on-screen action during the screening element of the event. The pre-narrative engagement also significantly expanded within this production. Before attendance at the event, audiences could engage with a host of digital materials including microsites for the *New York Evening Post*,[14] the Columbia University Institute of Paranormal Activity, the Ghostbusters' own website and a high-fashion magazine promoting the 1984 New York Fashion Week being hosted in the prestigious Sedgewick Hotel. These are all forms of transdimensional worldbuilding which drew from the existing story world, and then presented or re-created it in a different media form.

Audience costume instructions also evolved at this stage. No longer *just* 1980s attire (as in the first *Ghostbusters* event), ticket holders were now instructed to dress as either 'scientists' or 'fashionistas'. The Troxy venue was transformed into a re-creation of the Sedgewick Hotel in Manhattan and, upon arrival, augmentations included performers dressed as bellhops with heavy New York accents, who welcomed attendees to a New York Fashion Week party celebrating fictional designer Diane von Shattenburg. Participants were also greeted by the 'Mayor of New York', a scenario and setting previously established through online web engagement. There was also an increased use and visibility of cast members playing *Doppelgangers* of characters in the film; they would lip-sync the dialogue and mimic the on-screen action in a series of mirror moments. Augmentations advanced within this production to include a sophisticated, projection-mapped, animated sequence which played on the walls alongside the screen, replaying the famous scene of the three Ghostbusters using their 'proton packs and particle throwers' to pull a ghost into an awaiting trap. The climax of the film involves the inflation of a huge 'Stay-Puft marshmallow' figure which towers over the audience.[15] This was one of the first instances of the VFX (video-effects) techniques of film production being integrated into the experience, making it a highly creative moment and a significant step in advancing production values and visual ambition of the events.

The final FC-branded event followed in February 2014 – *Who Framed Roger Rabbit?* (1988), where the interior of the Troxy was re-dressed to recreate the fictional 'Ink and Paint Club'. The film's story is set in a 1947 version of Hollywood and is a mixture of live action and cartoon animation. The event augmentations included onstage live performances by dancers, singers and actors from Jessica Rabbit to 'Toon Patrol' mobsters roaming throughout the space, interacting with the audience and encouraging them to dance. Audiences were instructed on appropriate costume and etiquette via the microsite,[16] and via a mobile phone message given a secret password to enter the club. Reflecting the mixed-media genre of the film and its associated production approaches, the event also included a mixture of live action and cartoon animation. These included on-wall projections like a piano falling from a ceiling onto the stage and a very large silhouette projection of Jessica Rabbit.[17] Despite the phone ban at the earlier Laura Marling event, audiences could still be seen using their mobile phones and were particularly active in doing so to capture the spectacular effects. This was notably one of the few experiences which has accommodated children.

This passivity to participation period is shaped by a loyal SC audience who were willing to pay higher ticket prices, accept the secrecy and clandestine nature of the events, and dutifully follow the preparatory instructions and costuming guidelines. In this period, the pre-narrative formula now settled into a clear format which we lay out below (see Figure 3.1).

Pre-ticket promotion

The first opportunity for audiences to engage in the SC narrative world is when news of the experience breaks across social media channels and through direct email-outs to those who have subscribed via the SC website and from details gathered at previous experiences. SC have always included an email sign-up opportunity on the landing page of their website and this is their key mechanism for communicating and disseminating information. The look and 'feel' of the forthcoming production is established through the images, textured graphic design and the language, tone and scripting of these digital communications, which are all closely aligned to the intellectual property (IP) of the film.

These communications have been released in different ways and are usually preceded by a breadcrumb trail of clues to the film's identity across SC's social media accounts (Twitter, Instagram and Facebook), providing an indication of when the film's identity will be released. The targeted email usually directs the recipients to these channels. Within these communications, audiences are hailed as potential ticket buyers (not yet as a fictional character, which comes later).

The ticket release date is then identified on SC's landing page, often with a tantalising thematised countdown clock, and is accompanied by frequent reminders on social media. Tickets have been known to go on sale months before the actual date of the event, providing ample time to engage audiences and trigger audience-generated marketing opportunities.

Post-ticket purchase: pre-narrative experience and engagement

In addition to the event's main promotional web page, which is situated on the SC website landing page and gives basic details of the event – the title, dates and booking information with a link to an external ticketing site – there is almost always a dedicated, fictional, microsite that is designed to engage ticket holders in the narrative world of the film. These microsites are the central vehicle for what SC themselves refer to as 'pre-narrative' engagement; it is through this site, along with associated satellite social media accounts, that extensive engagement is fostered and facilitated. These are an intrinsic facet of the experience as well as a key tool for marketing, promotion and audience growth – and they now reveal a tried and tested formula.

The microsites always have a specific, fictional, thematised URL that relates to the themes or locations of the film.[18] The web addresses of these sites are 'secret' and are embedded in links within the email communications received by ticket holders, who are always addressed in a fictional register (the addresses are never publicised on the main SC site, for example), thereby

  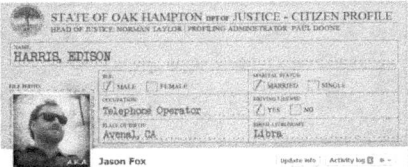

3.3 Examples of Secret Cinema audience ID cards. These are generated after a questionnaire has been completed. Audience members are instructed to print these out and bring them along to the events. From left to right: *Brazil*; *Saturday Night Fever*; *The Shawshank Redemption*.

sustaining the air of secrecy and exclusive access. The microsites are often designed under the guise of new organisations, institutions and corporations. These give the websites a corporate identity or 'sheen': e.g. Brave New Ventures for *Prometheus*.

In order to access the microsite, a log-in sign-up is required, often involving some form of questionnaire, where audience members are given a character name and a persona (often via an occupation or a key vocation). This can lead to the generation of a personal identity card (see Figure 3.3) which the holder is instructed to print and bring along to the main event. There is a clear aesthetic alignment with the fictional world, which requires the involvement of skilled storytelling and writers (this will be discussed further in Chapters 4 and 5). Identities are assigned fictionalised 'groupings' so that audience members are allocated specific affiliations with a costume/dress code which will enable recognition by other participants and SC performers.

In-world email communications ensue, pointing to maps of the venue, house rules and costume instructions in the lead-up to the main event.

The audience journey through these websites have become standardised as the following routine processes:

- audience-member questionnaire
- ID assignation (individual name, role and costume)
- connection to other users/participants through an in-world communications channel
- access to a newspaper or news channel
- receiving a map to the secret location of the event and
- opportunities to purchase merchandising and costuming items.

A key example of extra-dimensional worldbuilding – where the narrative canvas expands into the real world, and uses real-world signifiers and tropes – is the production of a newspaper (see examples in Figure 3.4). This is now a staple in the SC narrative toolkit as a key in-world storytelling device (as it is in many immersive experiences). The newspaper is made accessible digitally before the experience and/or in a paper version distributed at the event. For the early *Metropolis* screening in 2007, the post-experience promotional video end credits reveal that a newspaper was produced. In *Lawrence of Arabia* (2010), newspapers were made and distributed to the audience as part of the experience, such as *The Chicago Daily Courier*. In *The Red Shoes* (2011), a newspaper entitled the *Unknown Cultural Movement*, dated Friday 11 February 1948, with front-page news 'The Battle for the Freedom to Create', was distributed to audience members. Similarly, in *Bugsy Malone* (2012), the *Herald Tribune* was created. For *The Shawshank Redemption* (2012), *The Oakhampton Journal* was created; for *Ghostbusters* (2013), the *New York Evening Post*. These are always purpose-made for the SC production, with the exception of *The Grand Budapest Hotel* – *The Trans Alpine Yodel* newspaper created for this film as a prop (and website) also appears on SC's own secrethotel.org. It was created by the film's graphic designer, Annie Atkinson.[19]

Place, site and space

As the maps pictured in Figure 3.5 show, there is now an established formula for guiding audience members to the 'place' of the event. Audiences use the map to locate the meeting point, which is usually a tube or railway station. Upon arrival, the audience experience is narrativised and fictional experience is overlaid onto the real-world location. From this point, audiences are guided by in-character performers to the 'site' – the building or outdoor location where the screening takes place – in which the different story 'spaces' – the sets and staging – have been designed and built. We make a key distinction between place, site and space here and throughout the book; we use the term 'place' to refer the wider geographic context (e.g. district/region within London in which the site is situated); 'site' is the building/architecture/field that is taken over and repurposed; 'space' refers to the playable and navigable spaces that have been created through scenography, set design, lighting, sound, video, performance, etc. It is the expansive nature of these spaces that allows for the creation of a filmscape and the spatialisation of the film's narrative(s). Moreover, it is the tight control of these spaces that provides for but also determines the navigability of the experience.

The participant's arrival at the site and space will be discussed in the next section. For now, we observe that an emergent SC fan community both trust the organisation and embrace the format – and this will soon become entirely evident when we discuss the *BttF* event, where the core community clashed with the new, expanding and more 'mainstream' audiences.

... as format 73

3.4 Examples of Secret Cinema's in-world newspapers – a staple that has been routinely created for many productions. From left to right, clockwise: *Bugsy Malone*; *The Shawshank Redemption*; *Back to the Future*; and *Ghostbusters*.

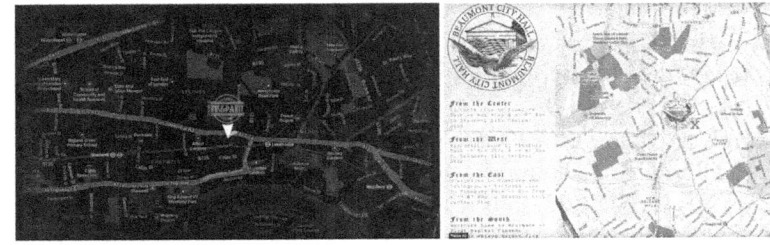

3.5 Thematised maps guiding audience members to the Secret Cinema site. Embedded links in emails or on the fictional website lead to thematic maps, which reveal the location of the designated meeting point. (Left) *Who Framed Roger Rabbit?*, (right) *Miller's Crossing*.

From clandestine to commodified (2014–2015)

A clear tension was emerging between an appeal to activism, exclusivity and countercultural aesthetics on one hand and the elaboration of a scaleable, replicable and commodifiable format that could entertain a 'mass' of participants and increasingly engage them in commercial, revenue-generating exchanges on the other. This became increasingly pronounced in this period in which a secret gig was staged by Riggall in protest against the cancellation of the Barbican Centre's Just Jam grime festival.[20] The impromptu event involved a performance by Ghetts – a young south London grime artist – in the housing estate within the Barbican Centre, exemplifying the original clandestine values of the organisation. So too did three one-off, smaller-scale screenings that took place in 2014 and 2015. Introducing these now takes us out of their original temporal sequencing (which can be referred to in Appendix 1). All followed the *BttF* production of 2014 that we will discuss shortly, but we introduce them now because, although they are central to the characterisation of the 'clandestine to commodified' era, they were not critical in the shaping of the SC format that we are framing in this chapter.

The three screenings all shared the following characteristics – they were impromptu, responsive and politicised. The first of these, *Dead Poets Society* (1989) in August 2014, was a commemorative set of screenings to mark the sudden and tragic death of the film's leading actor Robin Williams earlier that month. The film and its central themes of mental illness, professional pressure and suicide acquired an additional level of pathos in light of Williams' death. Set in 1959 in an American boarding school, *Dead Poets Society* tells the story of an English teacher played by Williams who inspires his students through his unconventional teaching of poetry. Augmented screenings were staged in multiple locations in the UK including the Troxy, London. These special screenings were delivered in partnership with UK charity Mind and US charity NAMI, and the augmentations included live music, poetry readings, enactments and special guests such as Neil Gaiman, Amanda Palmer and Bonnie Wright. At the Troxy screening, audience members sat at desks and premium-ticket holders were encouraged to act as participant performers and invited to stand on these desks to mirror the final scene of the film, during which the schoolboys stand on their desks as a defiant mark of respect for their teacher. Audiences were encouraged to dress in school uniforms, write letters and light candles in memory of Robin Williams.

A series of simultaneous screenings of *The Great Dictator* (1940) on 21 December 2014 took place to protest film censorship after Sony decided not to release *The Interview* (2014). *The Great Dictator* tells the story of Adenoid Hynkel's rise to power as the ruthless dictator of the country. Audiences were instructed to dress in dark suits and augmentations included live music, poetry and related short films before and after the screening. The #freedomtocreate hashtag made a reappearance at this event; it was previously used as a slogan in *The Red Shoes* pre-narrative campaign in 2011 (see Chapter 2, page 42).

The final screening of this period (and the launch of the SC X format)[21] was *Amy* (2015) in June 2015. *Amy* is a documentary which fuses archival footage with personal testimonials to present an intimate portrait of the life and career of British singer-songwriter Amy Winehouse. The event took place in a fictional 1960s-style jazz club called Round Midnight (named after a Thelonious Monk song which was reported to be a favourite of Winehouse). It was sited in her home borough of Camden, London in the renowned Koko venue where she had frequently performed. This was a smaller-scale 'secret' screening, which served as the launch of SC X in association with MAC UK, a Camden-based charity supporting mental health services for disadvantaged youth. The film's title was withheld from the audience and performers ushered them in through an 'artist's entrance' and green room, before they were seated by the nightclub 'owner' in the balcony or at low tables in the 'jazz club'. Augmentation took the form of a live band (who had all played with Winehouse during her career), DJs and other musical acts who performed before and after the preview screening of the documentary.[22] This event inaugurated the ambitions of the SC X brand – 'the strand aimed at growing the brand worldwide on a more intimate, transferable scale'.[23]

These three screenings all returned to the covert and clandestine roots of the event design in contrast to the large-scale commercial and commodified model which was inaugurated in the following productions.

The Grand Budapest Hotel (2014) (*TGBH*) – the first production to be released with a very explicit – an explicit 'SC Presents …' branding marked the beginning of this period, during which there was a notable shift to a more mainstream, conventionally marketed and formalised version of the SC brand. The film is an eccentric comedy set in a 1930s European ski resort, presided over by concierge Gustave H. (Ralph Fiennes) and his protégé Zero (Tony Revolori), a junior lobby boy. Running in February and March 2014, in all 21,000 people attended over the course of the event, with 350 attending each night. There was a significant jump in the published box office takings for this event, to £1.1m. The pre-narrative for the experience was offered via an extensive and detailed microsite which drew from the visual iconography created for the original film. It also included premium sponsorship and embedded branding.[24] This was the first microsite to show a list of corporate partners, including premium brands such as Penhaligon's and Moët & Chandon champagne. The microsite guided and instructed attendees to learn the waltz, fill in a guest card and bring pink flowers as props. It also moved towards a more sophisticated form of worldbuilding which sustains narrative and aesthetic coherence with the filmic text and a stylistic unification between all of the paratextual elements that are created. Worldbuilding techniques were central here: the visual look, feel and style of the microsites emulated the visual world and established IP of the film. The *TGBH* microsite mimicked a hotel booking system using the logos, colour scheme and 'look' already created for the film. The film makers had already engaged in their own worldbuilding activities through the creation of their Akademie Zubrowka website.[25]

The event itself included a highly detailed re-creation of *TGBH* at the Farmiloe Building, in Farringdon, London through a digital overlay upon the physical environment: an animated projection was mapped onto the front façade of the building simulating the external *mise-en-scène* of the hotel. Everyone entered the experience through a simulated train journey within the set. This 'travel' mode initiated upon entry was evidenced in many of the experiences and acts as a transition from the real world to the 'narrative' world. Such transitions are sometimes simulated, as this train ride to the Grand Budapest Hotel was, or achieved through travel on actual buses, as in *The Shawshank Redemption, Blade Runner* (2010) and *One Flew over the Cuckoo's Nest*. This is a common approach used in immersive theatre, as an SC stage manager explains:

> You transition via something – immersive theatre will always use something to make you feel like you've travelled much further than you have. Sometimes they throw you in the back of a van and send you round the block so it feels like you've been gone for ages.[26]

A snow machine evoked the Alpine atmosphere as the audience exited the train and prepared to enter the building where the lobby, reception desk and hotel rooms were all lavishly produced to emulate the narrative spaces of the film. Audience members were invited to explore these as well as the hotel's kitchen, bar, restaurant and spa, and to interact with actors, some of whom recited poetry, performed live music or led dances through the lobby space under the internal snow fall, before watching a screening of the film. As the lighting designer revealed:

> *TGBH* was all about pre-show and very little in the film. There's a few little moments in the film but that was a film premiere so the presentation of the film is very important.[27]

The online web design and digital extension and augmentation of these worlds became increasingly elaborate during this period. There was also an overlap between the end of the run of the SC Presents ... *TGBH* and the twenty-first SC Tell No One production of *Miller's Crossing* (1991), which ran from March to May 2014. This overlap will have required significant complex communication management around the distinctive elements of secrecy required for these different experience 'brands'.[28] *Miller's Crossing* is a Prohibition-era gangster film featuring two warring mobs. The preference for films with masculine themes and 'factions' continued across this period, enabling increasingly elaborate persona development and narrativisation that supported the development of distinct, 'experiencing' neo-tribes who could be instantly recognised at these events by strangers, who were immediately marked as game-like 'affiliates' and allies. A detailed map was provided which adapted a map of London to pinpoint the fictional location of the event, Beaumont City Hall. As an SC web designer describes:

> You could do this online betting on the boxing matches ... You would get an amount of money paid into your bank account that would come from an unknown source, and it turned out to be the mob. It was playing on tropes of how online banking works, even though it's just for a 1940s bank.[29]

Again, the pre-event narrative engagement provided opportunities for extensive audience interaction – here they were invited to register online with The American Union Bank[30] (a bespoke website designed for this event), to engage with electioneering and ultimately to vote for a mayoral candidate for Beaumont City. With the title of the film still unknown to the audience, they were assigned a name and job, and given costume instructions. Costuming was now an intrinsic part of the SC experience and increasing demands were made upon the audience to wear appropriate clothing and accessories. (See Chapter 6 for a fuller discussion of participant engagement with this element of the experience.)

Instructions were vaguer and looser for earlier events, but they have since become far more prescriptive, delineated and more closely linked to different character identities and groupings. For example, the costume instructions for *Miller's Crossing* contained the following simple, gendered distinction: 'Male dress code: A 1920s suit and trilby, please make sure you wear yellow in the brim of your hat. Female dress code: A 1920s afternoon/evening dress with a yellow fascinator or hat with a yellow feather.' Once at the event audiences were invited to wander a 1920s Chicago-esque city recreated in the disused Hornsey Town Hall, London while interacting with a cast of thirty actors, playing mobsters and mafia men. The post-experience video reveals that a boxing match was staged as part of the pre-screening spectacle and the audience members encouraged to place bets on the outcome.[31] This is an early example of multi-dimensional worldbuilding, where new story strands were created which exist in the same narrative universe, to draw out thematic but tangential threads from the main plot-line of the film.

The screening itself was situated in a space designed to emulate the jazz club setting featured in the film, with audience members sitting at crowded tables in front of a large stage, and live dance and re-enacted scenes accompanied the screening. The event attracted more than 16,000 attendees in all, with 450 attending each night.[32]

The post-experience promotional video also reveals extensive performances replete with fast-paced dialogue and staged shootings; it appears that they replayed the entire filmic narrative prior to the screening. The production values of the experiences here became the primary showcase focus of these videos, which moved to an increasing emulation of the stylistic qualities of the films as well as replaying their story and plot structures. This direction is exemplified in the approach taken to the *Miller's Crossing* video, which is a dialogue-led replaying of the film that showcases the high-quality performances of the actors as well as the scenography and stage direction.

Back to the Future

The 'clandestine to commodified' binary tension is epitomised by the largest production of this period, *Back to the Future* (*BttF*), where the impact of the shift from the organisation's clandestine roots to a more commercialised operation led to significant challenges, disruptions and discomfort for both the producers and audiences alike. The SC Presents ... *BttF* production in the summer of 2014 marked *the* turning point in SC's history; it shaped all events that followed (and has already been subjected to our own extensive analysis).[33] This much-loved 1980s cult favourite centres around the adventures of Marty McFly (Michael J. Fox), who is transported back through time to the 1950s in a modified DeLorean car, after an experiment by his eccentric scientist friend Doc Brown (Christopher Lloyd) goes awry. The event was hugely significant and we draw from it here to show key elements of the format: most notably, the adoption of worldbuilding strategies, including intra-, extra- and inter-dimensional techniques; and the technical evolution of the mirror moment and its aesthetic corollary of simulated liveness.

The event generated huge fan interest from audiences who had never before heard of, let alone attended, an SC event but flocked to buy tickets. *BttF* has a substantial and devoted fan community; the ticket site crashed within minutes of sales opening due to overwhelming demand. Tickets for SC events are often released using a phased strategy, with new dates added and the production timeline extended once the initially released tickets have sold out. This cultivates a sense of limited supply, scarcity and exclusivity (see Figure 3.6). *BttF* was no exception, and in this case the extension of the ticket sales was 'narrativised' using an 'in-world' newspaper headline.[34]

3.6 Phased ticket release strategy for *Back to the Future*: extra dates are added as the first dates sell out.

The pre-event engagement included increasingly elaborate, web-based activities,[35] and the most detailed example of *intra-dimensional worldbuilding* to date, in which Hill Valley High School and the various shopfronts from the Hill Valley Square – that only exist as a sign or a shopfront in the original film – were taken, expanded and elaborated on in the website and also at the event location. The fabric and iconography of SC's re-creation of Hill Valley was notably drawn from the entire *BttF* trilogy, for a deeper and more expanded frame of reference from which the SC creative team drew both textual and expositional detail.

As well as setting the scene of the event, the microsites also played a key role in directing audiences to engage in additional purchases of merchandise. They pointed to dedicated online stores that had been specifically set up for the experiences, to host and sell bespoke merchandise. Links to these stores often appear in the costume instructions that we will discuss in more detail in the next section.

Alongside the microsites, satellite social media sites – on platforms such as Facebook, Instagram and Twitter – also augmented the pre-narrative experience. Often-times dedicated, fictional, social media accounts are set up for fictional individuals and organisations; these accounts regularly post microcontent, images and film clips (including in-world news stories). Hashtags are routinely set up and audience members are encouraged to use these to post images of their interactions, preparation and planning for the main event. The pre-narrative engagement is a dual vehicle for experience design *and* promotion and it becomes increasingly difficult to discern where one ends and the other begins.

Instances of *extra-dimensional worldbuilding* included the creation of *new* fictional organisations and websites – we saw this in the creation of 'Utopia Skyways' for *Blade Runner* and the American Union Bank for *Miller's Crossing*. Here we see the creation of Hill Valley Stores – brand-new iconography was created for this imagined organisation. We also see this in the creation of new in-world radio and/or television news channels such as Radio Noir for *The Battle of Algiers* and Hill Valley TV (HVTV) for *BttF*. The trope of communicating via news and communication systems with in-world original content has been seen across all experiences since *Metropolis*. This contributes to the temporal framing of the experiences, usually invoking contemporaneity – with the exception of *BttF* which, appropriately, established a degree of anachronism aligned to the thematics of the film and its partial setting in the 1950s. A strategy of 'liveness' is also instantiated and invoked through live news and breaking news broadcasts communicating urgency and calls-to-action in the lead-up to the event. This narrative technique harks back to early radio drama where live news broadcasts were used as a dramatic technique to signify liveness and 'as-it-happens' – inaugurated by Orson Welles' *War of The Worlds* (1938), in which news broadcasts updating the situation of a live alien invasion interrupted what appeared to be a regular broadcast. This mixing of media is a well-established strategy of transmedia storytelling,[36] and plays with the real world/fictional world boundary which is a frequent and intentional blur in SC events.

Inter-dimensional worldbuilding occurs through the creation of an in-world communications platform for ticket holders to communicate with one another 'in-character' in the lead-up to the event – such a platform had previously been designed for *Brazil*. The web designer reflected on this being the most challenging and ambitious aspect of *BttF*:

> *BttF* was very complex because everybody was given a unique postal address, phone number, a whole phone system [was created]. So that meant your phone

number needed to be unique for the 45,000 people that were going. It was the same service that people like Uber use for their phone call managing systems to build the system for delivering all the messages to people. So if you phoned up your digital-answerphone the actors were recording messages to send out to people. So that was using an industrial product for a creative purpose.[37]

The first dedicated SC 'pop-up' store opened in east London in the weeks leading up to the main event, in which visitors were greeted and served 'in character' by actors playing Hill Valley residents. Pop-up culture – the emergence of temporary shops, cafés, venues and events in disused and vacant spaces, often in areas in need of or undergoing regeneration – was at peak fashion in London and other urban centres at this time. It has been subject to considerable critical interrogation, such is its association with gentrification and community displacement.[38]

The Hill Valley Stores combined a shop and café in which participants could buy clothes in preparation for the event, purchase 1950s-themed diner food and drinks, and have their hair cut in the adjacent 'Elite' salon. Participants had been instructed to wear 1950s costumes to the evening itself, where there were various props to assemble and tasks to complete. This pre-narrative engagement has evolved over time and is a key part of the production's 'worldbuilding' strategy, expanding the narrative canvas so that audiences are embedded into the film narrative. An SC head of costume revealed how:

> there was a big article that one of the daily papers ran about how we changed the face of what people wore in London because everyone was dressing in 1950s clothes because they were buying it all up because they were going to see *BttF*. It strangely changed the landscape of how people dress and what they do. It's become part of the public consciousness, particularly in London.[39]

Flash mobs also featured as an aspect of the pre-event promotional campaign for *BttF* – the film's famous time-travelling DeLorean made an appearance in London along with the SC actor dressed as Doc Brown providing a highly photographable opportunity (see Figure 3.7).

Flash mobs continue to be a key element of SC promotional campaign strategies; these are highly publicised through social media channels, fuelling awareness of and interest in the event and generating ticket sales. Where flash mobs have been used as a promotion and marketing tool by SC, pop-ups such as the Hill Valley Stores have provided an opportunity for initiating commercial exchanges.

Furthermore, they form part of the worldbuilding strategies that SC increasingly use to expand the narrative universe of the film. They all have

You built a time machine... out of a DeLorean?
#SecretHillValley #SCBTTF **Back to the future.**
#fluxcapacitor #Film

3.7 *Secret Cinema*'s Doc Brown pictured during a promotional flash mob. The actor playing Doc Brown made an unannounced appearance on the streets of London in July 2014 in the lead up to the *BttF* event – this was photographed by onlookers and several images then appeared on social media tagged by SC.

to fit in and cohere with the existing narrative world and, most importantly, the existing IP; they therefore take on an established approach and formula. New tangential IP has to be developed which is aligned to the core IP but does not have the status of official studio IP merchandise. Those for the *BttF* production included drinking cups and wristbands which featured 'in-world' Hill Valley branding.

SC Presents... *BttF* saw the extensive and hugely ambitious re-creation of Hill Valley in Olympic Park, London. The production included expansive sets, pyrotechnics, aerial stunts and multiple action vehicles. It attracted huge press interest when the opening night of the show was cancelled, just hours before the gates were due to open, leading to widespread anger and frustration publicly expressed on social media.[40] SC bore the brunt of intense criticism for their communication strategy, which was experienced as gnomic and opaque by the *BttF* fans who were new to the SC rules of engagement. These reactions were the source of much frustration among the SC 'core' audience and a clear conflict emerged between these two different groups as the SC audience asserted their cultural capital – a situation which we have previously interrogated in detail.[41] One of SC's production designers lamented:

> The stakeholders involved in dealing with the Olympic Park, I think most people didn't really have a clue what they were doing, they had never dealt with such a high-profile location and there was so much media attention and no one had ever dealt with it before. I think everyone was a bit out of their depth – including me.[42]

Riggall reflected on the difficulties of the situation (and the earlier *Brazil* cancellation):

> They were two really difficult situations, and [the reason people were so angry] is that it's heartbreaking to have to break the narrative, the fantasy and the magic. I should have cancelled it three days before. I was so bullish to think that we were going to open, [that we'd] persuade everyone we were going to be fine. We should have sent an email and cancelled it, but at the same time I thought I'm going to find a way. I thought how could they [the venues] do this?[43]

Riggall's perspective is tellingly naïve. An SC collaborator reflects on his approach, revealing that:

> he lives almost exclusively in this fantasy realm. SC is almost like a three-hour visit to Fabien's head on any given day. And it's chaotic. He's one of those people that fundamentally believes he's changing the world and can bend the world to whatever he wants it to be. So he's kind of operationally delusional.[44]

Through the PR debacle that followed the cancellation, we see SC momentarily lose control over their audience through a form of creative hubris, the second such moment in this period following the difficulties encountered with *Brazil*.

We now go on to introduce the next key elements of the SC formula: *arrival* at the place and site of the event; *pre-show* perambulation; and the *screening*.

Arrival

After arrival and ticket checks, the first and perhaps the most experientially specific action that participants are required to engage in upon arrival at the site is the surrender of their mobile phones. This instruction is clearly stated in the joining instructions for the event (i.e. via email) and any illicit use is forbidden and controlled by security guards. As Riggall proclaimed: 'We were one of the first shows to ban people from using their phones. It absolutely saved SC.'[45] The introduction of the phone ban was instantiated at *BttF* – although phones had been taken from the audience upon entry at the Laura Marling event, this was the first time that they had done this at scale. Riggall went on to state:

> I said we need to change this – we're going to build lockers for 5,000 phones, and again, my team looked at me, and said 'this is insane'. But I said, we have to do it, we have to take the phones off, otherwise the secret will be out, that there's a DeLorean, that there's a town hall, everything will be out … We can't do that every time [i.e. build lockers], we now have this amazing company called Yondr and you just trap in the phones.[46]

This became a major point of contention at the *BttF* event where participants were left without their phones as a result of the last-minute cancellations of the opening night, having complied with the instructions that phones would not be allowed.[47]

In addition to keeping the sites and experience secret, SC also frame the removal of mobile phones as a key facet of the 'being there' live experience of the event where audiences are 'present' and engage in an unmediated participation with their surroundings, the characters and each other. This is significant in managing or setting up the aesthetic of engaged participation.

Pre-show perambulation

Once inside the event, the audience have the opportunity to wander through a meticulously detailed re-creation of (for example) a Hill Valley fair (including locations such as the Texaco petrol station and Hill Valley high school), interact with actors, ride attractions (a ferris wheel at *BttF*), eat themed food and drink, and watch live music and re-creations of scenes from the film. The BttF site's re-creation translates into a 'film-set' aesthetic in which all buildings appear as façades fabricated through theatrical flats and materials, and illuminated by stage lighting. The sense of the simulacra of the film set, not of a real-world location, is further compounded by the context of the event site – for *BttF*, the highly visible, commercial environment of the (present-day) Westfield shopping mall and the UK's tallest sculpture ArcelorMittal Orbit, which loomed over the simulated 1955 landscape. (This sculpture was playfully referred to as 'Doc's Rocket Propulsion Device' on the accompanying map of the site.) This is an interesting juxtaposition between the fictional spaces of the narrative and the actual site. (This cacophony of styles and time referents unintentionally mirrors the intrinsic, post-modern, textual aesthetics of the *BttF* films, in which scenes contain simultaneous mixed period metaphors, cross-pollinating through costume, props, dialogue and *mise-en-scène*.)

The spaces started off as more open and exploratory in earlier SC experiences. The audiences were given the freedom to wander in and out of many of the spaces in an open narrative world in a 'sandbox' mode, where they could make their own discoveries and craft their own experiences as well as engage in opportunities for consumption. Audience members were asked to bring props that align with their new identity and grouping and to perform a specific preparatory task. The space became more advanced in *BttF* with the holistic re-creation of the sites of the film, and crucially, the story 'topology' – i.e. a structuring of a set that, if encountered linearly, replays the narrative of the hero's journey through the film.

The pre-show culminates in a hero moment, where all audience members are assembled at the screening (or pre-screening) space to witness a climactic moment; in the case of *BttF*, this was the Hill Valley parade where performers and audiences perambulated the square around the seated audience and a dance-along ensued with all audience members encouraged to engage.

The screening

During all SC's screenings (since *Bugsy Malone* in 2009), on-screen action is synchronously augmented by live performances, lighting, special effects and physical stunts including aerial performance, fight sequences and vehicle movements. Riggall indicated the intention on the part of the production, insisting that they 'don't distract from the movie – we amplify it, we mirror it, we shadow it, we silhouette it'.[48]

The screening environment is a hybrid of screen viewing space and theatrical performance space, with a different staging configuration depending on the location and on the film. The performance area is usually below and in front of the cinema screen, with a 'below the screen' second window where action is framed, structuring audience attention. This dual-screen format is clearly well established and features in the experience aesthetic of all live cinema, not just theatrical live cinema.[49]

For *BttF*, the film was projected onto the recreated façade of the Hill Valley Town Hall complete with clock tower. The screening included the most ambitious simultaneous screen augmentations to date, including action vehicles driving throughout the audience, high-wire stunts and pyrotechnics.[50] We have previously referred to these augmentations as 'screen-responsive performance',[51] and SC creative professionals refer to them as 'mirror moments'. These collective acts of cinephilia, which are a collaborative homage to the films, are now a prototypical feature of the SC format with three very specific technical and performance strategies (which have in turn led to a number of particular visual aesthetics). We categorise these in the following ways and will provide particular illustrations from *BttF* below:

1. Special effects created by lighting, sound and pyrotechnics to punctuate and enhance the on-screen events and action, and evoke affectively charged responses from the audience. This has become a formulaic and

routinised aspect of the production with technical processes established. This aspect of the production is now run to timecode, and some of the processes such as lighting are automated.

2. Two-dimensional action performed directly below the screen includes lip-synching of key dialogue, and mimicking physical interactions between on-screen characters. The actors who have been present in the pre-screening performances take to the stage to simultaneously re-enact on-screen action throughout the screening. These are meticulously pre-planned, as a senior stage manager explains:

> We'd have to nail down what scenes we're doing, and often that's much easier for the directors to work out far in advance, and they'd have to get signed off by the film company anyway about what they can do and what they can show, and what they want them to include.[52]

Performances are then highly rehearsed and carefully choreographed, as a regular SC performer and performance director explains:

> The thing that's specific to SC is the 'cinema element' rather than the 'show element' and what we call *mirror moments* or movie moments. The mirror moment elements distinguish the performers who were playing leading roles in the movie and have to recreate the original performances. The mirror moment is when you are imitating, mimicking, lip synching with the performers on screen at exactly the same time in almost exactly the same way.

He goes on to explain the creative process which involves:

> ... hours and hours of sitting down, watching the film in slow motion ... With *BttF*, technology was such that we had to watch YouTube in a mirror. To get that effect now, we have better tools ... The fact of the matter is it's a painstaking process of watching it frame by frame and trying to absolutely nail what your on-screen counterpart is doing.[53]

Although the dialogue moments are clearly very carefully lip synched, they invariably appear 'out-of-sync' to the audience as they simultaneously watch both the on- and off-screen versions of the characters. This invokes a sense of the uncanny, of the familiar made strange. Moreover, these moments of mismatched stunt doubles and out-of-sync dialogue reveal representational aesthetics of film production.[54] The filmic text(s) of the *BttF* trilogy also contain such moments during the repeated action, for example the re-enactment of the 1955 scenes in *BttF 2* include older (and sometimes different) versions of the actors. This acceptance by the cinema (and SC) audience of the mediation of film-making process has become the source of some cinematic fan practices (e.g. spotting continuity errors).

3. Three-dimensional action includes action beyond the stage. This can include action vehicles driving around the screening site and aerial stunts

... as format 87

3.8 Mirror moments from *Who Framed Roger Rabbit?* and *Back to the Future*'s post-experience promotional videos (here, dialogue 'mirror moments'). A comparison between *Who Framed Roger Rabbit?* (above) and *BttF* (below) reveal how these have become more sophisticated, more accurate and much more precise over time.

above the audience. These synchronised re-enactments have become more and more ambitious and technically challenging as the events have evolved.

In *BttF* there were a number of synchronous off-screen re-enactments of on-screen action in the expanded screening space. These included the opening sequence of Marty's trip to school set against the 'Power of Love' soundtrack, in which he is towed by a vehicle on his skateboard around the 1985 Hill Valley square; and a dramatic chase by the Libyan terrorists in the Twin Pines mall car park. Multiple stunt doubles were used for the main characters in these action scenes – although their costumes were identical, their physical appearances were clearly different. The repetition and replication of mediated action does not look 'quite right' due to the physical differences of the performers' appearances and the visibility of stunt wires, security personnel and stage management crew members. These render visible the aesthetics of film production, revealing the artifice and construction of the film-making process, particularly continuity errors as they are played out *live* in front of the audience for all to see. For example, when Doc Brown aerially traversed the audience on a zip wire, an unintentional continuity error occurred – two versions of Doc were in sight of the audience as the stunt version of Doc was still visibly uncoupling from his dramatic descent on the zip wire, whilst the actor-version of Doc appeared on the ground to deliver the next scene. This off-screen (SC) continuity error uncannily occurred as the same scene in *BttF 2* when two versions of Doc are also (albeit deliberately) visible on screen – the original 1955 Doc is seen setting up the electric rig to the clock from the point-of-view of the 1985 Doc. This striking moment signalled a shift towards the experiences becoming self-referential and playful texts.

The frequency of aerial sequences in SC's shows is not a coincidence. An SC production designer explained the value of these:

> There's an awful lot that we want to do overhead because it's such a great sight line for everybody. It's great to create that thing which everybody can see from any angle.[55]

The experience design has increasingly been led by larger audience numbers and expansive spaces, and the drive for these spectacular moments to take place in and amongst the crowds. The experience is structured to create awed engagement and not critical, evaluative reflection. The tightly enforced prohibition on photography and the removal of phones prevents any leakage, not just of the 'wow' elements of the experience but also of the mechanics and aesthetics of production. What is seen is both the performance and the mechanics of the performance. Although participants may spot the mechanics, their perception can be minimised by the 'magic' of the show and the absence of any record or evidence of the means of production. One of SC's technical managers reflected upon the challenges that need to be overcome in the 'live' moment:

> People are used to seeing the film, and in the film obviously those stunts are massively edited and there's loads of safety stuff which all gets CGI-ed out in the movie, and then you're trying to create the feel of peril and feeling of action in a theatrical environment, but you've got to have layers and layers

of safety around it because you can't have performers jumping off things without safety lines, as an example. And those safety lines take away from some of the aesthetic.[56]

Any signs of production are eradicated or occluded from SC-sanctioned imagery, including the post-experience videos, which we will discuss in a moment, from which the artifice of production is increasingly concealed.

All three of the 'mirror moment' strategies contribute to an aesthetic we refer to as 'simulated liveness' – animating on-screen (pre-recorded and post-produced) action with a live element in order to enliven and engage the audience and to contribute to the transformation of a film into a live event. This is the only form of transformation that takes place as the films themselves are left in their original state and copied/mimicked and enhanced, not altered or edited. As the SC experiences evolved, these engagements became increasingly built into the diegetic fabric of the film, such as singing and dancing to the final song of the film (e.g. 'Johnny B. Goode' in *BttF*). These are key moments in which the participants themselves augment the screening and become part of the live action. Participants are no longer individuals, but part of a collective of viewers who engage together in prompted and unprompted behaviours and aesthetic responses. Some of this participant behaviour is carefully crafted, such as the pre-screening 'dance-along' which is a fitting prelude to the stillness required for group viewing (in *BttF*, on a single-tier simulated lawn). During this aspect of the experience, the players are subject to a 'recombinatory aesthesis' as they are surrounded (literally enclosed within) screen and live-action re-enactments allowing for an 'amplification of affect and effect [as players respond to and experience] visual and kinaesthetic pleasure'.[57]

The *BttF* post-experience video followed what at first appears to be a linear narrative structure while simultaneously showcasing both audience engagement and the centrality of the 'live' experience.[58] The video also seamlessly blended the different contributing elements of the experience – those taken from the original film with those specifically created for the event. It starts with the inimitable incidental soundtrack effect that signals Marty's arrival in 1955, mixed with a voice-over from the fictional radio station created for SC that introduces the context of the Hill Valley Fair. We see the SC version of Marty stumble through the SC-created Hill Valley set. The soundtrack then segues into 'Mr Sandman', as the sights and sounds of the fair are intercut with re-enactments of scenes from the film. The video culminates in clips from the spectacular augmented screening and audience reactions which are set against the 'Power of Love' soundtrack (this is out of the linear sequencing of the original film). Post-produced effects include the speeding-up of the car chase and skateboard sequences. The video presents

3.9 The *Back to the Future* post-experience promotional video. The narrative structure mirrors that of the original film. Multiple mixed visual references are present – for example in the middle-left image, the presence of audience as spectators; at middle-right we can see film production elements such as rigging, lighting and the screen projection space.

a symbiotic mixture and overlay of referents of real-world location (place), film elements (titles), SC performance elements (performers and set), film production elements (lighting, effects), live event infrastructure elements (scaffolding, etc.) and the audience as both spectator and performer, both passive and/or participator. The audience inhabit a liminal space – they are neither 'in' the film nor 'in' its production space. This is a complex, interlayered, visual composition and most explicitly illustrates the experiential aesthetic qualities of SC – the experiences display multi-layered/multi-dimensional aesthetics which have become increasingly symbiotic, mixing real-world with in-world, film and film production aesthetics.

Conclusion

In this chapter, we have shown how the SC format has evolved through its negotiation of the key tensions that shaped this period of evolution – passive to participatory and clandestine to commodified. Whilst the newly inaugurated

'X' brand and the Secret gig attempted to retain the grass-roots, activist and community values of SC, the large-scale 'SC presents …' sphere of activity increased audience numbers with over 45,000 tickets sold, achieving the most successful recorded box office takings (at that time) of £3.5m. The film distribution industry began to notice; this recognition set the conditions for high-profile partnerships and venture capital investments that soon followed.

We have firmly established that there is a clear set of narrative and experience design principles, frameworks and aesthetics that play out in all experiences and these are increasingly being developed using worldbuilding techniques. The experience design and overall structure of the experience began to maximise opportunities for promotion, marketing and consumption at all stages. For example, the prohibition against bringing any food or drink on site, for an event that could now last up to five hours, provided a captive audience for in-world themed food and drink purchases. These purchases became much more obligatory and an expensive addition to the cost of participation in the overall experience.

In the following chapter, worldbuilding and multi-dimensional storytelling strategies became more involved and in-depth than ever before as brand engagement intensified and 'in-world' online stores were launched. Brands became increasingly embedded into narrative and experience design and the online store offered opportunities to purchase costume items, props and memorabilia within the verisimilitude of the fictional world.

Notes

1 When we approached SC on two occasions, to invite them to participate in a live cinema conference (2016) and to feature in a documentary (2019), they declined, stating that Secret Cinema is not a 'live cinema' format and that it has created its own format and art form.
2 Atkinson has previously referred to this as 'simulacinematic': see Sarah Atkinson, *From film practice to data process: production aesthetics and representational practices of a film industry in transition* (Edinburgh: Edinburgh University Press, 2018), 158–9.
3 Email subject lines are routinely titled 'A new world awaits'.
4 Charlotte March, interviewed by author, 16 September 2021.
5 Gavin and Jason Fox, 'Secret Cinema: *Brazil*', Death to the Flippers (blog), 23 July 2013, available at www.deathtotheflippers.com/2013/07/25/secret-cinema-brazil/ (accessed 13 December 2021).
6 Fox and Fox, 'Secret Cinema: *Brazil*'.
7 Gavin Fox, interviewed by author, 31 August 2021.
8 See chapter 2, page 44 for definition of hero moment.

9 Future, 'Terry Gilliam's *Brazil* | Secret Cinema', 23 June 2013. YouTube video, 3:31, available at www.youtube.com/watch?v=MS4cX-lAC6k&t=8s (accessed 13 December 2021).
10 Originally written by Ary Barroso, and re-recorded for the film in 1984 by Geoff Muldaur and Michael Kamen.
11 As a result of these, a screening of *Footloose* (1984) on 27 April 2013 at the Troxy was organised in around twenty-four hours as a complimentary replacement for the delayed opening night. *Footloose* is a 1984 American musical in which Ren McCormack (Kevin Bacon) discovers the small midwestern town he now calls home has made dancing and rock music illegal. Audience members attended the film dressed either in prom or cowboy attire and were instructed to bring balloons. Re-enactments played alongside the film, and audience members were encouraged to get up and dance – during *and* after the show. Branded as a 'Secret Screening' the post-experience promotional video shows an experience that reflects this 'last-minuteness'. It appears chaotic and somewhat disorganised in comparison with other events, but shows SC's nimble ability to respond quickly – rolling out their now tried and tested format in a very short space of time.
12 A full review of the experience can be found here: Richard Clayton, 'Laura Marling, Secret Cinema, London – review', *Financial Times*, 19 June 2013, available at www.ft.com/content/f54ebc90-d8c5-11e2-84fa-00144feab7de (accessed 13 December 2021).
13 Sarah McRuvie, 'Future Cinema present *Saturday Night Fever*', *Clash*, 14 June 2013, available at www.clashmusic.com/live/future-cinema-present-saturday-night-fever (accessed 13 December 2021).
14 This was http://nyeveningpost.com (accessed 13 December 2021).
15 Created by Gavin and Jason Fox.
16 This was www.inkandpaintclub.org/ (accessed 13 December 2021).
17 Created by Gavin and Jason Fox.
18 Although some are still accessible, many of the microsites have disappeared and are no longer maintained or hosted after the experience – these are never connected to or archived with the main SC pages, making this particular aspect of the experience particularly difficult to examine.
19 See Andreas Kofler, '*The Grand Budapest Hotel* poster and props', Fonts in use, 22 June 2014, available at https://fontsinuse.com/uses/7035/the-grand-budapest-hotel-poster-and-props (accessed 13 December 2021). *The Grand Budapest Hotel*: Akademie Zubrowka website was available in 2014 via www.akademiezubrowka.com/.
20 *London City Nights*, 'Ghetts at the Barbican Centre, Secret Cinema's secret gig', *London City Nights*, 9 March 2014, available at www.londoncitynights.com/2014/03/ghetts-at-barbican-centre-secret.html (accessed 13 December 2021).
21 'Secret Cinema X Tell No One are … much smaller-scale events revealing neither the film nor the location and usually feature unreleased films'; see this and other SC brand definitions of this period in Helen W. Kennedy, '"Join a cast of 1000s, to sing and dance in the revolution": the Secret Cinema 'Activist' brand and

the commodification of affect within experience communities', *Participations* (2017) 14(2), 682–96.
22 Which was formally released a few days later, on 3 July 2015.
23 Madison Antus, 'Secret Cinema X review: *Amy*', *Screen Daily*, 29 June 2015, available at www.screendaily.com/secret-cinema-x-review-amy/5089915.article (accessed 13 December 2021).
24 Available at http://secrethotel.org (accessed 13 December 2021).
25 Designed by WatsonDG, in collaboration with Wes Anderson.
26 Sophie Cairns, interviewed by author, 17 September 2021.
27 Terry Cook, interviewed by author, 15 September 2021.
28 Kennedy, 'Join a cast'.
29 Fox, interviewed by author, 31 August 2021.
30 Via www.americanuniobank.us (available in May 2014).
31 Future, 'Secret Cinema presents *Miller's Crossing*', 15 July 2014, YouTube video, 3:16, available at www.youtube.com/watch?v=gcOSt7LyMnw (accessed 13 December 2021).
32 BWW news desk, '*Miller's Crossing* completes run at Crouch End with Secret Cinema's Tell No One', *Broadway World*, 28 May 2014, available at www.broadwayworld.com/uk-regional/article/MILLERS-CROSSING-Completes-Run-at-Crouch-End-with-Secret-Cinemas-TELL-NO-ONE-20140528 (accessed 13 December 2021).
33 See Sarah Atkinson and Helen W. Kennedy, 'Tell no one: cinema as game-space – audience participation, performance and play', *G|A|M|E: The Italian Journal of Game Studies* (2015a) 5, 49–61, and Sarah Atkinson and Helen W. Kennedy, '"Where we're going, we don't need an effective online audience engagement strategy": the case of the SC viral backlash', *Frames Cinema Journal* (2015b), 1–24.
34 To manage and oversee the ticket sales process SC have often partnered with third-party ticket vendors and event promoters such as Universe, Eventim and See Tickets. In the latest production (at the time of writing in 2021) tickets for *Bridgerton* are available via their partner's website (Fever).
35 See www.hillvalleycalifornia.org (accessed 13 December 2021).
36 See Atkinson, *Beyond the screen*.
37 Fox, interviewed by author, 31 August 2021.
38 See Maria Vélez-Serna, *Ephemeral cinema spaces* (Amsterdam: Amsterdam University Press, 2020), 145–72; Ella Harris, 'Navigating pop-up geographies: urban space-times of flexibility, interstitiality and immersion', *Geography Compass* (2015) 9(11), 592–603; and Ella Harris, *Rebranding precarity: pop-up culture as the seductive new normal* (New York: Bloomsbury, 2020).
39 Susan Kulkarni, interviewed by author, 8 September 2021.
40 See Atkinson and Kennedy, 'Where we're going'.
41 See Atkinson and Kennedy, 'Where we're going'.
42 Ollie Tiong, interviewed by author, 20 September 2021.
43 Kaleem Aftab, 'Secret Cinema's Fabien Riggall on *Star Wars*, cancellations, and building galaxies', *The Independent*, 2 June 2015, available at

www.independent.co.uk/arts-entertainment/films/features/secret-cinema-s-fabien-riggall-star-wars-cancellations-and-building-galaxies-10292798.html (accessed 13 December 2021).

44 Interviewed by author, 14 September 2021.
45 Quoted in Rob Hastings, 'Secret Cinema gets the MI6 treatment with James Bond experience in *Casino Royale*', *i news*, 14 June 2019, available at https://inews.co.uk/culture/film/secret-cinema-casino-royale-james-bond-302049 (accessed 13 December 2021).
46 Yondr was founded in 2014. They produce sealable mobile phone pouches with a magnetic lock, and a device for unlocking them (similar to the security tag system used in shops and retail outlets). Fabien Riggall, 'Fabien Riggall and Secret Cinema', interview by Etan Ilfeld, The Etan Ilfeld Podcast, 14 July 2021, audio, 49:11, available at https://anchor.fm/etan-ilfeld/episodes/Fabien-Riggall-and-Secret-Cinema-e14cit3 (accessed 13 December 2021).
47 See Atkinson and Kennedy, 'Where we're going'.
48 Hastings, 'Secret Cinema gets the MI6 treatment'.
49 Katie Mitchell uses a similar screen and space configuration. See Sarah Atkinson, 'Synchronic simulacinematics: the live performance of film production', in *Image action space: situating the screen in visual practice*, ed. Luisa Feiersinger, K. Friedrich and M. Queisner (Berlin: De Gruyter, 2018), 191–202.
50 See Atkinson and Kennedy, 'Tell no one'.
51 Atkinson, 'Hangmen rehanged'.
52 Helen Smith, interviewed by author, 7 September 2021.
53 Male performer/performance director, interviewed by Natalie Wreyford, 11 February 2021.
54 Atkinson, *From film practice to data process*.
55 Tim McQuillen-Wright, interviewed by author, 3 September 2021.
56 Andy Barnes, interviewed by Natalie Wreyford, 14 October 2020.
57 Seth Giddings and Helen W. Kennedy, 'Little Jesuses and *@#?-off robots: on cybernetics, aesthetics, and not being very good at Lego *Star Wars*', in Giddings and Kennedy, *The pleasures of computer gaming: essays on cultural history, theory and aesthetics* (Jefferson, NC: McFarland Books, 2008), 31.
58 Secret Cinema Presents, 'Secret Cinema presents *Back to the Future*', 18 November 2014, Vimeo video, 3:15, available at https://vimeo.com/112151676 (accessed 13 December 2021).

4

Secret Cinema as immersive activism

This chapter captures a further turning point in the evolution of SC and its productions for three key, inter-related reasons – firstly the move into large, semi-permanent warehouse spaces led to the considerable increase in the range of specialists and professionals who were required to design and manage the scale of these productions and this, secondly, led to the creative advancement of narrative worldbuilding techniques and the sophisticated expansion of the now characteristic SC prequel narrative; thirdly, SC founder Fabien Riggall's increasing volubility in public and press accounts narrativised these experiences as responding to and/or intervening in real-world socio-political issues of their moment of production. These three factors were instrumental in shaping the very real elaboration and evolution of the professional requirements and expectations of the SC format (on one hand) and an attempt to shape the public corporate identity or 'brand' through which to communicate the value of their offer (on the other).

We combine the analysis of the five major warehouse-based productions of this period (*The Empire Strikes Back, Dr Strangelove, 28 Days Later, Moulin Rouge!* and *Blade Runner*); the two outdoor events (*Dirty Dancing* and *Romeo + Juliet*) and numerous smaller-scale 'X' events (including *Victoria* and *The Handmaiden*) with a consideration of the many press interviews, public appearances and conference presentations made by Riggall. Through this examination, we draw out the many tensions that exist in the organisation's communication of its corporate identity. These tensions are particularly acute in Riggall's multiple articulations of his identity as *both* a cultural entrepreneur *and* activist. A cultural entrepreneur is the name given to innovators in the cultural arena who create and produce new cultural experiences and new cultural products with the intention (sometimes, not always) of generating income. Riggall's frequent and very public articulation of a defence of artistic freedom and his fierce opposition to what he describes as formulaic cinema experiences is set against the backdrop of a specific period between 2015 and 2018. As we shall discuss, it was during this time that, paradoxically, a repeatable and commodifiable *formula* was being perfected through a series of commercially successful experiences. These increasingly drew upon principles of worldbuilding which incorporated 'brand activations' – companies promoting their brands through events or happenings. Within SC productions of this period, partnerships with external brands were a significant generator of income to support the increasing elaborations of the SC 'worlds' – and brand activations became increasingly embedded 'in-world'. In tandem, we see SC's public discourse of an emergent 'brand activism' – which we define as using the reputation and cultural reach of a brand to increase the visibility of political messages or social causes. We examine these contradictory forces in relation to wider macro-debates around the relationships between culture and industry, experience as commodity, social justice and the needs of the market.

Through this examination, we have identified the two binary oppositions through which the productions and the organisation's identity were shaped: 'intimacy to industrial immersion (2015–2016)' and 'audiences to activists (2017–2018)'.

From intimacy to industrial immersion (2015–2016)

The years 2015 and 2016 were characterised by three major productions which all took place in a large-scale *industrial* warehouse location – an abandoned printing press – which was itself a site of mass factory production.

This period also marked the completion of SC's significant transition from an utopian experimental 'start-up' to an investment-worthy producer of standardised and replicable experiences designed for a scaled-up 'mass' audience. This is a process that completed this 'becoming industrial' that we have traced throughout the organisation's evolution.[1]

Companies House records indicate that in January 2015 SC received £4.55m of 'later stage' venture capital investment from Active Partners, Social Capital and Neon Adventures. This category – 'later stage' investment – is reserved for companies that have evidenced significant growth in sales and have moved beyond a 'start-up' phase. We can presume that the scale of ambition and the audience figures for their 2014 production of *BttF* played a key role in demonstrating this 'readiness' for investment of this nature. The investment clearly underpinned some highly significant scaling-up in technical and creative ambition of the productions of this period along with an important and strategic investment in the fitting-out of larger sites that would later be available for re-use.

This period initiated the use of warehouse space rather than the 'found' locations which SC had initially used and from which the film title would emerge (for example, using school buildings to stage *If …* and *The Shawshank*

Redemption). The practices for these earlier productions were 'site-responsive', an approach that was appreciated by previous SC creatives:

> We had the most amazing buildings – a hospital, a church, a school, Victorian buildings. Those buildings give you so much.²

This later period was instead characterised by a 'site-neutral' approach, where a site was built from the ground up inside an empty, and in some cases semi-derelict, shell. The vast empty warehouses and the large outdoor sites provided the most flexibility, adaptability to any *given* film narrative. An SC location manager explained that 'working in a warehouse is more enjoyable as everything is contained, controlled and it's just a more structured experience' and that it provides 'a blank canvas for the creative team to work from'.³

This new approach led to a change in practices and in collaborations – SC began to commission and hire key immersive events and location development teams to oversee this specialist area of work: the technical complexities of developing and delivering a live event in an undeveloped venue. Their first major collaboration was with Wonder Works, who had a leading reputation in this area: their technical director Piers Shepperd led the London 2012 Olympic opening ceremony. Significant creative and technical advances were achieved in the design and delivery of experiences situated within expansive, and increasingly detailed, spatialised narratives within complex, robust and interactive models of familiar film environments. This period also saw the further extension of bespoke microsite design and social media sites through which to deliver online narrative, building participant engagement and directly linking to the in-show experience.

The Empire Strikes Back (1980) became SC's longest running production to date – from June to September 2015. This – the original sequel to *Star Wars* – included an extended audience pre-narrative engagement strategy. The evening experience also lasted five hours from the moment of entry until the conclusion of the screening (discounting any after-show party, which was a feature of some of the weekend events). This was the first SC experience to take over and completely repurpose the vast abandoned printing press (18 acres in Harmsworth Quays, near Canada Water in London, UK). The event sold 100,000 tickets (these were priced at £75 for a standard ticket – the highest standard price to date) generating overall box office takings of £6.45m ($9.8m).

Once audience members had bought a ticket, they could visit two thematised physical spaces in the lead-up to the main event: the 'Rebel Stores' and a Secret Cantina nightclub. At the Rebel Stores pop-up shop near Brick Lane, London costumes and accessories such as scarves and badges could be purchased, and at the nightclub (housed in Hoxton Hall, London) participants could engage with performers dressed as aliens, Jawas and other members of the rebel alliance. New iconography was developed around 'Rebel X' – the rebel alliance. This new organisation directly linked to the themes of the film, but did not reference anything directly taken from the film. The 'conceptual merchandise designer' described the process behind developing the merchandising strategy for *The Empire Strikes Back*:

> It was part of their props and props game, and that was what I came in to research. Look at the characters, what we could do, then source the products, and work out a way to sell them to the audience, to sell them as part of the range. We're building an entire costume and merchandise range. Then it became a shop, we had a physical shop. I think we got it open in something like five or six weeks from when I started, which was crazy but a brilliant experience. I've never learned so fast on my feet![4]

Many practitioners reflect on the tight time scales for SC productions – their highly temporary, 'pop-up' nature (which has been subjected to academic critique)[5] imposes a particular, fast-paced mode of working. For *The Empire Strikes Back* there was also a pop-up launch event – a dance party at Alexandra Palace, London, UK, on 4 May 2015 – the day on which the second 'phase' of tickets were released. This was strategically timed to coincide with national *Star Wars* day ('may the fourth be with you'), ensuring maximum publicity since this is a well-used hashtag in the *Star Wars* fan community. This event provides further evidence of SC's ability to mobilise existing *story* fans and the existing SC network of experiencers. For this particular event they successfully recruited 3,000 compliant audience members, who all arrived dressed in the required white boiler suits that marked them as members of the 'rebel alliance'; they were all photographed in an iconic flash mob moment outside (see Figure 4.1). Participants were then allowed entry to the event itself, which included DJ sets from artists including DJ Yoda, Nightmares on Wax and Jamie Jones. The launch event was simultaneously promoted as a fundraising event in support of the Refugee Council, raising £11,000. This was a significant event in relation to the production of a particular audience identity and the SC brand identity and we shall return to a discussion of the fundraising event shortly.

The site of the main production – the abandoned printing press – was transformed by Wonder Works into an infrastructurally suitable space for mass participation and the elaborate story-world setting of the *Star Wars* universe. Their promotional materials made significant claims regarding the nature of their expertise in designing experiences: 'both large and small, anywhere in the world. We have a 25-year history of transforming complex creative concepts into extraordinary live experiences; reliably producing work that wows clients and audiences alike.'[6] They provided complex

... as immersive activism 99

Rebel X
@WithYouRebelX

The circle is now complete. We are one #RebelX

4.1 The 4 May 2015 flash mob for Secret Cinema presents ... *Star Wars: The Empire Strikes Back*. A promotion for the upcoming event, which coincided with *Star Wars* Day and the release of the second round of SC tickets.

technical production, overseeing lighting, audio, video, scenic, staging and automation. The base-line infrastructure that they put in place went on to underpin two more major events (*Dr Strangelove* and *28 Days Later*) and, at the time of writing, the transformed building is now a fully operational nightclub and events venue.[7] As an SC location manager explained:

> At SC anything under 1,000 a night wouldn't be financially viable – the sweet spot was between 1,000–1,500 a night so that impacts the space as with all the production and sets that had to be installed, you still needed enough space for up to 1,500 people to roam about without it being too crowded.[8]

As the following comment from an SC production designer makes clear, the shift in the scale of the experiences – the space available and the audience size – created very different design and creative challenges:

> Once we got to that level, we had to think very carefully about the flow of people ... because you had these great ideas about what you expected the public to do at certain timings, but you never quite knew whether it was going to work out. So we often had to change things after the first couple of shows because the flow wasn't quite working and people weren't getting to a certain point for certain key acts, we just weren't getting the attention that we wanted ... That is an integral part of the design process that *doesn't exist in any other genre.*[9]

What the production designer also captures here is a view commonly held by many of the creative teams behind these productions – that they often find themselves in uncharted territory with these experiences.

The entire *Star Wars* story world was drawn from in order to provide the settings, the look and the feel of the space, which expanded far beyond the on-screen universe of *The Empire Strikes Back*. For example, the Mos Eisley space and the Cantina were dominant features of the SC setting, within which other multiple spaces were created in the building, including narrow corridors, small openings to crouch through, a cavernous spacecraft hangar, prison cells, shipping containers, stairways, space shuttle interiors and a flying X-wing space craft.

The production designer explained how the wider *Star Wars* universe was drawn from in order to inform the production and set design:

> There had been a 'zine or comic where it described all of the characters that lived in this town of Mos Eisley. So we wanted different buildings, but we had more buildings than we had characters from the film for, so each set was from another character that we took from this comic book that was part of the *Star Wars* canon. We could officially say that George Lucas has said that this is part of the world.[10]

A team of more than seventy actors and performers populated the space and stage interactions and re-creations of key scenes from the film. These performers included actors dressed as the characters from the film with whom audience members could become embroiled in direct interactions and dramatic situations. So, audience members might be locked in a cell with Han Solo or take breakfast with Luke Skywalker and his uncle, or embark on a rescue mission to free Princess Leia (see Atkinson and Kennedy, 2016 for an in-depth audience study of this experience).[11]

Wonder Works revealed the challenges of managing audience's expectations 'in-world':

> We had things where we arrested people and put them into prison where they could then hang out with various other members of the cast. But of course they didn't like getting arrested because they thought they were missing out on the show, not knowing that eventually Han Solo and Chewbacca would rescue them but that they had to wait ten minutes. There were a few instances of people getting annoyed that they were missing the show when actually they were in one of the most exciting parts of it. [12]

SC also incorporated a large auditorium environment for the screening of the film during the latter part of the evening, with three separate screens, configured in an elongated corridor arrangement necessary to accommodate the large audiences each night. This multi-screen approach had only previously been used for the *Prometheus* production. The mirror moments also became more detailed and technically advanced during this period, with new expertise brought on board, as the lighting designer explained:

> For *Star Wars*, we had two-and-a-half-thousand lighting cues in the film alone. The sci-fi films are a wonderful thing, they are a gift for a lighting designer because the colours are cool and funky, there's lots of flashes and flickers.[13]

The details of the deal between SC and Disney, who hold the rights for *The Empire Strikes Back* IP – which allowed access to the film and the permissions to design an experience around this – are not public knowledge. However, the comments below from an earlier creative director do offer some insight. Firstly, they make it clear that SC paid Disney a share of the ticket price; secondly, they reveal the extent to which this highly elaborate, creatively and technologically ambitious project was a research and development activity which informed Disney's *Star Wars* experience (Galaxy's Edge), which opened in the USA in 2019:

> With *Star Wars*, they [SC] developed the whole project, but they were still giving Disney an enormous allocation per ticket. Disney used the SC project of *Star Wars* as the development for their *Star Wars* experience. Disney got paid to develop their own concept and it was ridiculous – it was the research and development money that they would have otherwise paid for – the amount of money that went into it![14]

This was an extraordinarily ambitious project, occupying a space more than twice the size of the already expansive setting for *BttF* in 2014, drawing on the talents of some 400 professionals, realised through considerable venture capital investment and delivered through a significant professional partnership with Wonder Works. What this creative director also reveals is that this was a high-level, proof of concept R&D project for a major Hollywood studio (Disney) and brought about considerable advances in the creative and technical infrastructure central to immersive event design – particularly lighting, sound, set and narrative design. Although the price of this event drew some negative commentary, the experiential elements received considerable praise in mainstream and industry press,[15] as well as positive coverage in fan-oriented publications. Every indication here supports the notion of an organisation that was moving towards or aspiring to mainstream visibility and audience reach.

The post-experience promotional video returned to the earlier approach: showcasing the success of the event through its audience figures (as previously seen with *Prometheus*, chapter 2, page 52) but this time blended it within a fictional register.[16] The opening graphic title states: 'Summer 2015 … Over 100,000 left earth … To unite in the battle against the galactic empire …' – this graphic used the same text and interface as that used in the productions' dedicated microsite. This marks a shift in the approach taken to these videos – the pre-narrative, not the film itself, provides the structuring principle. The story of the rebellion and Rebel X was intercut with scenes showcasing the expansive scenography and the spectacular effects of the experience.

Rebel audiences and an emergent activist branding

Running alongside this process of professionalisation and 'scaling up' of the experience was the further consolidation of a defined SC brand identity discursively produced through the figure of Fabien Riggall. His identity as a celebrated cultural entrepreneur was joined with that of a socially responsible cultural activist in 2015 when a series of activities and public statements aligned SC in opposition to anti-refugee policy. The public statements intensified around *The Empire Strikes Back* experience; the discourse of rebellion and participant identification as 'rebel' were continuously emphasised through all communications. The Rebel X communication channel provided SC's in-fiction response to the real-world UK general election, May 2015: 'Territories across the galaxy woke up to shocking news this morning. Against all projected outcomes, the Empire has increased its strength following yesterday's election.' The audience participants were here addressed as politicised and potentially 'radical' subjects sharing a particular interpretation of these external/real-world events. Wonder Works reflected on the pre-narrative campaign which had effectively:

> ... encouraged people to rebel and rise up against the Empire. What we then found was that people would drink quite heavily prior to coming to the show. They would then see a Stormtrooper and punch them. Or they would have some kind of weapon with them, which had been encouraged as part of their costume, and then they'd hit a Stormtrooper straight across the head. Of course, however menacing these Stormtroopers look they are just actors ... so it was quite hard to find the right level of excitement.[17]

Later the same year, 'Secret Protest' was launched: this involved a screening sited at the Calais Jungle, accompanied by a 'Secret Screening Protest' campaign, with numerous other simultaneous screenings reportedly happening at multiple venues across the UK, USA and other locations. The initiative was launched via SC's website and through social media channels:

> This Saturday, 12th of September 2015 at 7pm BST, we will stage a secret screening protest in a Central London location and simultaneously in the Jungle Refugee camp in Calais. Standing in solidarity with the tragic plight of refugees in the biggest crisis since the Second World War. We are building a makeshift cinema in the Calais Refugee camp for this event and with your support, we want to build further cinemas in camps worldwide, screening a wide cultural programme for both adults and children. We will send a powerful message to those that need to listen and ask you to join us in large numbers.[18]

This announcement was picked up and covered in the publication *Fad Magazine* – an art and culture edition that covers art happenings and subcultural events in the UK and internationally.[19] The hashtag #loverefugees was set up to communicate and disseminate information and participation in the secret protest screening. This new initiative does not appear to have extended beyond 2015, but the brand work performed by these actions and declarations was significant – positioning SC in a particular relationship to mainstream politics and mainstream culture and articulating an oppositional anti-establishment identity. We have previously analysed how, during this period, SC:

> aligned themselves with dominant mainstream media narratives through the inclusion of refugees into the opening narrative of the experience and their sponsorship of their partner charity the Refugee Council for which they raised £28,000. SC furthered this alliance through a high-profile screening at the refugee camp in Calais.[20]

This alignment achieved a great deal of publicity for both Riggall and the refugee crisis in the wider press coverage around this event. For instance, David Pollock wrote in the *Guardian* detailing this wider political context and Riggall's activist motivations in a review essay that featured an interview with Riggall.[21] Dougal Wilson provided in-depth background to the crisis, outlining the process of staging the pop-up screening in the Jungle camp and providing a detailed, first-hand account of the 'protest' in the *Creative Review*.[22]

In a post in 2016 written by Eli Goldstone for Run Riot,[23] Riggall publicly reflected on both his cultural activist intentions for SC as an organisation and his own personal activism. Goldstone introduced Riggall as:

> founder of the 'hyper-social, communal' immersive screening events SC and co-organiser of the March for Europe, Fabien Riggall has combined his passion for films and ideas about community in increasingly imaginative ways over the last few years.

The March for Europe was held in London on 3 September 2016 and was the largest anti-Brexit protest of the period. Riggall's discussion of the March mixed his personal viewpoint with the organisational vision of SC:

> We can all use the power of *cultural activism to harness political change*. SC is a *socially responsible* organisation which believes in bringing people together to *tell the truth through culture*. Creative groups like us have a responsibility to act during these uncertain times, and like many people I felt passionate enough about the Brexit vote to try and do something about it. [our emphasis]

Although this was a personal project for Riggall he leveraged his growing SC network to promote the event and his discussion of it here further sutured an anti-establishment position to both himself as an individual and to SC as an organisation and brand. Looking beyond the March for Europe Riggall reflected on the motivation for SC's intervention in the refugee crisis:

> Along with many others, I felt incredibly angry and frustrated with the government's reaction to the worst refugee crisis since the Second World War. Millions of people across the globe have been displaced and many of them find themselves in refugee camps like those in Calais. From my visits, I found out that, along with crises in healthcare and providing shelter, one of the biggest problems in the camps was boredom, contributing to loss of hope. We set up a screening of a Bollywood film for about 1,000 refugees and for a few hours they could take themselves away from the harsh realities of the 'Jungle'.

Here the entrepreneurial drivers of SC are largely absent, as is the discourse of innovation in film experience. What comes to the fore in Riggall's proclamations is this drive for 'truth'. During this period the *Moulin Rouge!* production was in its pre-planning stage and the experience was very much framed around this notion of 'truth' and authenticity through culture. In the same article, Riggall went on to reflect upon the close connections between the choice of productions and the socio-political context of the moment:

> Since we began, SC has always been inspired by the political mood of the country, and the wider world. We staged *Battle of Algiers* during the Arab Spring, taking 20,000 people into the dark underworld of the film, very much inspired by political events. We screened *28 Days Later*, the Danny Boyle film about the outbreak of a deadly virus, during the recent junior doctors' strike – in solidarity, we seeded-in the narrative of an understaffed health service into a mock-up St Thomas's Hospital, hosted a special free screening for NHS workers, and publicised the doctor-led Justice for Health campaign throughout the month-long run.[24]

Here we have the return of an assumption of the idea of activist and an embrace of activism which is aligned to the *Zeitgeist* – 'inspired by the political mood of the country, and the wider world'. The post was entirely dedicated to the subject of cultural activism and was featured on Run Riot – a website that covers 'happenings' in London that are largely differentiated from mainstream cultural events, featuring queer performance, radical and experimental art, for instance. This is a discursive space within which Riggall clearly feels comfortable with an activist identity: Riggall has internalised these accolades of influence to adopt a public persona for himself as a *brand* with the cultural authority to change behaviour or to shape engagement.

Assuming the identity of the countercultural entrepreneur, Riggall marked out SC as a socially responsible *brand*, deploying its assumed cultural authority to boost particular messages. There is considerable research that examines the complexities of cultural brands intervening in or contributing to political debate, or appropriating countercultural sentiment or attitudes to promote their own goods and services,[25] practices that can significantly backfire if the alignments are perceived as inauthentic. This engagement is considered to be an appropriate use of influence or *power* in some circumstances, as Christine Moorman explains:

> Brand political activism is justified because brands are powerful cultural actors. This status imbues brands with cultural authority and this authority, in turn, offers the license to or establishes an expectation of involvement in social issues.[26]

In this context, Riggall's approach to aligning the SC brand with these political issues can be conceptualised as a process of 'activist entrepreneurship'; the activist entrepreneur is a concept that emerges from within business and organisation studies. It is used as a deliberate attempt to distinguish a set of socially and politically engaged practices and identities from existing entrepreneurial frameworks.

SC's discourses of responsibility and activism recurred throughout this period across a number of different contexts: 'Our current world situation is so uncertain and as members of society we often just watch it go by in some respects', said Riggall. 'I think we have a *responsibility culturally* to debate these things and *become activists* through exploring film' (our emphasis).[27] He repeated this sentiment in an interview for *Screen Daily*: 'SC is committed to creating powerful experiences in which *audiences become activists* in stories that matter during these uncertain times' (our emphasis).[28] This invitation, or interpellation of the *audience* as activists through their participation in SC experiences, is something that we shall return to below.

Cultural critique as formula

This cross-cutting relationship between film text and contemporary cultural context intensified for the next major SC 'Tell No One' event, *Dr Strangelove or: How I Learned to Stop Worrying and Love the Bomb* (1964) in February and March 2016. The promotional materials for the event positioned it in support of the charity War Child UK – with a similar opportunity for publicity, and an invitation to make donations. The event attracted 20,000 attendees and earned box office takings of £1.24m ($1.8m).

Another entirely bespoke, thematised microsite was established through which ticket holders were given detailed costume instructions and issued elaborately conceived identity papers by the fictional Department of Cultural Surveillance (D.O.C.S.).

This experience was staged in the same location as *The Empire Strikes Back*. This time the large warehouse was transformed into a Cold War-era Burpelson Airbase, filled with actors, vintage props and rooms that costumed audience members could explore while completing tasks such as tracking down specific characters or passing letters to the 'communists'. We see the formulaic aesthetics of control and militarisation used in the last period return here.

The screening itself utilised six screens, four of which showed 'complementary images' while actors on a central stage silently mirrored the film action. The video projection designer offered a sense of the scale of both the artistic and technological interventions underpinning the development of these highly elaborate spatialised narrative environments:

> The 360[°] screens made it tricky because you're suddenly trying to create a world from footage that doesn't exist, and not really having the assets that exist either ... With *Star Wars*, we were able to at least get assets and all of the different CGI bits and pieces, whereas with *Dr Strangelove* everything was made from scratch, and that took a lot of time.[29]

The intentional and overt signalling of a connection between the Cold War thematics of the film and the contemporary moment was maintained across social media channels and brought directly into the pre-screening experience, which was replete with images and references to Donald Trump and Vladimir Putin. The highly detailed reproduction of the original film set included further iconography that drew explicit parallels between the historical context of the film's setting and the contemporary political landscape, including allusions to a renewed fear of nuclear warfare.

The mirror moments also advanced to a sophisticated state in this production, as one of the actors describes:

> There was a moment in *Dr Strangelove* where whenever there's a war room scene – which of course the majority of it is – the actors were all doing it live and mouthing along to it, which you know some people thought was fun, other people thought that less impressive, but an incredibly impressive moment was when the screen cut out, and the cinema fell silent. The actors took a beat and then just played out the scene, live in real time. They did a good five minutes because they've got this stuff in their bones. Then of course the screen re-set and it all came back up, and there was an eruption. It went from the cinema and came back into a live theatre moment – which was gorgeous.[30]

The post-experience promotional video mirrors the style and themes from the original film, and blends film elements with SC staging.[31] Graded in black and white, the narrative arc of the video follows the storyline of the film. It is the first of these videos to show SC performers lip-synching during the mirror moments, celebrating the skill and prowess of the performers which was highlighted by the actor above. This is intercut with shots of the audience singing along to 'We'll meet again' at the end of the screening, and real-world news clips of Donald Trump and David Cameron.

SC returned to its anti-establishment, festival and dance-culture roots in a one-off small-scale 'SC X event' in March 2016 – which characterised the 'intimacy' element of this period. *Victoria* (2015) – a break-through independent film shot in one continuous take, with one camera and no cuts – tells the story of one night. The events centre on a young Spanish woman who has moved to Berlin and who inadvertently becomes involved in a bank robbery. For the SC X event, the Berlin dance club location was entirely recreated at the internationally renowned Ministry of Sound dance venue in London. With the title of the film withheld, the 500 audience members were emailed the day before the screening and told they were on the guest list for 'Club Schwester'. They were instructed to wear clothes for dancing, and to meet the next night at Newington Causeway in Elephant and Castle – this once again harks back to the original roots of the organisation, inspired by the secret, illegal raves of the 1990s. This is not immersion on an industrial scale – and reveals a further tension between the organisation's values and aspirations, which ran at odds with the commercial size and scale of all other productions in this period.

Massification and gamification

The elements now so well established through *The Empire Strikes Back* and *Dr Strangelove* formed the basis of a clear, replicable formula; the core elements, design techniques and tropes were now stabilised; and we move through a period of refinement and consolidation. The next major experience took place between April and May 2016 and was once again staged in the Harmsworth Quays warehouse. This next project was based on *28 Days Later* (2002), a low-budget horror film in which London bike courier Jim (Cillian Murphy) wakes up from a coma to find a post-apocalyptic London overrun with zombie-like victims infected by the highly contagious 'Rage' virus. More than 22,000 people attended this event and box office takings were £1.33m ($1.9m).[32] The experience that was developed around this film included further audience massification and greater adoption of game-like mechanisms to control participant movement through the space and the narrative elements.

The warehouse location became a reconstruction of the St Thomas's Hospital 'Rage Treatment Unit' as well as providing a detailed spatialisation of the film's key narrative pivot points, complete with replica environments and models of crucial locations. Prior to attending the event, the online engagement established the post-apocalyptic context (the Rage virus has broken out, there are widespread deaths and chaos), and invited ticket holders to sign up for online Rage testing. It instructed attendees to wear scrubs and face masks (conveniently available to purchase from the microsite as a 'kit' – see Figure 4.2) and directed them to carry an identity card. For this event, the costume 'kit' included no variety and upon arrival at the event it became clear that this costume was not 'optional'. Anyone arriving without the appropriate costume was taken to a vendor and required to purchase and quickly dress in the required scrubs. The creative choice behind this approach is explained here by the conceptual merchandise designer – a role developed specifically to support the SC format:

> That was the first time I'd ever made kits for the audience. And I love doing that, because for me it was such an effective costume, because you basically came to the show looking like Jim, and so you immediately understood why you'd been asked to dress like that. And being a kit it was really easy for you to purchase and go and dress up, and people just looked amazing, turning up *en masse* in these scrubs, and you see them walk across the Quays and be like 'oh!'.[33]

... as immersive activism

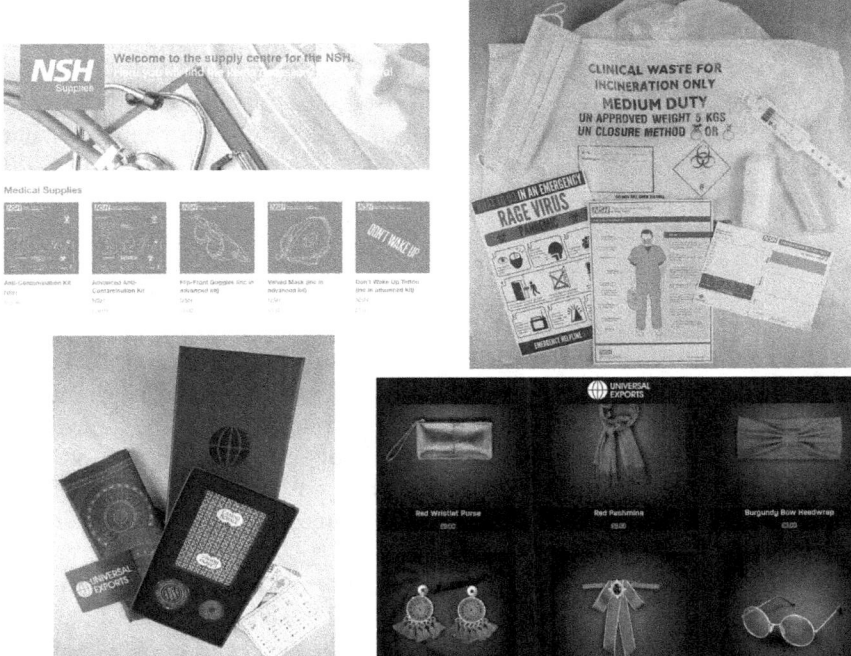

4.2 Secret Cinema bespoke costume kits for *28 Days Later* and *Casino Royale*. Entire costume kits and accessories are now routinely manufactured for audience members to purchase.

The choice of the single costume created a further visual spectacle in the spaces outside the experience itself such as on the streets, on public transport (as the conceptual merchandise designer notes above) and has echoes of the flash mob interruptive aesthetic that was deployed so effectively as a promotional device in the *Star Wars* event. The movement of this audience through these spaces added significant promotional value for the event in particular and for SC as an organisation in general. The other consequence of this uniformity and the sheer numbers of participants was the strong sense of a *mass* and undifferentiated audience.[34] The designer expresses the importance of distinguishing between the assigned costumes:

> we have to have that distinction between what the audience wear and what the cast wear, so that we can recognise cast 'in-world'.[35]

Here we also see instances of extra-dimensional worldbuilding, a term that we introduced in Chapter 3 to denote when something additional is created outside or beyond the existing world but parallels the themes of the film.

In this case, new, fictional organisations and websites were created; for *28 Days Later* this was an 'NSH' website which used the same branding, colours and logo design as the National Health Service (NHS). This was not something that featured in the film itself, but made it relevant to contemporary audiences. This was a sophisticated ARG-type technique that enabled audience members to relate to and engage with the narrative world in their own context and environment through making cultural connections and recognising familiar reference points. These strategies were further enhanced by the contextualisation of the event in real-world socio-political contexts, i.e the refugee crisis for *The Empire Strikes Back*, political upheaval and the rise of Trumpism with *Dr Strangelove* and now for *28 Days Later* the young doctors' strikes. An 'RBC' news channel was also established for the *28 Days Later* pre-narrative campaign and bulletins updating the status of the virus outbreaks were regularly posted on social media channels. A strategy of 'liveness' was instantiated and invoked through the use of these live and breaking news broadcasts, which had now become a characteristic facet of all SC experiences, communicating urgency and inciting calls to action in the lead-up to the event.

Once participants arrived at the site, the augmentations included registering for vaccination, being assigned to a hospital bed, then being 'chased' through that expansive spatialisation and re-creation of the film locations in a temporal sequence that roughly tracked the film storyline. The emergent experience design of the tight control of movement through space reached a new-found intensity here.

The mass audience watched the screening lying on camp beds (those that bought the higher-priced VIP tickets were given sprung hospital beds) with the film projected on twelve screens hanging from the ceilings above them. In a subsequent interview reflecting on the experience, Riggall lamented:

> *28 Days Later* was special ... it was during the time that Jeremy Hunt was fighting the junior doctors, and so we created this story that, due to the junior doctors' pay cuts, ... a zombie apocalypse had taken over England, and everyone was sent to these mass vaccination centres where we put them to sleep; but the vaccinations don't work, and they wake up, in this apocalyptic part of London, and they have to run through corridors [with] zombies attacking them. Much to my accountants' and technical directors' dismay, where we were going to do the screening with seats, ... I just suddenly said, no we shouldn't do that, let's buy 1,000 camp beds, and then let's put all of the screens on the ceiling, so that you're lying down and the blood can trickle around you ... It was an amazing production, but it was quite expensive.[36]

Here, Riggall is introduced as a recognised cultural entrepreneur and an innovator in this particular immersive experience space. His comment reveals something of his creative process and also makes a direct reference to how expensive some of the key experiential augmentations really are. Riggall has often referenced the complexity and the expense of the production in interviews as a form of rebuttal of some of the negativity regarding the pricing structure of these events.[37]

Activist formulation

In this interview Riggall also described how he intended this contemporaneous social and political context to connect with the overall experience communication and worldbuilding. As he describes, the pre-screening discourse around the *28 Days Later* event re-cast and re-presented elements within the film narrative to suggest that the rapid transmission of the deadly zombifying virus Rage was an outcome of the current UK junior doctors' strike. SC publicity images became iconic for the junior doctor strikers; SC offered reduced ticket prices to NHS workers during this run and 400 junior doctors reportedly attended a special event.

For the event itself, *all* participants were guided through the space-as-story. Both *The Empire Strikes Back* and *28 Days Later* mark a specific progression in the design of these internal spaces; in particular, there was a shift towards the creation of a three-dimensional version of the film, through which the participant journey was designed in a way that is closest to a computer game's mechanics. *The Empire Strikes Back* allowed for moments of free 'wandering' through these spaces, within which participants could trade items and pursue multiple missions. For *28 Days Later*, however, this was essentially an experience 'on rails' or, to put it another way, participant movement through the story space was very tightly controlled as though on a single track; there was little or no opportunity for exploration except in carefully managed moments of narrative exposition set in lavish re-creations of iconography from the film – such as the mountain of shopping trollies at the base of the block of flats – and there was a wall of photos and messages with participants encouraged to post their own images. During these moments of stillness on the part of the participants actors performed key scenes from the film. The speed of this journey through the story space was dictated by music and other auditory prompts and began with the participants 'catching up' with the main character's journey as he woke up in a hospital bed and (for the SC participant/player) the zombie chase commenced. The soundtrack was commissioned from the electronic music producer Danny Nolan. He described the creative process behind composing the forty-minute piece which contributed so much to shaping the experiential quality of the event:

> First you have something nice and tranquil, and then suddenly you're woken up and you've got the first chase down the corridor, which was a very dramatic beat-y piece. There's a lot of up and downs like that. You went into someone's bedroom at one point, and again, there's some quiet, nice music, and in another

moment in a church which was choral. The drum and bass would come in for the zombie chases – it's very much light and shade. This is for two reasons – to manage stuff audibly smashing into each other, but also for the sake of contrast – when the beats come in, it has much more impact if the thing before it's been quite mellow.[38]

There was just a single 'forking path' moment in this otherwise one-railed experience, which pivoted around a key plot point – when arriving at the military base the women were taken to one room and the men to another, which mirrors the film's plotline. Afterwards, audience members were free to roam a club space until the climactic moment – a highly charged music and spoken-word performance of 'Do Not Go Gentle into that Good Night' by poet Dylan Thomas. The model of an intense physical chase through the space, interspersed with slow moments of spectacle or narrative exposition, mapped very clearly on to game design mechanics and cut-scene dynamics – for instance, a period of frenetic gameplay activity broken up by periods of short, non-interactive, narrative videos that advanced the story. Many participants and the designers themselves referred to the *28 Days Later* experience using the language of game and play.[39]

The sound designer for the *28 Days Later* production provided further evidence of the artistic and technological advances taking place through the development of these experiences. Here they articulate the complex work behind the sound and light design. The language used by the sound designer here is also noteworthy in the way in which they draw on the language of theme parks and games to describe the experience:

> *28 Days Later* was the first one where we developed this concept that everything is controlled by the sound and that actors follow the soundtrack. The lights and the video are all triggered by sound. We had lots of different two-to-three-minute time-code sections and when we had amassed thirty people, I would hit the button. You do your three-minute run very much like a theme park and I think that was then when it was a necessity because it had to be so tightly controlled. That was when the concept of the show control grew.[40]

In the post-experience promotional video real-world footage of news broadcasts was mixed with fictional broadcasts created for this experience from the fictional news channel, RBC.[41] This was intercut with footage from the event emulating the story arc of the film. Using music excerpts taken from the event for the forty-minute soundtrack, we see the audience arriving at the vaccine centres as everyone is processed, before going to sleep, then being abruptly awoken for the dramatic zombie chase sequences, before being placed under screens like lab rats – *subjects* of experimentation and surveillance. The passive/participatory dimension that we discussed in Chapter 3 is played out most explicitly here with compliant participants subjected to the greatly heightened levels of control and coercion. The post-experience promotional video is the only enduring medium that provides a visual account of the event, the only record of the secret internal spaces that were created. In this case it is also the most explicit demonstration of audiences as performers, directed through the live experience as if this video was the end in sight; it offers a stark reminder that the 'mass' audience are the performers without whom the event could not unfold, nor could the video itself exist as a document and as a promotional device for future experiences.

The purported *brand activism* was somewhat muted here in comparison with the examples of the March for Europe and the screenings at the Jungle camp in Calais and did not go beyond this alliance with the junior doctors' strike and the 'signal-boosting' that this afforded. However, even the shallow engagement indicated here did act to maintain the identity of SC as an organisation with a specific social conscience and oppositional values.

Utopian outdoor events

Alongside the intensive and expensive creative and technological advances taking place through the repeated use of spaces like Harmsworth Quays, SC continued to stage outdoor, festival-style events which were shorter in duration and considerably less expensive, so therefore more profitable. The second iteration of the SC Presents ... *Dirty Dancing* (1987) experience took place over two weekends in this same summer of 2016.

For this experience there was not the same level of activist discourse, either explicitly or implicitly evoked, through any of the publicity; in fact the countercultural discourse was largely absent from the *Dirty Dancing* promotional materials. However, values of freedom and self-expression were highlighted, and SC's social conscience was evidenced through explicit high-profile fundraising and associating this event with a specific charity – Women's Aid – that aligned with the target audience which, as SC confirm, was 95% women.[42]

For this short run, an outdoor re-creation of the film's central location – Kellerman's Holiday Resort – was simulated in Leyton Jubilee Gardens, London and, like the event in 2013, this followed a similar, expansive, festival-like formula. This was also billed as a thirtieth anniversary edition of the film – following a now established strategy where many of the films in SC's slate are aligned to anniversaries or forthcoming new releases of related films in the franchise. This was definitely the case for *BttF* – the SC production coincided with the thirtieth anniversary of the original film's release date – and also for *The Empire Strikes Back* – the new film in the *Star Wars* franchise (*The Force Awakens*) was due for release later in the year of the SC event. These strategic temporal alignments clearly maximise synergistic promotion opportunities for both SC and the film's studio and distributors.

The repeat production of *Dirty Dancing* evidences the establishment of a formula within a formula – these cult classics have an established, engaged fan base that is easy to reach, so are scheduled as a key summer income stream, in this case with more than 30,000 attendees generating £1.9m ($2.5m) at the box office. The organisation demonstrated a canny ability to engage a mass audience in their vision of an engaged collective of people, and to continually advance an ethos of belonging to a community while clearly adopting a profit-driven, formulaic model of experience design. These outdoor events were suffused with the utopian affect of the music festival or carnival. Audience members were drawn into the hedonistic atmosphere of a party, encouraged to sing, dance and engage in play, and to quote-along to their favourite dialogue – this is a well-worn film formula.[43]

The third SC *Dirty Dancing* production was set to run in summer 2022, having twice been postponed since 2020 and 2021 due to COVID. The fact that the SC 'festival' formula has also been emulated by an organisation in Australia offers a further indication of both the replicability and the profitability of the event.[44] It also signalled the increasing industrialisation of the experiences and the wider sector, which shaped this period – and will go on to do so in the next. However, we will now consider the particular discursive formation of *intended* audience subjectivities which run counter to these commercial imperatives – as they are encouraged to become activists.

From audiences to activists (2017–2018)

Another large *industrial* location – this time in a series of connected warehouses close to Canning Town underground station – was used to house the two major productions of this period. The alignment with underground movements and notions of resistance continued to shape and influence the productions: it was central to the performance and experience design and, as we have already noted, was most explicitly underscored by Riggall in his desire for audiences to become activists.[45]

As with the previous period, the number of different productions started to slow, they were situated in buildings which had now become established, and the productions became ever more complex and ran for longer periods. The scripted performances and interactions also became even more elaborate and increasingly professional – qualities that matched an increased level of expectation from immersive audiences.

For *Moulin Rouge!* (2001), which ran from February to June 2017, SC worked with Entourage Live to develop the Canning Town site as a 'meanwhile use' for these buildings. A detailed account of these site developments and place-making strategies is provided in our earlier analysis of the UK immersive cinema sector.[46] Entourage Live became the technical production lead on all experiences mounted at this site from this point onwards.[47]

This cult film, a modern take on the classic Hollywood musical in which contemporary pop songs are reimagined, is set in Paris in 1899 and features a young, poor, English writer who becomes infatuated with Satine, a singer at the Moulin Rouge. Reportedly more than 70,000 people attended the lush, lavish re-creation of the over-the-top Luhrmannesque re-visioning of late-nineteenth-century Montmartre in Paris during the sixteen-week run, and box office takings were £4.48m. Luhrmann himself came and took part – a key turning point in the organisation's status and recognition according to one associate producer:

> I think when Baz Luhrmann started showing up to *Moulin Rouge!* and *Romeo + Juliet*, it really helped SC because people were really engaged with the fact that it had support from the director.[48]

The SC event made a clear alignment between the film's values and wider political and social debates, with a particular, direct reference to refuge and the plight of refugees. A charity was nominated – the Help Refugees campaign – and the societyoflove.org website drew explicit connections between the values of 'truth' and 'love' espoused in the film and support for refuge in general. During the performance itself a key speech given by the actor performing the role of Zidler made a direct reference out to this wider contemporary context.

This was one of the most expansive audience interaction developments to date, as one of the creative producers explained:

> Every single person had their own character, so we actually wrote something like 1,200 different profiles of people and created a family tree of how they were all connected to each other – who was whose uncle, so-and-so murdered a prostitute. It was so complicated.[49]

This description shows the complexity of the creative labour involved in the development of these experiences of mass individuation, within complex environments populated by a 'mass' of individuated or distinct stories. The experience was characterised by its extensive audience embeddedness, shaped by increasing ticket stratification in which the lower-paying Creatures of the Underworld ticket holders (standing, £49) were the source of entertainment for higher-paying Children of the Revolution (seated, £59) and Artistocrats (£130).

A number of creative and technical practices were advanced with this production. The sound was an intrinsic feature of the internal locations, became increasingly elaborate, and techniques were drawn from film production and the aesthetics of cinematic sound design. The sound designer gave us some interesting examples of how the space was sonically spatialised through the use of sound effects and directional audio:

> We had an overall sound system in surround where we had various voices of distant Parisians, street scenes and then prostitutes coughing and all sorts of things. We also had a lower tier of speakers which were hidden around behind props with sounds like cat meows, pigeons flying overhead, somebody playing piano in a bedroom behind a window ...[50]

The global performance director explained how he engaged all of the bar/security and front-of-house staff in the show's narrative, in a further creative layering of the experience:

> For Paris I used a great one – it was 1899, so we're on the cusp of a new century and Montmartre is like Shoreditch, where basically all the rich people want to hang out where the artists are ... It's just a place for rich people to hang out and the artists get pushed out so then you've got an instant identity for people to work with.[51]

In-film audience participation was at its most extreme with the Creatures of the Underworld faction of the audience becoming performers during the screening of the film, commanded and conducted by the character Zidler to stand, sing and dance throughout.[52] They were rewarded for their lively interactions through their participation with, and proximity to, the action and the performers: the action occurred directly above their heads and in amongst them. As a production designer explains, 'overhead's just great: a sight line for everybody ... The trapeze in *Moulin Rouge!* was great from an audience experience point of view.'[53]

This proximity and the intimacy of these performance spaces also led to challenges, particularly in light of the risqué themes of the film, which include prostitution and promiscuity, as reflected on by one performer:

> I often had to walk through the crowd from the very back to the very front, to just get up onto the stage. By the time the film goes on, everyone's had their fair share of drink and so people would just be very handsy and grabby ... I just moved fast enough so people didn't really have a chance to do it. But that's the weird thing – it wasn't in a nasty way, it was just like they really felt that was okay because we created that world. I felt we can't really tell them off for doing that – we've just spent two hours trying to get them into a place where they're feeling crazy enough to do these things.[54]

4.3 The evolution of dancing mirror moments: *Wings of Desire* – a solo aerialist performance (top left); *Saturday Night Fever* – a couple dance (top right); *Dirty Dancing* – the climactic lift sequence (bottom left); and *Moulin Rouge!* – a choreographed, multi-couple dance sequence (bottom right).

In Chapter 5 we will look in more detail at how safeguarding performers has been prioritised and managed in later experiences.

Within *Moulin Rouge!* we also see more complex and synchronised mirror moments – particularly in the re-enacted choreography of dancing sequences. These have evolved over time from single performances, to couples dancing, to the synchronised re-creation of demanding physical stunts (such as the climactic lift in *Dirty Dancing*), to the multiple-dancer sequences that we now saw in *Moulin Rouge!* (see Figure 4.3).

These technically perfected moments of synchronised choreography and aerial sequences are all showcased in the *Moulin Rouge!* post-experience promotional video,[55] which emulated many of the film's aesthetics. It also provides another visual demonstration of the audience as central to the performance – without them the event could not unfold.

This particular production signalled a shift away from the previously overt control of audiences into a more free-form mode of play and exploration. It also returned to the burlesque roots that we saw in the very early productions. However, high-end brand partners were now in place, which in this instance reinforced the 'French-ness' of the film's setting – these included French luxury beauty brand L'Occitane, the French purveyor of vermouth

Noilly Prat and exotic French cocktail brand St-Germain. These brands were not as apparently embedded in the narrative world – nor 'activated' – as others that followed.

The tension between industrialisation and intimacy persisted with two smaller-scale productions in the intervening period before the next major, warehouse-scale production. Both offered higher levels of intimacy, in their smaller screening environment – both returned to the Troxy.

The first was an SC X Tell No One production of *The Handmaiden* (2016) in April 2017. The South Korean erotic psychological thriller, based on the book *Fingersmith* by Sarah Waters, was the last production to be held under the SC X banner. These were a series of preview screenings for the film, which went out on general theatrical release the following week. In the lead-up to the event, a series of emails were sent instructing guests to bring love letters, notebooks and a pen to communicate, and instructed them to maintain absolute silence until given permission to speak by 'The Master'. The event recreated the film's 1930s eastern setting with three differently priced and themed tiers of seating – Gallery, Salon and Library. On the stage below the cinema screen ran a large, back-lit, Shoji screen, which the actors used throughout the film to recreate mirror moments – walking through the door, or using silhouettes to discreetly re-create some of the more erotic scenes appearing on the screen above. The production involves the creation of a bespoke production soundtrack – first initiated by *28 Days Later* – in this case it included a live performance in a return to the experimental live cinema scoring which was a feature of Secret Cinema's sandbox period detailed in Chapter 2. The sound designers explain how:

> silence was enforced for an hour prior to the screening, during which we scored the drama on stage. Sohyun Park and Sohjin Park performed on piano and violin, amidst our dark and schizophrenic interpretation of Park Chan-wook's beautiful tale.[56]

The second small-scale production of this period was a series of screenings for *I, Daniel Blake* (2016), both at the Troxy and at the Blackfriars Ouseburn Cinema, Newcastle in June 2017, in the days leading up to a general election. Branded as a 'Secret Youth' initiative, a special ticket price was offered for 16–25-year-olds: just £3.50. Ticket holders were invited to share the message across their networks, to encourage as many young people as possible to attend these screenings. Held in partnership with SB.TV (an online urban music platform) speakers, artists and performers included Ken Loach, Rebecca O'Brien, Paul Smith and Goldie. The stated aim of the screenings was 'to empower young and first-time voters as part of the Secret Youth initiative'.[57] This initiative was launched earlier in 2017 by Riggall at various forums in the UK.[58] There is no evidence to suggest that this branch of activity was sustained after the initial flurry of press around the launch. Later that year

Riggall announced a related initiative – #WeDreamArabia at the Misk Global Forum in Riyadh – in November 2017.⁵⁹ Speaking to 1,000 Saudi youth about the vision and history of Secret Cinema, Riggall explained:

> The goal is to empower youth to take control, to become hyper creative and develop a new cultural landscape in the Middle East. To explore new forms of entertainment where audiences become participants and activists in the stories being told. During these uncertain times, it's projects like these that are paving the way for artists to tell the truth and imagine a more hopeful and compassionate society.⁶⁰

Again, the progress and outcomes of this initiative do not appear to have been followed up nor documented after this launch. At this particular forum, Riggall was joined on a panel by representatives from two global media powerhouses – AMC Entertainment and Discovery Networks – a clear signal that SC were being considered as key players influencing and shaping international film cultures. Reporting on the event and Riggall's input, *Arabian Business* stated that 'following the conference the Saudi entertainment authority announced a new portal that would fast-track application for event permits'.⁶¹

These alignments with youth activism returned yet again with a later venture launched by Riggall, displaying a now characteristic form of peripatetic hyper-activism, moving from one hashtagged social initiative or political cause to the next. There may be more that we have not referenced here, since their history is just as scattered and difficult to track as are all of the past screening events. Despite this fragmented and dispersed approach, Riggall always engages in consistent messaging – a call to reject mainstream digital culture, and to engage in community-led, grass-roots creativity.

The constant tension between these core values and the drive towards commerciality was ever-present – the latter funds and subsidises the former – Riggall confirmed this as an approach within his own business strategy:

> I put on bigger shows like *Star Wars* to fund smaller shows like *Battle of Algiers*, and *Dr Strangelove*, I was using the power of the IP to create secret shows, so I knew what I was doing, roughly ... The product is always driven by purpose, a need for social change.⁶²

This same tension also played out internally within the larger productions – which manifests in the way that SC integrate partnerships with external brands into their model, as we shall see in the next section.

Becoming brand: SC, brands and worlds

As we have seen, SC engaged in a broad spectrum of brand development activities, whether through their carefully managed 'secret aesthetic' or through Riggall's frequent public proclamations about the values and *intentions* of the organisation. This period of time – between 2015 and 2018 – also marked the considerable elaboration and development of the way in which brands and branding operated as part of the worldbuilding for SC experiences, in three key ways. What has already been described above is the first layer of brand work, which defines SC and their audience as a distinctive consuming community with a utopian spirit and a strong belief in the power of culture and engagement, through the right kinds of cultural event, to bring about social and political change. This is a *world view* within which inconsistencies between a drive for profit and libertarian or activist principles are effaced. The second layer of brand engagement is a more direct form of creative practice where brands such as those shown in Figure 4.4 are created to support the film-specific worldbuilding activities – these include Earth Cargo Airlines (featured in *The Empire Strikes Back*) and the NSH (for *28 Days Later*). The third form of brand activity is building alliances with brands that can be embedded in the experience in a way that *augments* the authenticity of the world being created. The *Blade*

4.4 In-world corporate logos and branding created for fictional organisations in pre-narrative experiences. Clockwise from top left: Utopia Skyways (*Blade Runner*, 2010); Brave New Ventures (*Prometheus*, 2012); D.O.C.S (*Dr Strangelove*, 2016); NSH (*28 Days Later*, 2016). Centre: Earth Cargo Airlines (*The Empire Strikes Back*, 2015).

Runner experience is the moment when this element of the SC approach became well established, extending film product-placement practices and in this case also replicating many of the *same* brand alignments chosen for the film.[63]

Blade Runner (1982) made its second appearance in the SC slate, this time on a much larger and more elaborate scale and branded under the tag line 'A Secret Live Experience'. It ran for more than sixteen weeks from March 2018 in the same Canning Town warehouses as *Moulin Rouge!*, attracting similar audience levels – approximately 70,000 – and taking £4.8m at the box office. There was an expansive and extensive pre-narrative digital and in-show experience with the most detailed, reverse-engineered worldbuilding to date. *Blade Runner* represented another turning point in the approach to the 'show' element of the experience, by advancing multi-dimensional worldbuilding techniques – new story strands were created which existed in the same narrative universe but were tangential to the main narrative. As one writer explained:

> My work basically involved building a detailed 'pre-narrative' story architecture – what's happening in the world in the immediate timeframe leading into the film. And then, within that overall story arc, we needed to create a detailed journey for every single member of the cast, from Deckard, Batty and Tyrell right down to the most fleeting extra (forty of them in total). And once all those weaving, interlocking story arcs, motivations and countermotivations were set, we then had to weave ten different audience journeys through the whole thing.[64]

The term pre-narrative has already been used in previous chapters – according to this writer, it refers to the 'prologue to the film'.[65] This has been contested by other creatives:

> Whenever I was there and even up until now I despise the term 'pre-narrative' because it implies that the theatrical bit is less important than the film, so it undermines the work. So I always say, no, it's *the* narrative … the amount of work that goes into this bit! The work there [in the film] had already been done and all we're doing is copying it.[66]

The pre-narrative story for the *Blade Runner* experience was infused by themes of activism and rebellion. After buying a ticket, audiences ('citizens') were first invited by 'The Utopia Group' (part of the film's Tyrell Corporation) to emigrate to an off-world colony for 'the chance to begin again' (an invitation also issued in the first SC *Blade Runner* experience: see Figure 4.4). When attendees gathered at the site – the 'World Terminus' district – they discovered that a resistance movement called 'Blackout' was rising up within the 'scavenger' community, seeking to steal and destroy citizen data owned by the corporation (and therefore erase records of replicant identities). The SC writers drew this narrative from the blackout event that is mentioned in *Blade Runner 2049* – a disaster that occurred thirty years before the period of that film, caused by an electromagnetic pulse that led to a power outage lasting days, which resulted in the deletion and corruption of all digital data – including that owned by the Tyrell Corporation. The cause remains unknown and unexplained in the film, although there is speculation that it was carried out by rogue replicants. This narrative strategy follows a well-worn ARG trope where a nefarious corporation is established (e.g. the Utopia Group) and a resistance group rises up in response (Blackout).[67] This strategy also reveals how SC's worldbuilding draws from the extended narrative universe of *Blade Runner*, which spans the original novel by Philip K. Dick,[68] two feature films, a short animé film (*Blade Runner Blackout 2022*), as well as the speculations of extensive online fan communities. As the SC writer explained: 'We created this imaginary film that exists in the space between the two films [*Blade Runner* and *Blade Runner 2049*]'.[69]

The site featured the most spectacular production design yet seen – a re-creation of Ridley Scott's neon-lit, rainy Los Angeles 'of 2019', fused with aesthetic influences from *Blade Runner 2049*. The sets included a Los Angeles police department, a whiskey-fuelled snake-pit bar, a departure lounge, Hannibal Chew's laboratory (in the film, he designs replicant eyes) and a number of hidden rooms – one of which included replicant testing. The writer explained how the food and drink was also themed and 'scripted': 'We came up with the names of the cocktails and the noodle dishes – we'd give him a name that would make sense in that world'[70] (see Figure 4.5).

The centrepiece of this production, for which it is renowned and remembered, was its *internal weather* system in which rain fell from the roof onto the crowds in the main internal arena. Audience members were instructed to wear transparent coats and bring umbrellas, and to wear goggles to 'protect from the acid rain'. This was the most technically spectacular – but operationally challenging – element, as the senior stage manager reflected:

> Everyone ended up so bloody wet. That was a big headache for the wardrobe department. Also, the floors became very slippery, and of course, as soon as you put a drunk audience in, there's beefburgers in it, there's drink spilled into it. The operations department dealt with the water, thankfully.[71]

There was also expanded video projection design which included more than sixty screens and monitors, LED walls, projections, holographic special effects and interactive touchscreens. The video projection designer explained the process for the on-screen content design:

> A really good example of this is the most iconic image, which is the geisha on the billboard. You only see it for ten seconds [in the film], so you don't

4.5 Secret Cinema presents … *Blade Runner* production designs for in-world food outlets. These show how the food and beverage offer was designed to fit with the themes of the film.

know what it's advertising. So we're going to have a big LED wall that's going to have a geisha on it, and we're going to have to film that, so someone would have to figure out what they're advertising. You're backwards-engineering from a limited amount of data.[72]

The advanced, multi-screen video design also expanded into the auditorium space where three separate screens accommodated the high volume of audience members and delineated the viewing environments. Those on the lower-priced tickets – the Scavengers – reported cramped and uncomfortable seating conditions in the auditorium space allotted to them.

Embedded branding

SC production sponsors' logos may feature on the main SC web pages – the nature of these partnerships have evolved over SC productions from product placement to *embedded brand engagements*. For example, early SC productions in 2008 were sponsored by Nokia, and Windows Phone sponsored productions in 2009 and 2010. Their integration was rudimentary and very

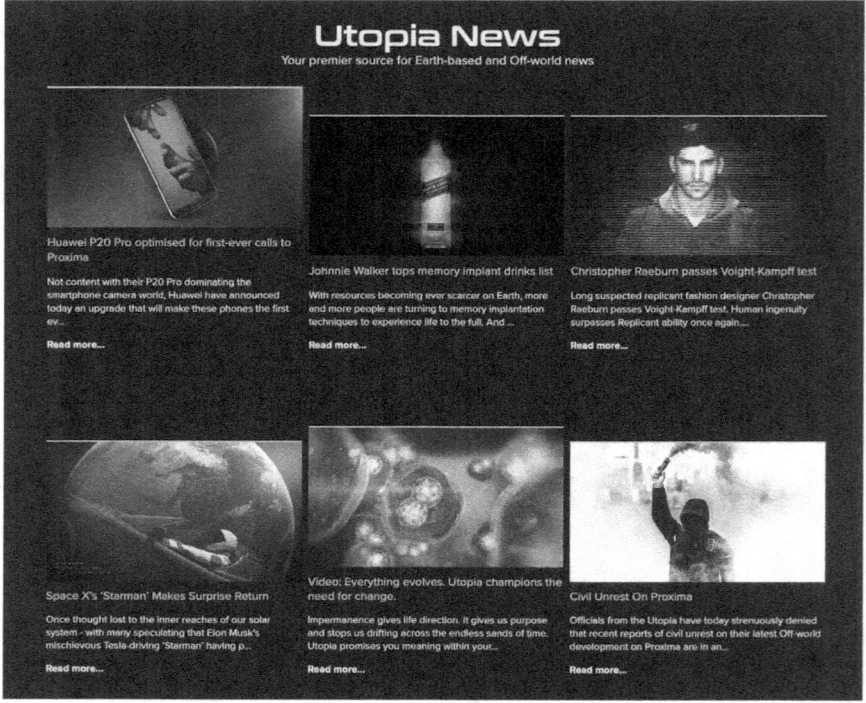

4.6 Embedded branding in Secret Cinema presents ... *Blade Runner*. The participating brands were blended into the in-world pre-narrative campaign through news stories on the website.

often out-of-world, such as social media tweet walls on which audiences commented out-of-character (see Chapter 2, pages 33 and 40). A good example of more advanced and sophisticated brand embedding can be seen in *Blade Runner* where the partners Huawei, Johnnie Walker, Asahi, Dr Martens, Tesla and JCDecaux were integrated into the pre-screening narrative experience in numerous ways. Firstly, they featured in narrativised in-world news stories in the lead-up to the event (see Figure 4.6).

Secondly, *narrative re-versioning of existing branding* featured on the screens within the event itself. The video projection designer provided an illustrative example:

> We needed to find a way of taking Asahi's [a premium beer's] modern, current branding and then convince them that it looked much better if you made it this Retro 1985 version, but that still complies with their brand guidelines *and* also looks like it's in *Blade Runner*.[73]

4.7 Secret Cinema presents … *Blade Runner* production designs showing Asahi branding embedded into the set design.

In relation to the SC brand partnership, Laura Mitchell, director of brand marketing at Asahi UK Ltd, is quoted as saying:

> When we relaunched Asahi Super Dry … we wanted to ensure its marketing would reflect the identity of the brand and put us at the heart of forward-thinking experiences, with a mix of Japanese culture. We're delighted to be partnering with some truly exciting experiences that feed consumer curiosity and showcase the brand in a contemporary manner.[74]

Figure 4.7 is an example of an in-world brand activation. SC had previously honed these approaches through 'brand-work-for-hire' projects such as deploying their immersive worldbuilding skills to develop a Cadbury Milk Tray brand activation experience.[75]

The other selected brand alignments worked very well with the thematics of the film – fusing Asian elements with high-tech aesthetics. Bringing together the gritty punkiness of Dr Martens with the elite branding of Johnnie Walker chimes with the overall cyberpunk aesthetics of the film. The futuristic brand appeal of Tesla further supported the aesthetic design through its in-world incorporation as one of the LAPD cars. The writer explained how: 'It was kind of advertising, but advertising through the lens of the IP.'[76] Riggall justified this practice to meet creative aspirations:

> This is certainly a new form of advertising and, as long as it is the right film, the right association with the film, and we can weave brands in to the world that we've created, then we are open to these partnerships.[77]

The descriptions of the narrative and creative design elements that our interviewees have shared provide an insight into the complexity of the artistic and technological processes that underpinned this particular SC experience. They also provide an insight into the narrative practices that underpin the *individualisation* of participant experiences. The writer described how:

> different audience members will remember different pre-narrative moments that have informed the film. So when an audience member sits and watches the film, there'll be certain moments that they will realise: 'I met that guy in the bar and he made me an origami thing' ... but they won't have all of the pieces unless they go every night and follow every track.[78]

The different audience journeys related to the grades of access to the experience conveyed by the ticket type – there were three tiers of ticketing in *Blade Runner* with a clear stratification of experience, as with previous productions: Orion (regular), £45; Phoenix (advanced), £59; and Black Galaxy (VIP), £115 – the VIP ticketing level included two cocktails designed for the event and a secret meal. Some audience members were assigned a scavenger identity, whilst others were members of the LAPD (those holding VIP tickets). These identities were assigned within a now established pre-narrative format – the routine in-world 'questionnaire' which, in the case of *Blade Runner*, was again framed as a Voight-Kampff empathy test but is always thematised in a manner appropriate to the film narrative.

The elements that constitute the VIP experience have shifted over time – VIP ticket holders have sometimes been allowed into 'exclusive areas' (for example in *Moulin Rouge!*). For *Blade Runner*:

> We had the VIPs going straight up to LAPD and it actually became so efficient that they went straight into the building and missed everything. So what we did was put the VIPs in the pen with the scavengers. Then suddenly they were undercover cops and had to break into the building, they had the best time. So actually we learned from that and know the VIPs want to be in the heart of the action, so rather than having a VIP parlour that's closed off ... we put the VIP areas within the heart of the story. The VIPs might meet some of the main characters and receive a little extra bit of narrative or *Easter eggs* that others don't get. [Our emphasis][79]

These 'Easter eggs' included being awarded 'Blade Runner' papers, and becoming embroiled in a climactic raid of the 'snake-pit bar', an activity designed to move everyone into the central arena for the hero 'blackout' moment which culminated in an aerial performance. Characteristic SC themes of control and rebellion were centralised into the performance and experience design. The post-experience promotional video showcases the blackout narrative and spectacular scenes of rain falling onto the crowds below.[80] An experience-based soundtrack was created by the artist Rival Consoles and this features as the soundtrack to the video. *Blade Runner* was a landmark production for SC, excelling in its complex and detailed immersive rendering.

The final production in this period was an outdoor event, based around *Romeo + Juliet* (1996) and staged over a short run in August 2018 in Acton, west London. Like *Dirty Dancing* this experience attracted a large audience over its thirteen-night run – a reported 60,000 people attend, almost the same numbers as for the sixteen-week run of *Blade Runner* on account of the extensive outdoor location, garnering £3m at the box office. There were two tiers of ticketing – Young Hearts & Rogues (£49–64, for different nights) and Nobles & Underbosses (£85). The audience were framed as the warring Montagues and Capulets and instructed to wear clothing which was either red or blue to denote their allegiance. The pre-narrative was comparatively shallow; a 'stock' website – 'the story was that Father Laurence has interceded in the city-wide violence and has organised a summer festival where the feuding Capulets and Montagues can come together in peace at the Truce of Two Houses'[81] – supported by a flow of promotional social media content, boosted by a flash mob on the South Bank in London where a number of the characters and a gospel choir from the show delivered an impromptu performance. Clothing and accessories could be purchased in advance from the online shop.[82] As with the *Dirty Dancing* experience little overt activist rhetoric was deployed in promotional materials but the alignment with thematically or content-appropriate charitable activity continued: here SC continued their ongoing partnership with young people's mental health charity MAC-UK. The SC reports show that this production was the only one that generated a profit within this financial reporting period. We surmise that this evolved format for expansive, outdoor, 'festival'-style events has far less overheads and significantly reduced costs than the indoor experiences.

The post-experience promotional video is a fast-paced trailer,[83] only thirty-four seconds long, using the opening title track of the film – 'O Verona' by Craig Armstrong. It intercuts clips from the film with SC clips that directly mirror these, using the same title graphics and freeze-frame aesthetics to introduce the main characters (see Figure 4.8). There is a further aesthetic blurring between the original film and its representation where both production values and the skills of convincing 'copying' are showcased. An actor commented on the technical accuracy of the mirror moments performed during the screening:

4.8 *Romeo + Juliet* post-experience promotional video. The aesthetics of these videos are increasingly brought closer to the look and feel of the original film; on the left-hand side are screen grabs from the original film, and on the right are screen grabs from the SC video.

The actor, James Byng, who played Tybalt, the work with his guns that he was doing! Not only could he do the flips and throws, but to do that in time with what John Leguizamo was doing on screen – he's matching [Leguizamo's] tempo and doing the exact same moves while performing a skill; these flourishes of gun play were very impressive.[84]

Conclusion: from freedom to formula

The last two major productions of 2018 – *Blade Runner* and *Romeo + Juliet* – epitomised the now matured SC experiential aesthetic format for both indoor and outdoor productions. Across both we have seen an increasing of the intimacy and the performers' proximity to the audiences; the oscillation of audience subjectivities between mass-consuming audience and activist; and that mirroring reached a point of perfection.

What evolved over this period are two distinct formulae, a creative and technically intensive indoor model and a highly profitable, less demanding outdoor model. The latter may well work to provide the funding to support the former. This period also marked the *industrialisation* of the SC activity; it could no longer be positioned as a niche brand but was now established as a profit-making organisation that would require a level of consistency not only in the experiences offered but also in the identity of the brand itself. As part of this process, activism fell away after this period, marking another turning point for the company. Max Alexander was appointed as director on 8 January 2018, and a later-stage venture-capital investment of

$6.55m occurred in October 2018. As a consequence of this further investment, the scale and nature of the experiences that we will explore in Chapter 5 take another profound turn.

Notes

1. Here we are of course referring to the 1947 critical framework for defining 'cultural industries' established with considerable negativity in the early twentieth century by Max Horkheimer and Theodor W. Adorno in 'The culture industry: enlightenment as mass deception' (see *Dialectic of enlightenment* (Palo Alto, CA: Stanford University Press, 2020), 94–136). SC is a fascinating case study of this process of 'becoming' industrial and the processes of commodification that slowly undermine the more utopian discourses originally espoused by the founder.
2. Garrett Moore, interviewed by author, 8 October 2021.
3. William Ma, in an email exchange with author, 19 November 2021.
4. Conceptual merchandise designer, interviewed by Natalie Wreyford, 11 December 2020.
5. Vélez-Serna, *Ephemeral cinema spaces*, 160.
6. Wonderworks, https://wonder.co.uk (accessed 13 December 2021).
7. The Printworks, https://printworkslondon.co.uk (accessed 13 December 2021). A consulting report commissioned by SC and undertaken by BOP highlights the benefits and impacts of this particular Secret Cinema residency: Alex Homfray, Douglas Lonie and Joshua Dedman, 'Changing the scene: the impact of a Secret Cinema residency', BOP Consulting (2017), available at www.secretcinema.org/charity-and-community (accessed 13 December 2021).
8. Ma, email exchange with author, 19 November 2021.
9. Ollie Tiong, interviewed by author, 20 September 2021.
10. Tiong, interviewed by author, 20 September 2021.
11. Sarah Atkinson and Helen W. Kennedy, 'From conflict to revolution: the secret aesthetic, narrative spatialisation and audience experience in immersive cinema design', *Participation: Journal of Audience and Reception Studies* (2016) 13(1), 252–79.
12. Collage Arts, 'Wonder Works interview', *Collage Arts*, 11 July 2016, available at www.collage-arts.org/wonder-works-interview/ (accessed 13 December 2021).
13. Terry Cook, interviewed by author, 15 September 2021.
14. Moore, interviewed by author, 8 October 2021.
15. Including: Benjamin Lee, 'Secret Cinema: *The Empire Strikes Back* review – the force is weak with this one', *The Guardian*, 12 June 2015, available at www.theguardian.com/film/2015/jun/12/secret-cinema-the-empire-strikes-back-review-the-force-is-weak-with-this-one (accessed 13 December 2021); Rebecca Hawkes, 'Secret Cinema: *The Empire Strikes Back* review: "ridiculously fun"', *The Telegraph*, 12 June 2015, available at www.telegraph.co.uk/film/star-wars–the-empire-strikes-back/secret-cinema-review/ (accessed 13 December 2021); Michael

Rosser, 'Secret Cinema: *The Empire Strikes Back*, review', *Screen Daily*, 12 June 2015, available at www.screendaily.com/news/secret-cinema-the-empire-strikes-back-review/5089352.article (accessed 13 December 2021); Steve Wright, 'Secret Cinema *Star Wars: The Empire Strikes Back* review', *SciFi Now*, 6 July 2015, available at www.scifinow.co.uk/blog/secret-cinema-star-wars-the-empire-strikes-back-review/ (accessed 13 December 2021).

16 Secret Cinema Presents, 'Secret Cinema presents *Star Wars: The Empire Strikes Back*', 17 December 2015, Vimeo video, 2:45, available at https://vimeo.com/149302612 (accessed 13 December 2021).
17 Collage Arts, 'Wonder Works'.
18 'Secret Cinema presents #loverefugees: a secret cultural protest', available at https://secretprotest.org (accessed 13 December 2021).
19 Mark Westall, 'Secret Cinema presents a secret cultural protest', *Fad Magazine*, 8 September 2015, available at https://fadmagazine.com/2015/09/08/secret-cinema-presents-a-secret-cultural-protest-loverefugees-to-stand-in-solidarity-with-refugees-worldwide/ (accessed 13 December 2021).
20 Atkinson and Kennedy, 'From conflict to revolution'.
21 David Pollock, 'Secret Cinema in Calais: "We can offer a break from the constant reality of living in tents"', *The Guardian*, 11 September 2015, available at www.theguardian.com/film/2015/sep/11/secret-cinema-in-calais-jungle-fabien-riggal-secretprotest (accessed 13 December 2021).
22 Dougal Wilson, 'Dougal Wilson reports on Secret Cinema's "secret protest" at the Calais Jungle camp', *Creative Review*, 19 September 2015, available at www.creativereview.co.uk/dougal-wilson-reports-on-secret-cinemas-secret-protest-at-the-calais-jungle-camp/ (accessed 13 December 2021).
23 Eli Goldstone, 'Q&A: SC founder Fabien Riggall talks cultural activism', Run Riot, 29 August 2016, available at www.run-riot.com/articles/blogs/qa-secret-cinema-founder-fabien-riggall-talks-cultural-activism (accessed 13 December 2021).
24 Goldstone, 'Q&A'.
25 See for instance Frank Thomas, *The conquest of cool: Business culture, counterculture, and the rise of hip consumerism* (Chicago: University of Chicago Press, 1997).
26 Christine Moorman, 'Commentary: brand activism in a political world', *Journal of Public Policy & Marketing* (2020) 39(4), 390.
27 Catherine Chapman, 'Kubrick's *Dr Strangelove* meets immersive theater in London; Or: How I learned to stop worrying and love the Secret Cinema', *Vice*, 21 March 2016, available at www.vice.com/en/article/4xqpmm/dr-strangelove-secret-cinema-london (accessed 13 December 2021).
28 Cited in Rosser, 'Secret Cinema'.
29 Duncan McClean, interviewed by author, 6 September 2021.
30 Daniel Dingsdale, interviewed by author, 27 October 2021.
31 Future Shorts, 'Secret Cinema presents *Dr Strangelove*', 10 June 2016, YouTube video, 2:29, available at www.youtube.com/c/futureshorts (accessed 13 December 2021).
32 See Kennedy, 'Funfear Attractions', for further analysis of this event.

33 Conceptual merchandise designer, interviewed by Wreyford, 11 December 2020.
34 Robin Mansell and W.E. Steinmueller, 'Denaturalizing digital platforms: is mass individualization here to stay?' *International Journal of Communication* (2022). ISSN 1932–8036. In press, available at http://eprints.lse.ac.uk/105619/ (accessed 13 December 2021).
35 Conceptual merchandise designer, interviewed by Wreyford, 11 December 2020.
36 Riggall, interview by Mishcon de Reya, *Jazz Shapers*.
37 Stuart Heritage, '*28 Days Later* at Secret Cinema: a bloodthirsty attack on the wallet', *The Guardian*, 15 April 2016, available at www.theguardian.com/film/filmblog/2016/apr/15/28-days-later-secret-cinema-bloodthirsty-attack-wallet (accessed 13 December 2021); *Londonist*, 'Secret Cinema's *28 Days Later* lacks bite', *Londonist*, 20 April 2016, available at https://londonist.com/2016/04/secret-cinema-s-28-days-later-lacks-bite (accessed 13 December 2021).
38 Daniel Nolan, interviewed by author, 16 September 2021.
39 See also Kennedy, 'Funfear Attractions', for a further analysis of participant experience as game.
40 Luke Swaffield, interviewed by author, 22 September 2021.
41 Secret Cinema Presents, 'Secret Cinema presents *28 Days Later*', 17 August 2016, Vimeo video, 3:04, available at https://vimeo.com/179181953 (accessed 13 December 2021).
42 Fabien Riggall, 'Keynote speech', REMIX conference, London, UK, 19 January 2017.
43 See for instance Barbara Klinger, 'Once is not enough: the functions and pleasures of repeat viewings', in Klinger, *Beyond the multiplex: cinema, new technologies, and the home* (Berkeley and Los Angeles: University of California Press, 2006), 135–90 and the authors' own typologies of Live Cinema (enhanced, augmented and participatory) that capture the full range of these activities, in *Live cinema: cultures, economies, aesthetics*, ed. Sarah Atkinson and Helen W. Kennedy (New York: Bloomsbury, 2017), 243–64.
44 See Chapter 1, note 1 relating to Underground Cinema.
45 Cited in Rosser, 'Secret Cinema', and also Riggall, 'Keynote speech'.
46 Sarah Atkinson and Helen W. Kennedy, 'The immersive cinema experience economy: the UK film industry's third sector' in P. McDonald, ed., *The Routledge companion to media industries* (London: Routledge, 2022).
47 Entourage Live are now important players in the field, having overseen the digital development of the Jeff Wayne *War of the Worlds* immersive experience in 2020 as project directors.
48 Charlotte March, interviewed by author, 16 September 2021.
49 Charlie Dixon, interviewed by author, 24 September 2021.
50 Emmet O'Donnell, interviewed by Natalie Wreyford, 4 November 2020.
51 Global performance director, interviewed by author, 6 October 2021.
52 In the film and as 'performers' in the space, the Creatures of the Underworld are revolutionary underdogs. In these terms this audience segment is aligned with a 'faction' of dissenting performers. See Kennedy, 'Join a cast of 1000s', for a more detailed analysis of the aesthetics of activism and audience stratification.
53 Tim McQuillen-Wright, interviewed by author, 3 September 2021.

54 Simon Gordon, interviewed by Natalie Wreyford, 11 November 2020.
55 Secret Cinema Presents, 'Secret Cinema presents Baz Luhrmann's *Moulin Rouge* – trailer', 20 December 2017, Vimeo video, 3:08, available at https://vimeo.com/248180966 (accessed 13 December 2021).
56 Elsham Music, available at www.elshammusic.com/secret-cinema-x-tell-no-one (accessed 13 December 2021).
57 Secret Cinema, Facebook, 20 July 2017, available at https://m.facebook.com/SecretCinema/videos/to-inspire-the-younger-generation-to-vote-in-the-recent-general-election-secret-/10154679821506053/ (accessed 13 December 2021).
58 Including at the Young Progress Maker's Day, Roundhouse, London on 25 January 2017.
59 Held on 15 November 2017.
60 Secret Cinema Facebook site.
61 *Arabian Business*, 'Global giant keen to swoop if Saudi Arabia lifts cinema ban', *Arabian Business*, 16 November 2017, available at www.arabianbusiness.com/saudi-arabia/culture-society/383726-global-giant-keen-to-swoop-if-saudi-arabia-lifts-cinema-ban (accessed 13 December 2021).
62 Riggall, interview by Mishcon de Reya, *Jazz Shapers*.
63 Janet Wasko, Mark Phillips and Chris Purdie, 'Hollywood meets Madison Avenue: the commercialization of US films', *Media, Culture & Society* (1993) 15(2), 271–93.
64 Lee Brotherhood, 'Behind the scenes – Secret Cinema presents *Blade Runner: The Final Cut*', Lee Brotherhood (blog), 16 October 2018, available at https://leebrotherhood.com/2018/10/16/behind-the-scenes-secret-cinema-presents-blade-runner-the-final-cut/ (accessed 13 December 2021).
65 Lee Brotherhood, interviewed by author, 14 September 2021.
66 Dingsdale, interviewed by author, 27 October 2021.
67 Atkinson, *Beyond the screen*.
68 Philip K. Dick, *Do androids dream of electric sheep?* (New York: Doubleday, 1968).
69 Writer, interviewed by author, 14 September 2021.
70 Brotherhood, interviewed by author, 14 September 2021.
71 Helen Smith, interviewed by author, 7 September 2021.
72 Ian William Galloway, interviewed by author, 1 October 2021.
73 Galloway, interviewed by author, 1 October 2021.
74 *Convenience Store*, 'Asahi hosts "Remastered by Japan" campaign', *Convenience Store*, 30 April 2018, available at www.conveniencestore.co.uk/products/asahi-hosts-remastered-by-japan-campaign/566411.article (accessed 13 December 2021). The article reveals that Asahi also brand-partnered with another immersive experience at the time – *Somnai* – the creators of which are also behind the *War of the Worlds* immersive experience.
75 On 6 October 2016. As another form of ephemeral experience very few traces remain beyond this event promotional blurb: 'fans will be required to register on Yplan before details of their mission are revealed. Guests will be given a new identity, co-ordinates of a "Cadbury Milk Tray command base" meeting point

and details of appropriate attire to wear in order to get into character on the night. At the evening itself, guests will take part in interactive experiences, such as learning the art of thoughtfulness in a bid to show there is a Milk Tray Man in all of us. And of course, there will be the opportunity to sample delicious Cadbury Milk Tray throughout the evening itself!' All in London, 'Join the new Milk Tray Man on his first official mission', *All in London*, 5 October 2016, available at www.allinlondon.co.uk/whats-on/event-188616-join-the-new-milk-tray-man-on-his-first-official-mission (accessed 13 December 2021).
76 Brotherhood, 'Behind the scenes'.
77 Yasmin Arrigo, 'Secret Cinema's Fabien Riggall on a decade of creating new worlds', *Campaign*, 26 March 2018, available at www.campaignlive.co.uk/article/secret-cinemas-fabien-riggall-decade-creating-new-worlds/1460405 (accessed 13 December 2021).
78 Brotherhood, interviewed by author, 14 September 2021.
79 Thomas Maller, interviewed by Natalie Wreyford, 6 November 2020. 'Easter egg' is a term widely used in games design to denote a special mission or bonus that is hidden within a game to be found by expert or skilled players.
80 Pascale Neuschäfer, 'Secret Cinema presents *Blade Runner – The Final Cut*, a secret live experience (2018)', 9 January 2019, Vimeo video, 2:53, available at https://vimeo.com/310372174 (accessed 13 December 2021).
81 Brotherhood, interviewed by author, 14 September 2021.
82 Available at www.veronaforpeace.org or https://shop.veronaforpeace.org (both accessed 13 December 2021).
83 Secret Cinema, 'Secret Cinema presents William Shakespeare's *Romeo + Juliet*', 9 December 2019, Vimeo video, 0:34, available at https://vimeo.com/378328807 (accessed 13 December 2021).
84 Dingsdale, interviewed by author, 27 October 2021.

5

Secret Cinema as industry

> It's a huge machine when we do the big shows.
>
> SC performance director.[1]

> It's a big factory now.
>
> SC props maker.[2]

The years 2018–2021 can be best understood as SC's final phase of development from an artisanal production (and passion project) to an established and profit-motivated industrial practice. From being dubbed 'the true pioneers of *petit* cinema' by *The Guardian* in 2006[3] to becoming 'a cultural phenomenon, transforming ordinary spaces into filmic dreamscapes' in the view of *Attitude* in 2018,[4] the organisation and its productions went through incredible growth and expansion – from the scale of its locations, to the size of its audiences, to the significant box office takings and the increasingly complex and detailed staging and narrative design. By foregrounding industry observations as a lens through which to understand SC's two most recent productions (at time of writing) – *Casino Royale* (2019) and *Stranger Things* (2019–2020) – in this chapter we examine how the professionals are engaging in new working practices in order to solve problems and innovate within unique cross-sectoral collaborations. As one of SC's senior producers explains:

> We are at the intersection of three industries. There's the *events industry*, the *theatre industry* and the *cinema industry*. If you imagine a three-circle Venn diagram, we lie at the intersection of those three.[5]

While as an experience SC has significantly evolved and matured over the past thirteen years, so too has the organisation, its working practices and processes, and the professionals that work within it. This chapter looks at how the productions currently run, while also looking back and reflecting on how this has evolved and developed over time. As those who have worked for SC for a number of years reflect upon its significant growth and evolution:

> when I started I think there were eight of us, full-time, working in the office in SC; now I think there's about forty, so that just gives you a sense of the

scale and how it's grown. When I started, SC was working very much as an underground player that could very well pass under the radar of the big studios.⁶

the budgets have got bigger, the fan base has got bigger, the office has got bigger ... We've absolutely learned how to create this crazy organised chaos, how to start to work and find a routine because what we create isn't like everything else.⁷

There are two key points of significance to be drawn here – from the first observation, the increasing importance of the (big) film studios in SC's model of production (they worked *with* Eon and Netflix on the latest two productions); from the second, the emergence of an established way of working that is specific to large-scale and (crucially) *transferable* immersive productions. Both *Casino Royale* and *Stranger Things* were built at scale in warehouse locations and both were later transferred and adapted to an international location and audience – *Casino Royale* to Shanghai, China in 2019 and *Stranger Things* to Los Angeles, USA in 2020 for an adapted 'drive-into' experience. This followed SC's business strategy as laid out in their annual reporting by the director and CEO Max Alexander:

to continue to develop shows to be initially launched in the UK, which are then transferred to international markets. It is in the early stage of international expansion and launched its first show in Shanghai, China, in late 2019. The increase in overheads in the year reflects investment made to support this growth strategy.⁸

This statement was made in the context of SC reporting a significant financial loss, against the backdrop of their highest turnover to date: £15,768,942 for 2019 against losses of £4,242,148 (before taxation). As Alexander indicated, this was due to increasing overheads which, as we shall reveal in this chapter, involved the substantial labour costs required for the multiple specialists who design and deliver the major productions, as well as the large number of on-site personnel that are needed to run them over extended periods.

The two experiences discussed in this chapter reached an apex for SC (and for the immersive sector at large) in terms of their venue size and audience numbers, whilst at the same time they made sizeable leaps in the quality of production values. These leaps were evident in the impressive set design, spectacular effects and the highly detailed re-creation of the film and television IP, in both cases translated into expansive 'worlds'. The ability to build the two worlds to this level of detail in these two particular cases was made possible through the expanded 'hyper-diegetic'⁹ landscape that already existed for both *Casino Royale* and *Stranger Things* – both properties had already been extended across multiple films, episodes and merchandising.

Furthermore, they already brought with them huge fan communities, willing to engage in repeat viewings and document their engagements in online forums – for which the SC experience was increasingly designed. Within these two experiences, we see the most sophisticated narrative design to date with multiple narrative 'tracks' – the name given to the different routes made available for the audience to take throughout the experience – in an attempt to ensure that every individual participant has the opportunity for a distinct experience. We shall go on to explore the attempted unification, in this final period of activity, of what would usually be considered two divergent imperatives that we identified in Chapter 4 – massification and individualisation.

Through our interviewees, who reflected on their experiences of working on these two productions, we reveal the different specialisms, collaborations, languages and specific terminology that SC use. These can also be applied in the wider immersive sector – of which all of the professionals and their sector networks form a part. As we noted in Chapter 1, there was a huge proliferation of immersive experiences in 2019, and many of those working for SC at the time were also working in other immersive productions and transferring their techniques and approaches with them.

In order to capture the scale and complexity of these productions in terms of those who were responsible for their creation, production and delivery, we have developed our own immersive experience production model to show how both the organisation and the productions were structured, organised and managed. Moreover, we use this model to show how the three different industries within which SC operate – events, film and theatre – intersect and collaborate.

In Figure 5.1, the sector key shows where industry expertise was drawn from in the two most recent productions. Broadly, the three industries and their contrasting influence and input can be summarised as follows: the *Film* sector licensed original IP, a legal and distribution infrastructure, and production management; the *Events* sector provided expertise in logistics, site infrastructure and site management; and the *Theatre* sector provided the most directly creative elements including performance, production design, video, sound and lighting design. There were of course natural cross-overs where professionals worked across both theatre and film sectors (such as costume, hair and make-up). Other sectors were involved, including hospitality and music. The sector key shows a more detailed breakdown of the professional backgrounds of each of the departments. The increasing influence of theatre within the creative (inner) aspects of the production became far more pronounced in the two productions of this period, but has not been the case throughout SC's history – set designers were originally drawn from

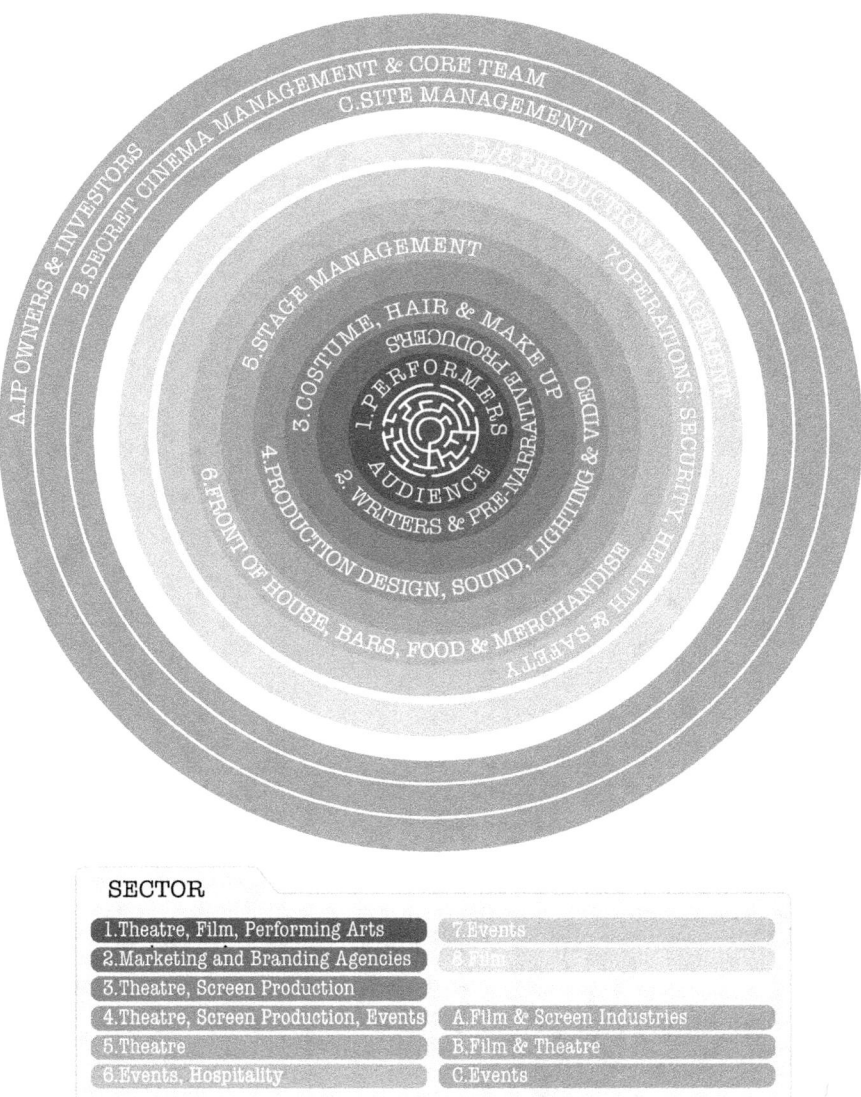

5.1 The immersive experience production model. The organisational structure of labour and collaborative relations within SC productions.

A. IP Owners & Investors	B. Secret Cinema Management & Core Team	C. Site Management
IP Owners include: Disney EON Productions Lucasfilm Netflix Twentieth Century Fox **Investors:** Active Partners Neon Adventures Social Capital UK Government	**Executive Team** Founder Chief Executive Officer Executive Assistant to CEO Chief Operating Officer & Chief Financial Officer **Management & Core Team** Commercial Director Director of Slate Head of Business Development IP Asset Manager Global Head of Partnerships Director of Partnerships Partnerships Manager Partnerships Executive Account Manager Sales & Marketing Director Chief Marketing Officer Head of Marketing Senior Marketing Manager Digital Marketing Manager Digital and Content Manager Social Media Manager Content Editor Customer Service Executive Marketing Executive Operations Director Senior Producers Operations Manager Financial Director Financial Controller HR Director Office Manger Accountant Finance Assistant **PR & Marketing** Social Media **Core Creative Team:** Creative Director(s) Associate Creative Director(s) Creative Producer Head of Content Head of Graphics Graphic Designer(s) Head of Web Development Conceptual Merchandise Designer	Wonderworks/ Entourage Technical Director Senior Production Manager Production Manager(s) Health & Safety Advisor Site Services Comms and Networking Power SFX, Pyrotechnics Rigging Scaffold Structures Plumbing

D/8. Production Management	1. Performance	2. Writers & Pre-Narrative Producers
Producer Associate Producer(s) Production Manager(s) Production Administrator Production Assistant Production Coordinator(s) Community Manager Social Community Manager Locations Manager Production Accountant Bookkeeper	Performance Director(s) Global Performance Director Specialist Directors: • Casting Director(s) • Choreographer/Dance Captain • Music Director • Movement Director • Fight Director • Stunt Director • Action & Stunt Coordinator • Aerial Director • Magic Consultant • Voice Coach • Parkour Consultant • Cast (40+) Dancers Singers/Choirs Aerialists Musicians Stunt Performers Illusionists Resident DJs Guest DJs	Pre-narrative Producer Writer Pre-narrative script writer Pre-narrative writer(s) (8+)

5.2 Secret Cinema departments involved in a Secret Cinema production and the different roles that can exist within them.

3. Costume, Hair & Make up	4. Production Design, Sound Lighting and Video	5. Stage Management
Costume Costume Designer Costume Co-Designer(s) Costume Supervisor Costume Design Assistant(s) (6+) Costume Maker(s) (9+) Costume Milliner Wardrobe **Hair & Make up** Hair & Make up Designer Hair & Make up Artist(s) (7+)	**Production Design** Production Designer Design Director Design Assistant Set Designer **Art** Art Director Set Décor Production Buyer Props Master Props Buyer(s) Set Decorator(s) Head Set Dresser Set Dresser(s) Graphics Assistant Art Department Assistant(s) Illustrator(s) Art Carpenters (+10) Graphic Designer(s) 3D Pre-Visualisation **Video** Video Designer(s) Systems Designer Animator(s) Video Programmer Video Operator(s) Video Technician(s) Video Production Engineer Video Projectionist Editor **Lighting** Lighting Designer(s) Lighting Programmer(s) Assistant Lighting Director Lighting Crew Member(s) (10+) Production Electrician(s) (17+) Follow Spot Operator(s) **Sound** Sound Designer(s) (Creative) Sound Designer (Technical) Composer Music Producer Music Director Senior Production Sound Engineer Production Sound Engineer(s) (6+)	Senior Stage Manager Company Manager Deputy Stage Manager Show Caller Assistant Stage Manager(s)(8+) Props Consultant
6. Front of House, Bars, Food & Merchandise	**7. Operations: Security, Health & Safety**	
Front of House Manager Deputy Front of House Manager Front of House Supervisor Duty Manager(s) (5+) Front of House Assistants (50+) Health and Safety Management Merchandise Manager Merchandise Assistant(s) (12+) **VIP Hospitality** VIP Producer Guestlist Coordinator VIP Coordinator VIP Supervisor(s) VIP Team Member(s) (14+) Bar Manager(s) Duty Bar Manager(s) (3+) Logistics Manager Multiple Independent Food Traders	Site Operations Manager Site Operations Deputy Operations Coordinator(s) Operations Assistant Logistics & Site Manager Crew Chief Crew First Aid Medical Lead Medical Team Leader(s) Medic(s) (7+) Head of Security Security Supervisor(s) Security Officers (50+) Cleaning Team (12+)	

5.2 (Continued)

a film background, for instance. An SC performance designer working from 2010–2013 explained:

> On *Lawrence of Arabia* [2010], it was still very much the film industry designers working on the set. Toby Stevens was the lead production designer and he would design the set. Then he would work with up and coming people within film production to do each of those sets.[10]

Film professionals continued to be central to the production design and art departments up until 2015; a production designer who worked for SC between 2011 and 2015 explained how:

> it was mad because [the sets] weren't meant for people [i.e. film sets designed for on-screen action are not made to be walked through by hundreds of audience members]. Most of the guys that I worked with, in the art department, they all tended to be feature film background people. So they were all working in the film industry and that's how I approached it ... I think a lot of the creative management was from a film background as well.[11]

Since around 2017, theatre professionals increasingly became involved in the creative aspects of the productions, as a video animator explained:

> I think in recent years I am starting to recognise a lot more people from theatre within the immersive sector; as it's started to become a little bit more recognised, but also the theatre pool has, because of the history of putting on shows and production knowledge and the familiarity with tech, I feel like they've started to come in to streamline how these productions actually work. Whilst maybe initially the sort of people making immersive events would have been more within the music and festival industries where everything happens very quickly but is not necessarily ... at least at a grassroots level ... particularly organised or run in the kind of strict framework that a theatre tech environment would be.[12]

Our model has not been officially endorsed by SC, and the department listings in Figure 5.2 are not exhaustive – different productions will require different skills and departments depending on the themes of the show, and indoor and outdoor settings, also have different requirements. It is meant as a general, illustrative guide to highlight the highly complex and multi-disciplinary nature of the productions, showing how many different specialisms and skillsets are involved and how they interact and collaborate with one another. It helps us to understand the workflows and connections and the different sector specialisms that come together, as well as highlighting the 'specialist' roles that are unique to these types of experiences. The design of this model was explicitly informed by our interviews with thirty-eight individuals who have worked for SC, and a further fourteen leading professionals in the wider UK immersive sector. These provided key insights into the work of the individuals and their departments and the coordination and collaboration across and between them. The interview data was augmented by information taken from five credit listings[13] – although it should be noted that some of these lists are only partial; the most comprehensive is that produced for *Romeo + Juliet*. The consistent factor is that they all included a full *cast* listing, which came about because SC are working more closely with Equity, the trade union for performance professionals, directors, designers, stage managers and other creative workers in the UK. As Equity's industrial official revealed:

> that nuanced understanding of what a credit and a profile means to a performer has [previously] been lacking, and so we've had a number of conversations with them [SC] about it, and they are much more relaxed now ... We've reached a compromise position whereby people are able to talk about the work in industry-facing places such as their Spotlight profiles. But they can't be on social media sharing the secrets of the show.[14]

As SC have matured, they have improved working practices considerably. In their early history, SC worked with unpaid students, volunteers and interns and in the past they have received criticism about this,[15] but they frequently come out in defence of their position as this is no longer a practice that they engage in.[16] Central Saint Martin's College, London originally provided a key talent pipeline into productions with many interviewees making their first link with SC there. It is by no means unusual for creative and cultural organisations to make connections with higher education institutions, to provide students with applied learning opportunities. One such student who went on to be employed by SC as a props maker described their first experiences when working on *Ghostbusters* [2013]:

> Those collaboration often happen because it's a renowned school, Saint Martin's School, they liked the link. Also, there is something with the students where the project would be a bit cheaper for big companies, and they would have very creative input, but we are working for them. But we were designers. They own the project and we were agreeing with them and working with them.[17]

This individual was keen to underscore the value of these engagements, and this provides a counternarrative to the criticism that SC have experienced, noting how they provided important opportunities in 'creating a portfolio, getting to know industry, looking for what's new'.

Other practitioners reflected on the enjoyment of working with the organisation during its informative stages when the identity of the film remained a secret:

> at the very beginning it was unbelievably creative, interesting, cool. We were all doing interesting things and it was very, very underground and very engaged

in a very creative world. It was a great crowd ... There was a lot of creative freedom to be *inspired* by a film, but not *dictated* by a film.[18]

The rich, collaborative atmosphere was foregrounded by a number of our interviewees, as were the much-valued opportunities to experiment. This reflects back on Riggall's values of artistic and creative freedom discussed in Chapter 4:

> A lot of it came internally from the people that were actually working on the ground and on the floor, rather from above down, because that's where it was all happening. You know that it came from, like, you know, a very loose structure.[19]

These observations chime with the sandbox mode of creation and experimentation that we examined in Chapter 2, present in SC's initial phase of development. The organisation have clearly formalised and professionalised since this time, but as we shall see as this chapter progresses opportunities for ground-up, creative experimentation remained ever-present. The formalisation of the organisation was triggered by the first round of VC investment in 2015,[20] and this was made apparent by the triggering of notable shifts in production scale, ambition and quality.

The individuals and organisations who inhabit the outer three rings (A, B and C) of our model form what a senior producer referred to as the 'magic triangle':

> In parallel to the creative feasibility, we start with the venue feasibility, so looking into whether the venue can work financially with health and safety ... And then, once *this sort of magic triangle comes together, which is IP rights, creative treatment and venue,* that's when we'll move into sort of the pre-production phase [our emphasis].[21]

These sides of the triangle form the outer three rings of our circular model, to retain the visual relationship of this important triumvirate and because of the critical influence that they wield across all other departments within the model.

A: IP owners and investors

In 2021, there are four active VC investors in SC: Active Partners,[22] Neon Adventures,[23] Social Capital,[24] and the UK government.[25] The investors are situated in the outermost ring A of our model as those with the most influence on a production and those who are also the first in the 'production timeline' – their input is key to the production taking shape and getting off the ground. Within this outer ring are also the IP owners; securing IP is a crucial factor in determining which projects are able to proceed, as the senior producer explained:

> Some titles we'll be able to get really with ease by talking to the studios; there's some titles that we'll never get because they're tied up in so many rights.[26]

The IP owners vary from production to production – for the productions considered in this chapter these were Eon (who own *Casino Royale*), and Netflix (who own *Stranger Things*). Previous productions have included titles owned by Lucasfilm and Disney (*Star Wars: The Empire Strikes Back*) and 20th Century Fox (*Moulin Rouge!*). The IP owners hold the key to how their particular property is treated, creatively, and are a sustained influence throughout the entire development and design process. Numerous IP representatives are consulted constantly throughout the production process and negotiations have become increasingly complex as the experiences have expanded and intensified, as our interviewees explained – IP considerations are highly production-specific. For *Moulin Rouge!* the costume designer explained how IP is:

> … a negotiation with every single project so with *Moulin Rouge!* we weren't allowed to copy anything, but we could be 95% close to it. But obviously with the can-can girl, it's just that whirl of colour and corsets and excitement and big hair and, like, fabulousness … every single show – What are the parameters for us, are we allowed to copy it or we allowed to pretend that they're in the same world?[27]

An increasing number of stakeholders might be involved, for example:

> there were two versions of *Blade Runner* [the original and *Blade Runner 2049*], and so you had all of the people that were involved in the first film and all of the people that were involved in the second film.[28]

For *Star Wars: The Empire Strikes Back*:

> I would have a 1am call with them every day to review all of the content we'd made that day, and then I get notes from them … it was just the pressure that you're under to create this brand, that everyone knows so well … It was basically Lucasfilm, 20th Century Fox, Disney, a visual effects producer of *Star Wars* … five people every night on this call. And the stuff they would note … I remember there was this one shot of the Millennium Falcon banking round to come back towards the camera; they said, 'It would never move like that'. And I replied, 'What? We're talking about a fake object here', but they said 'No, if it's going to do it, it would tilt this way, and turn and rotate at that angle'.[29]

There are clear tensions expressed here between creative freedom and the extensive workload implications in satisfying the protectors of the source IP, where corrections such as those described above require significant time and effort to address. This relationship between the studios and SC has evolved over time. In *Casino Royale*, Eon was reportedly heavily involved in the design of the prequel narrative. The SC head of slate was quoted as saying:

> It's very much a live approvals process. We see them very regularly. They have very strong opinions on how Bond is portrayed. We are guided in how we portray him and the other characters, and how we portray the world.[30]

There is clearly now an acceptance and formalisation of how interrelations between SC and the IP owners function. It is clear that this turn to the development of 'transformative' works – i.e. an original, extended, pre-narrative – signalled a more business-oriented approach for SC as an organisation. This shift enabled the development of SC-specific IP which was independent of but directly related to (and, *importantly*, authorised) by owners of the IP in the film. It is abundantly clear that IP and licensing were absolutely critical to the creative possibilities, and impacted significantly on the practical progress and the cost of a project.

B: Secret Cinema management and core team

The core SC team are led by *the Executive Team* who are in turn accountable to their investors. At the time of writing, there are four members of the executive team and six board members. These are represented by the public-facing figure of Max Alexander who came onto the board as chief executive officer from 2018.[31] Alexander routinely undertakes all press activity related to the organisation. One current board member is founder, Fabien Riggall. Alexander and Riggall sit on both the executive team and the board. The other members of the executive team are a chief financial officer (who is also chief operating officer) and an operations director. The board is made up with a chairman, a commercial director and two non-executives. Other SC officers include a head of business development, a global head of partnerships and a chief marketing officer. The management team also includes a 'head of slate' who manages all of the relationships with the studios.[32]

The senior producer explained how many roles, previously outsourced, have been brought 'in house':

> we've integrated all of those functions which you traditionally find in any business into the company, but that SC being a small arts organisation didn't have. So partnerships, marketing, ticketing, customer service, all of these operations that are needed to make a company grow and thrive. And now that we have put all of these in place, we're in a position in which we are top of our game and we're sitting now at the table with the studios.[33]

The core SC team of 2021 covers business development, marketing, HR, operations, finances and partnerships. In the senior producer's articulation here, we see a significant shift from a collaborative artistic 'troupe' that structured early SC experiences, to the more *industrial* structure with separate departments presented in our model. What the senior producer also underscored is the role this process of *industrialisation* has played in achieving credibility, critical success and that coveted place 'at the table with the studios'.

The permanent employee base was forty administrative staff members in 2019 and forty-five in 2020.[34] Other personnel are brought on board for productions – contracted individual freelancers and smaller specialist companies. The total number of personnel listed on the credits can run to as many as 400 named individuals.

C: site development and management

The site is the third element of the 'magic triangle' that needs to be in place for a production to go ahead. Both productions during this period were staged within sites that required significant infrastructural development (and appropriate planning permission) before elaborate sets could be built and dressed. This process was overseen by an external company contracted by SC – as we outlined in Chapter 4 (Wonder Works and Entourage Live). These were headed up by a technical director who had practical and technical oversight of both the creative and logistical elements of the production including construction, design and management, planning and licensing, applications, regulations, building control, safety of the performers, scenic dressing, lighting, sound, video, any technical practicals, pyrotechnics, flying, rigging and overall health and safety.

The 'site' is particular to these forms of immersive production, which have rapidly grown in scale and complexity – an emerging priority is to identify more permanent (or semi-permanent) premises that can be re-purposed for multiple experiences since, up to now, all of the sites that SC have used are taken apart and decommissioned at the end of the productions (with the exception of the site used between 2015–2016, which has since become the Print Works, an established and operational nightclub).[35]

The key distinction between the three outer rings and the eight inner rings is that those in the outer rings are semi-permanent or permanent employees of the organisation, whereas roles in rings 1–7 are all specific to a production (see below for ring D/8). As the show moves into pre-production – the recruitment of the extensive creative team and crews for the production begins – these are all contracted organisations, or freelance individuals who are commissioned and hired to work on a particular production. This temporary and project-specific collective of creative, technical and logistical talent brings considerable insight and expertise honed through their employment across multiple immersive projects.

D/8: production management

Alongside preparing the physical site and infrastructure for a production, a production management team is established and led by the permanent senior producer,[36] to put all of the personnel of the production in place. The production team replicates the structure of a film production team, with executive producers, associate producers, production administrators and production assistants.

In our model, the production management ring is presented as an interface between the outer, management teams and the production teams. For example, an SC location manager explained how they:

> ... work with all departments especially the creative team and production teams as the creatives will feed into how they want the building to 'be' and the production and operations team tell them what is actually possible with the money we have.[37]

Production management are separated from the inner core of personnel because they do not play a role at show level and are not embedded in the experience, unlike those in the seven inner rings who all sustain a presence throughout the run of the production.

We will now look at the work of those in the inner rings, in 'audience experience' order – i.e. from the centre of the model outwards. Common to all accounts is how creative practices and crafts have to be adopted in the context of immersive experiences. The audience are at the heart of the experience and have direct contact with the performers, who guide them both spatially and temporally. They have the least influence upon how their experience is shaped although they are offered multiple opportunities for interaction. Both audience and performer behaviours and choices are governed by pre-designed and pre-destined narrative tracks that have been created by the writers and pre-narrative producers. These are visually represented by the maze in the centre of the model – all tracks lead to the show's hero moment, followed by the augmented screening.

We will outline the creative contribution of those in ring 2 first – although they are not at the centre with the audience, they govern the choices and behaviours of both audiences and performers.

The inner rings

2: Writers and pre-narrative producers

As we shall see, across many of the creative departments, creatives and producers work side-by-side in the content-creation processes. For the pre-narrative design, the writer undertakes the creative aspects – writing new storylines, extending existing characters, creating new characters and producing the fictional copy for the web-based channels. The producers work to populate the social media channels, creating new content and encouraging ticket holders to engage in these channels.

Casino Royale (2006) was SC's biggest production to date in terms of scale, box office and global reach. Running from May to October 2019 in Dagenham East, London, 120,000 audience members attended, generating £8m at the box office.

The pre-narrative experience launched with a prolonged advertising campaign and pre-event narrative engagement referred to as 'Operation Wildcard'. Ticket holders were addressed as 'operatives' and invited to engage in a top secret mission. They were assigned a particular identity and could then purchase relevant costuming and identification items from an online store, entitled 'Universal Exports' (a cover name for the British Secret Service in Ian Fleming's books, adopted into the 007 filmic universe from 2008 onwards and here conveniently deployed as branding for the SC storefront). The logo already existed – it was designed in 2008 and features in a clip in *Casino Royale*. The narrative set-up for the event involved targeting a network of corrupt underground financiers with links to terrorism. Ticket holders could access training videos including mental recall and lie detection.

As *Casino Royale* was under way, *Stranger Things* tickets were launched on 22 May 2019. Running from November 2019 to February 2020, 110,000 people attended, with a wider age range than usual, including special screenings with a 15+ age-rating. This production signalled the organisation's first foray into television through a partnership with Netflix, to create a production described as a '3+ hour immersive experience exploring the town of Hawkins and storylines centered around *Stranger Things* season 1–3 ... incorporating 360-degree projections and special effects ...'. This marked a significant departure from the seated screenings and proscenium arch which had dominated SC productions up until that point, and opened up opportunities for new experiments within an expanded, *standing*, viewing environment. The pre-narrative experience invited ticket holders to join one of six youth sub-cultures denoting different 'classes': rockers (1978), punks (1979), hip hoppers (1980), movers & groovers (1981), New Romantics (1982) and pop kids (1983). Those holding a VIP ticket were called Media Hot Shots (1977). The pre-narrative involved tracing children who had mysteriously disappeared, which segued into the opening narrative set-up of the first series of the TV show.

Populating the voracious social media streams with content was a constant requirement for the pre-narrative producers who worked hand-in-hand with the story elements. These included live news broadcasts for *Stranger Things* and the different dispatches and briefings for *Casino Royale*.

In addition to the extensive narrative communication that was generated by this department, through emails, the microsite and social media channels, we see enhancements in communications around audience preparations and expectations. Within these communications, preparatory instructions became far more detailed, as the industrial official at Equity explained:

> we had a number of concerns raised by our members working on the production about the lack of clarity in the messaging that was going out to audience members before they were coming to the show. You know, they were being told in advance that the dress code was 'X' and this is what time to arrive and that sort of thing, but there wasn't enough in place around what standards of behaviour were to be expected from them. SC – to their credit – worked really well with us on addressing that and putting some proper measures in place.[38]

Once the show was launched, the social media streams were populated by audience responses to the event; these were highly managed and curated by the SC team. The pre-narrative producer explained how:

> One of the main drivers [of pre-narrative] for SC is so they can sell more merchandise because you need to have your costumes and more visibility, and the pre-narrative very quickly turns into audience-generated content once the people started [to] showcase their costumes.[39]

1: Performers

Upon entering the space in *Casino Royale*, 'operatives' were given an in-character briefing in the grouping to which they had been assigned online through the Operation Wildcard website, and instructed to approach a person wearing a flower in the colour given to their grouping. In *Stranger Things*, audiences were directed to the podium denoting their assigned subculture to receive their briefing and first clue, to set them on their journey. These 'missions' or 'tracks' to pursue depended on the participant's subcultural identity – different tracks for each grouping. This was the first moment when audiences came together with the performers and were set upon a particular narrative track.

The extensive group of performers is led by the show's performance director, who oversees the work of other specialist directors – such as movement, stunt and fight directors, and choreographers – as well as all of the performers, the main cast members, singers, dancers, aerialists and stunt performers. This is perhaps the most demanding area of work – where professionals work across multiple spaces and scenes for a prolonged period, in and among a sizeable and excitable (and very often inebriated) audience. The creative and logistical approaches to the performance have evolved over time, as have the professionals working within this space. An early performance designer reflected on how they broke new ground, and on changing practices in response to the specific demands of large-scale, immersive environments:

> One director really didn't get it until we opened – how the audience entered the building is absolutely their top concern, not the one-on-one actor moments that only three people will watch anyway, whereas everyone will remember what it's like to enter the space, to go to the courtroom at *Shawshank Redemption*, to be tried, to be transported, to be processed. That is the focus. It requires a shift and a different emphasis of expertise.[40]

The growth in audience numbers pointed to the particular challenge of engaging all audience members in the narrative, the performance director explained:

> how else do we engage the audience with these key characters – a thousand audience members but there's only five key characters in the film? Let's create other characters in our world that have a similar feel. So I don't have to be around James Bond, I can meet other agents in the world.[41]

As this interviewee alludes, while these experiences were designed to be interactive, they also required specific skill in organising and managing bodies through a meticulously designed temporal narrative. The performance director described the complexity of the performance design in *Casino Royale*:

> I would say to the actors, this is your two-hour track and within these two hours you have these four key narrative beats, which might happen every ten minutes, fifteen minutes, twenty minutes. I'll give you a timeline. So [I prepare a] big sheet [showing] every actor moving around every five minutes, every location, which is like a *maze*. So it takes me hours and days to do that with the stage management.[42]

This points to a key experience design strategy – worldbuilding and the creation of multiple storylines, coordinated by a large group of actors – in *Casino Royale* and *Stranger Things* there were casts of up to forty performers situated throughout the performance space. Here, we see the emergence of sector-specific language – the word 'tracks' refers both to an actor's performance (the plot line that they are following) and the audience's journey through the narrative (the mission that audience groupings are pursuing). A performer described this in more detail and revealed how this has evolved as a creative practice:

> what's certainly changed now is the deepening and development of an interest in personal character, story, and narrative, what we'd call the *track* of the character, the beat of where they would go, what they would do ... how you go through the two hours is now created and refined and honed in an interlocking spider web, where potentially in the past you'd be having a wonderful time, but that interlocking wouldn't happen as much, but now that's how they set up shop and how the rehearsal rooms will run.[43]

The audience engagements were also designed to invoke a sense of play, particularly in these recent experiences. Within *Casino Royale* the idea of going on missions became highly explicit and literal – the narrative arc of the show involved tracking a deal through a global financing network – a briefcase containing £100m was making its way to the casino, along with nine other, 'dummy' briefcases that were empty. Audiences could be pursuing any of these, depending on the track they were following, but each would reach its own narrative conclusion; and no one would discover the full briefcase – this would only ever be revealed in the climactic hero moment.[44] The performance director went on to explain how the audiences were led to feel within these interactions:

> the audience needs to feel like they're in the driving seat of an experience or even an interaction. However, *the house always wins, the actor is always in control*. So if the actor needs you to say yes or no, they're going to look like they need the answer coming from you and you'll feel like you generated the answer but it's all been orchestrated by a clever, smart performer.[45]

Here the director borrows from the language of casino management and gambling to articulate the extent to which the audience participation and sense of freedom of movement were illusory within this tightly controlled, regulated and managed experience design. This had evolved over time throughout previous productions, but came to the fore in the *actual* environment of a casino. The ability to navigate a dual role – both a convincing performer and an effective crowd manager – clearly requires a specific specialism and expertise, which is highly distinct from film and theatre performance. Many of our interviewees described the skills and talents required within these demanding roles:

> it's a really special skillset, I think, for an immersive actor, particularly the level of energy that you need to stay in character and maintain that and be able to ad lib and work off the cuff. Senior creative producer.[46]

It's improvisation. It's sometimes stand-up comedy. The range of creative skills you need as an immersive performer is massively different from your standard actor. Technical director.[47]

The centrality of the audience is underscored:

you also need to be generous and understand that you're not the star of the show, they are. Performance designer.[48]

3: Costume, hair and make-up

Costume is a necessarily expansive department (between fifteen and forty employees comprising designers, makers, a supervisor and assistants) in order to provide a costume for every single member of the cast, crew, front of house and bar staff, which can total between 600 and 800 costumes for each show. A majority of the costume designers and costume makers work across both stage and screen and recognise the distinctiveness of what they need to produce for this format. The costume designer explained the level of detail required when designing costumes for immersive environments:

for immersive, you have to think of everything, because people are literally breathing on you. So everything has to be correct. But it also has to be really durable and you also have to make sure you keep hold of your costume because the audience see your costume as a prize so often they get nicked, so it's such a kind of an immediate costuming, I guess it's very tangible and every single detail will be noticed.[49]

Furthermore, where the production has a long run, all costumes have to be bought or made; they cannot be hired. The costuming instructions that the audience members received prior to attending the event were designed to ensure performers could be discerned amid the audience; the costume designer explained how they worked with SC's merchandise department to achieve this:

We guide them and it guides us as well to basically ask questions of how to be better than the audiences, so you believe *our* actors. It's a very fine calibration! we hopefully do a better version than the audience just to help people buy into it.[50]

The simultaneous presence of performers and audience in elaborate costumes is a unique quality within immersive experiences more generally, and contributes significantly to the distinct pleasures and the distinct challenges of the production. The challenge of distinguishing audience from performer is made more manageable in Punchdrunk masked shows, for instance, as all the audience are wearing masks.

What the SC costume designer also further illuminated here is the extent to which the performers work in very close, very intimate moments of interaction where audience members may *need* to be managed and controlled. For instance, as we saw in Chapter 4, an actor described how audiences could get 'grabby';[51] here we see him reflect on the difficulties of responding to or intervening in these situations:

> the first time it happened was one of the first few nights. And I remember just thinking, like, 'that was way too far'. And I told security what happened and there is nothing really they can do unless I give a really accurate description. Everyone's in a costume and they all look similar.[52]

The challenge of distinguishing between performers and audience members has become much more carefully managed over time and there is now much greater attention given to ensuring the safety of performers. We will see just how far this has evolved when we discuss the role of the operations team.

4: *Production, sound, lighting and video design*

This is the largest section of the ensemble with four major departments who are responsible for the design and creation of the expansive narrative space. The individual departments combine both creative and technical expertise – video *content* creators and editors work alongside video *systems* engineers and video designers; creative sound *content* designers and technical sound *system* designers and engineers work very closely together. It is within these close working relationships between creative and technical departments that a unique collaborative quality is highlighted by the senior producer:

> I don't think there's roles that you wouldn't get in any other industries. I think what you'll find is probably these roles wouldn't necessarily work together as they do at SC.[53]

The performance director explained the importance of both operational and creative synergies within and across these four departments:

> there's a very clear concoction and chemistry balance that makes an immersive show. I don't want to see the light in the roof if you don't have to because it takes away from the theatrical environment. The sound has got to be full enough to engage ... say we've got a thousand audience members but I've got forty actors, which means probably 50% of the audience are actually engaging with an actor. What are the rest of the people doing? They need to be encased, enclosed and immersed within the soundscape and environment. So sound needs to be a certain level; however, the actors need to be able to perform and not ruin their voices within the first week. The sets need to be tangible, they need to be physical, I need to open that door, I need to go somewhere.

I don't want to have a film set which looks incredible but that I can't touch or it feels hollow.[54]

Production design

This latter point is particularly insightful since it indicates the specific requirements of production and set design within immersive environments – both to enable participation on a practical level, and to ensure narrative immersion on an imaginative level, to be real and believable, and to ensure verisimilitude with the world that has been created. This is in distinction to theatre 'flats' and film and TV 'sets', which are usually two-dimensional façades, designed to be viewed only from the front, with nothing behind them but the props that support them. The technical director also emphasised this requirement and the practical implications of set design for immersive experiences and performances:

> designers who have come in from theatre, having spent the last twenty years designing sets for proscenium arch stages, have to get their head around the fact that now the audience are going to be all over their set, so what they're designing is actually a mixture between theatre and an exhibition stand. Not only does it need to be creatively interesting and communicate where the scene is, but it also needs to be ramped for wheelchairs, and it needs to be tough, and it's going to be kicked by hundreds of people every night, so therefore the finishes need to be built for public use. The way it's laid out needs to be in line with building control and fire regulations. Materials we use have to be fire retardant in a way that proscenium arch [scenery] doesn't because you've got the fire curtain that just drops down at the first sign of a problem.[55]

In the *Punchdrunk Encyclopedia* this quality is referred to as the 'minute detailing within touch-real installations' (page 245), capturing that sense of the tactility and interactability of immersive scenography. Furthermore, there is not just one single stage in immersive experiences – multiple different spaces, rooms and sets need to be designed in 360° detail which brings with it a particular set of demands. The art director explained the nuance of their role in immersive experiences, compared to the other sectors in which they work:

> Art director is not a traditional theatre role, it's a very film and TV role but with a slightly different job description [in immersive]. I've kind of developed my own job description over the years because it's such a niche role – you need an art director because it's so large-scale with twenty-five to fifty different sets. A production manager just can't keep up with that, and so you need an art director to be able to basically protect the set designer's vision, whilst making it happen and working within the budget.[56]

5.3 Secret Cinema presents … *Stranger Things* production designs. A functioning bar situated within the context of the Hawkins High Reunion Fair.

In addition to these important practical concerns relating to set design, the production designer explained the approach to designing the sets:

> They [the IP owners] seem to be very understanding of the fact that this is a different experience. We can reimagine things to [enhance] the theatricality of the experience. So, that's great for me because, apart from anything else, there isn't always the budget to do a museum-like copy. But there's a lot of things obviously you want to get in. Because it's like a little Easter egg. If you went into Murray's in *Stranger Things*, it's really nice to try to find some of the exact props because the hardcore fans will spot the mistakes. They're always very appreciative of the effort.[57]

Other sets for *Stranger Things* included re-creations of the Starcourt Mall, a fortune teller's tent, an archive/library and a mayoral campaign tent. The location of the Hawkins Fair was created with various stalls and entertainment; there was also a secret 'cabin in the woods' and a hidden industrial area accessed by those who successfully pursued the right 'track'.

Important aesthetic considerations related to commercial imperatives of some of the production's stakeholders. The production designer explained the implications of these considerations:

in order to finance these things, there's a lot of partnership involvement with food, beverage and merchandise, and to give them a decent deal you need to make sure ... In SC particularly, we love hiding things away, and that's all very well and good for an audience experience but for someone who has a quota to hit, you've got to be really careful that hiding it doesn't damage that... it's got to improve their sales.[58]

A member of the video department talked about the specific challenges of working with other departments in immersive:

The biggest skillset is learning how to navigate relating to other departments, which I think is something you do within traditional theatre anyway. You're doing it across a much larger space and also having to take into account that you have audience and cast members moving through in a completely different way. I'd say the biggest intersection is probably with the spatial design for things like galleries.[59]

The art director is responsible for enacting and implementing the production designer's vision while also ensuring that these commercial interests are protected:

It's not just the designer and the performance directors you have to work with – it's also the food traders who are all different people who have their own identity and want to be seen and they have to function as well. It can't just be all designed for design's sake. Then we've also got bars and they are all sponsored by different companies. So then you're almost getting into the corporate world of 'I want my Pantone Green on this thing', but you've also got to make that mesh with the actual world of the film. So I'm sort of the protector. 'Oh, you want to put that in there? – that doesn't make sense in our world.' I've got the bigger picture that they don't – they're just looking at their bar. So it's not just traditional theatre, there's absolutely a more corporate side, which has to happen to order to afford to put on the shows. There's a lot more aspects and also things like toilets, the design of toilets, and what does a bin look like in the 1980s![60]

Here, the art director revealed how all elements of the site are subject to set design – even the most functional and mundane spaces. In *Casino Royale* the toilets in 'Miami International Airport' were designed to look and feel like airport toilets. The *Casino Royale* site included re-creations all of the key locations of the film – Madagascar, Venice, London, the Casino, the Ocean Club, the Lahore bathroom and the Secret Intelligence Service (SIS) Building, including the Q Branch surveillance unit. These were recreated in meticulous detail, with explicit reference to the source texts, and in addition to the extensive design of the physical sets this also involved extensive and detailed video content and video systems design.

Video design

The video designer explained that in the film of *Casino Royale* Q Branch is not seen. The video designers therefore carefully studied where it appeared in previous films and *Skyfall* became the primary point of reference. Eon reportedly supplied some of the original graphics from that film; although these were only designed to be on the film screen for three seconds, they required extensive development work by the video design team.[61]

Studying the source IP – the film or the TV programme – in meticulous detail is a key part of the process for many creative departments. The global performance director explained:

> I don't know how many hours I spent just looking at documents that are in the backgrounds. When you see someone walk into a room and you know there's a board there or something, then that's gold for us, because then you really want to zoom in trying to understand what the writing looks like; if there's newspaper cuttings; to get a sense of the vibe – we created the Hawkins newspaper, for example, so we wanted to get the same tone.[62]

As noted by the performance department, consideration of audience flows now dictate much of the creative experience design, as here described by the video and projection designer who explained how a particular element of the *Casino Royale* experience:

> I think we realised in London that Q Branch was a really useful way of automating and keeping people on story tracks. They would come to Q Branch a couple of times in the night with their new clue and the system would randomly generate where to go next. So you could actually throughput loads of people ... For the first few previews everyone tried to go to Q Branch at once. It was a thousand people trying to cram into one-tenth of the site. So we doubled the size of Q Branch, we did a lot of work on audience flow to figure out how many game points you could do with someone before you sent them there, because once you sent them there, they were on their own track from that point.[63]

Video design involves a high degree of innovation in practice through its interface with immersive productions, particularly in relation to systems design which has started to embed and facilitate gameplay within the experiences. For example, in past experiences the obligatory ID card rarely played an intrinsic role in the experience itself; however, they became far more integrated into the narrative and game mechanics of *Casino Royale*, where 'operatives' were required to collect them from characters and they were used as currency to access the next part of the narrative. The *Casino Royale* experience used key mechanics of the computer game. The video designer explained:

People could get information from business cards with phone numbers, then go to Q Branch, type the phone numbers in, which would consult the show track and locate that actor on the site. And then provide the actor in the Q Branch three or four leads that they could then choose to give to that group of audience members to send them off to find the actor. *It's like a mix of software development, game design and aesthetic design.*[64]

This example shows how the field of video design has evolved from the aesthetic design of screens to advanced interaction design. The video designers collaborate directly with the lighting department, who explained their extensive remit:

Not only are we installing the lighting, we're installing the lighting positions of power, the distribution [of] the emergency lighting, the exit signs, we're creating something much, much more.

They are responsible for both the sets and the film screening itself – which involves a number of specific aesthetic practices. The lighting designer explained their creative process:

I take the film and I put it into a piece of software that I use that allows me to literally go frame-by-frame through the film ... I run through the film and I find the lighting moments – so the flicker of light in the background of the shot or, in James Bond, the twelve-minute airport sequence where he's rushing through the airport to stop the bomb going off on the plane. There are beacons that flash on airport support vehicles. There's red dots that flash on the airport door as it opens – they're the magic for me, they are the moments.[65]

They also explained how their work on immersive productions differs from theatre requirements when it comes to the augmented screening and the mirror moments:

That's very unique, because that doesn't follow anything that we do in theatre. Of course, we put someone on stage and you sit in the auditorium and watch them, but you don't really have to balance them to anything. I have to balance them to a film ... and I want you to believe that you're looking at exactly what you're seeing on the screen.

The expansive and detailed sets also serve as a literal film set in the creation and filming of the post-experience promotional videos. These have proved to be a staple in the SC marketing machine throughout its history – capturing and communicating the excitement, energy and dynamism of the productions in a highly mediated and visualised way. These are also the place to see the most explicit showcase of the increasing production values of the shows – the expansive sets, atmospheric lighting and spectacular effects. The *Casino Royale* video is a rapidly paced montage of the different sets and scenes, capturing the drama, chase and fight sequences and culminating in the spectacular aerial hero moment.⁶⁶ The *Stranger Things* post-experience promotional video is a fast-paced sequence cut to 'Kids in America',⁶⁷ showing elaborately costumed audiences arriving in Hawkins Mall, showcasing the many sets and sequences, and the exceptionally convincing *Doppelgangers* playing the characters. As well as serving as a promotional film, these are likely to feature in the show reels for the professionals who have worked on the productions, as calling cards for future work opportunities.

Sound design

Sound design has become an increasingly important facet of the experience in recent productions. An SC head sound designer explained their process:

> Essentially thirty to forty small shows all running together. The basic scenario is just isolating all of those different elements so that rather than just having, like, a stereo file that we just play in a room, we can have a crackly fireplace over there, a ticking clock over here and just being able to spatialise things a little bit more in that 360° environment that we're working with.⁶⁸

One of the creative sound designers provided insights into the importance of collaborations to ensure that effective spatialisation is achieved across the visual, sonic and lighting elements:

> we want to do something clever with lights here under this tunnel, like a train going overhead, so I might create a train rumble going overhead so that they can plot lights to that. And again, for the video department, I work ... certainly recently, a lot more closely with those guys because I'm cutting audio to their video picture.⁶⁹

The lighting designers work particularly closely with the sound designers during the show itself, where they share the automated cueing system – based on a show control system called QLab. As the creative sound designer explained:

> it's a theatre cueing software primarily for sound, but you can also control lights and video from it [by] sending MIDI cues, sending a little bit of data information along the network and so everything's all cabled in there. So, we can control lighting and everything – if we need an explosion and a flash and a smoke effect we can trigger all of that from QLab.⁷⁰

The lead sound designer explained in Chapter 4 how, since *28 Days Later*, the system has become more centrally integrated into the running of the shows.⁷¹

In summary, this set of departments – production, video, lighting and sound – have evolved a unique set of collaborative working practices that are specific to immersive productions and are in distinction to both film and theatre. Although both theatre and film *are* frequently described as multi-disciplinary and highly collaborative fields, across a traditional film production pipeline creatives do not necessarily communicate or collaborate with one another, as the norm is to engage in a linear hand-off process where they work on separate aspects in separate departments. Although this has recently been disrupted with the advent and rapid adoption of virtual production techniques, the linear approach to production is still the norm across the sector.

5: Stage management

The stage management (SM) team are responsible for the running of the show and the performers' and audience's co-navigation of it. The SM team are a cross-over department who straddle logistics and performance. SM work very closely with lighting and sound to build an integrated cue system that combines the automated cue system for sound, video and light described above with the human elements of performance and action. A tight working relationship is articulated between stage management, video, lighting and sound, and the 'show caller' – the person responsible for verbally calling out all of the cues to the cast and crew across the internal communications system – is consistently praised for managing what is regarded as exceptional complexity. This group consists of theatre professionals – it is a department that has evolved to respond to the complex demands of immersive production – they have evolved, tuned and adapted processes from traditional theatre to respond to the genre-specific elements of immersive theatre, which include repeat scenes, multi-layered narratives and simultaneous, multi-sited performance across different spaces. The SM and deputy SM/show caller work in a control room utilising an expansive CCTV system with multiple monitors across the space, whilst numerous assistant SM are positioned across the site, in costume and on communication devices. The senior stage manager talked through the complex preparatory process:

> The timeline is unique – it's a big grid. That will be very unique to this, because normally you'd have a script, or you'd have a storyboard that existed in advance. They call it a paper tech, where we sit down and I go through and say, 'This is the show, and this is what the technical moments are'.[72]

The deputy SM explained the difference in practice when working on immersive production:

> with immersive, you don't have a script … There's no point of reference in that sense, but also there you're not cueing off lines, you're not cueing off movement, particularly because it's all about time. So suddenly it's a very different way of putting a book together.[73]

'Book' refers to a working document which lists all cues and instructions that relate to action, effects and any changes in lighting, sound and video (see sample section in Figure 5.4).

19:26 "Over & Out"	SC ➜➜	S/B- Tarrick, Q48 & 49, Q Branch Q48................GO Q49................GO	LIVE COMS Sophie- Tarrick in Skyfleet Rose- Ronnie Activate video (camera 1) Restore
19:31		S/B- Q50 Q50................GO	SECURITY BREECH 3
19:31:30	OPS	S/B Secret Room 1...GO *Take ropes out of sandpit in Madagascar*	SM gives Dan the G.O Calin exit
19:33:30 f/o		S/B Q51- 100 & Secret room 2,3&4 Secret Room 2..GO Q51...................GO	SM- Katherine (goes to Alex) and Marko (goes to Christina A) Triggers live in Q Branch
19:34		S/B Madagascar..........GO	Faye- Calin, Paul & Glenn
19:35 f/o		S/B- Dani DANI........GO Q52..........GO	Filipe FIGHT 3 LX change and music dip
19:35:30		Secret room 3....GO	SM- Dan (goes to Anouk)
19:36:30		S/B Secret Room 4......GO	SM- Kirsty or James
19:37		S/B Bahamas, Montenegro & Tunnel..............GO	Sophie (Bahamas) - Christina A Filipe (Montenegro) - Alex & Violet Rose (Tunnel) - Sam & Caroline
Gun shot in Madagascar		Q53..................GO	PAROUR LX Sam firing at Caroline
Alex arrive in Miami Airport		Q54..................GO	LX change for fight in Airport
f/o		S/B- Cristina & Dancers in Casino	Filipe (if Montenegro shots Have fired)
Alex off carousel		Q55..................GO	Alarm on baggage carousel

5.4 A sample page from the show caller's book. This includes cues for all actors and actions, video, sound and light changes, which are occurring simultaneously across multiple spaces.

The separation of the different sets and performance spaces as a way of managing the complexity was described by an assistant SM – one of a number who are 'on the floor' during the performances:

> You manage zones and everything that comes in and out of that zone is yours to look after ... you should know when a character is arriving in that zone for a scene, you get used to their rhythms, and if they're not there, then you start to use your radio and call to another ASM ... your role is not to look like a stage manager, which can be difficult if you're wearing these really ridiculous headsets, but you get used to giving the nod or a tap or just communicating with just signals and no language whatsoever.[74]

The performance director explained how SM interface with other departments to ensure the safety of both performers and audience members throughout the performance:

> As well as the people with radios for the actors and the safety of the show, they're also there for the audience as well, the safety of the audience. If anything was to happen, they're there to look after you and we use the security at front of house to shepherd the audience into safe areas if there were to be some aerial [performance] or a fight or a chase or action. So they're also trained to put people in the right places.[75]

This is another distinctive feature of immersive entertainment: creative performance and operational logistics have to work simultaneously, hand-in-hand, across all aspects of the process and experience. We have observed this ourselves when attending events where stage management are in costume but their real function is revealed only through the presence of a communications headset or walkie-talkie. They deftly appear and disappear through hidden apertures as they manage scenes where performers are present. In *Stranger Things*, just prior to the appearance of the Demogorgon, there was a palpable sense of 'something about to happen' as the volume of the audio increased significantly (a dance track accompanied by a frenetic keep-fit instruction scenario), and as stunt security and the stage management team appeared around the site to clear a pathway, suddenly shouting at audience members to get back, as the Demogorgon burst through the door, ran through the crowds and jumped onto the stage. The performance director explained this as a core dramatic technique, and it describes our own experience as audience members:

> You can let people know with your voice first that you're coming, so I have a thing called *a beep before the beat*. If there's a piece of action, I put a small beep before the big fight kicks off. Just so the audience goes 'oh what's going on over here?' but there's enough time to react.[76]

There are also simultaneous (and often multiple) performative vignettes, which is unique to SC, and immersive experiences where complex creative direction and stage management are required. The senior SM explained the complexity of the *Casino Royale* hero moment, which involved a complex aerial stunt involving two performers, a helicopter, a rope ladder, shootings and the case spilling open to scatter bank notes on the crowds below:

> ... that happened across the whole space at once. And they're pretty tricky to put together, because you need to have everybody in the three warehouses interacting at the same time ... That led on from a chase of suitcases and shootings that happened across four spaces. So the cast had to hit those spots at exactly the same moment, and not get stuck behind audience members.[77]

In *Stranger Things*, there were actually two simultaneous but separate hero moments and audience members were marshalled to one of two areas for these climactic moments to play out. They were then led into the huge screening space from two different directions, perambulating in a circular configuration, chanting 'together we are one' as white dust particles were emitted across the audience to signal their entry into the 'upside down'. The immersive show culminated in a performance montage of all three seasons played out around and above the audience, with numerous aerial performances and multiple 'mirror moments' in a 360° space.

The *Casino Royale* experience included one of SC's most spectacular introductions to the screen space following the hero moment. The huge screen, which had been disguised through the projection of a chandelier onto its surface, slowly descended as the ranked seating area was revealed from behind dropped curtains and a count-down clock was projected. The moment was suffused with excitement and awe-inspiring spectacle, and a red confetti cannon was fired above the crowds to signal the opening of the casino. An augmented screening followed, characterised by dramatic lighting effects, pyrotechnics and action vehicles including the Aston Martin, which circled the area in front of the screen, synchronised with the multiple occasions where it features on-screen.

6: *Front of house, bars, food and merchandise*

Drawn from the hospitality sector, these are functional roles performing hosting and serving duties. A dedicated front of house (FoH) team manage guests as they arrive and are fully integrated 'in-world'. In traditional theatre FoH are a distinctive, separate group of individuals usually marked out by their own uniform, but in SC they blend in with the performance and performers and play a crucial role in maintaining the verisimilitude of the narrative world throughout all aspects of the experience. There are specific

... as industry 163

SC roles designed in support of this endeavour, as the senior producer confirmed:

> The one role that is really specific to us is the *global performance director* – who leads *not* the cast itself – [this is the role of the performance director] but who leads rehearsals and trains up from a creative point of view, our in-front-of-house staff, security staff, bar staff. So it's their task to then train them up and make sure that they know who they are *'in the world'* (our emphasis).[78]

An FoH manager explained the preparatory work required to develop their staff team:

> ... the performance director will consult with me about what the tracks will be for the front of house and what those responsibilities will be, and then when we do our global orientation, as it's called, we train them and do workshops, teaching them how to do that. We give them character profiles. Here's what your main concerns are. Here are the passwords that you need to know. Here's how we're going to change *that* here. Concentrate on getting people from this point to *this* point and they're given a lot of freedom in how they can do that, as long as they're accomplishing the goal.[79]

The global performance director contextualised and described their own role and how the front of house team are developed:

> There's normally about 120 other staff on site in the world, so it's integrating them into the world; but then also integrating them with the cast as well so they can start to have those interactions. You really want to start to extrapolate more, and obviously the actors do a lot in the rehearsal process as well to develop those characters further, but you want to give him a certain amount of information in advance to help them. For example, we said with Mayor Kline, he's got an upcoming election so that creates an interesting game for us to play, but also it's something for him. That's his pressure to make sure he gets these votes from people who are arriving into Hawkins. So this is a great tool for us to be able to use.[80]

The FoH team also include VIP assistants, led by a VIP producer; the VIP experience includes exclusive access to performances, meals, drinks and transport unavailable to other participants. VIPs are looked after by a dedicated team of in-character performers who escort them throughout the performance.

Merchandising is also a central part of operations throughout the experience – right from the moment of ticket purchase. As we have described in previous chapters, SC use the term 'merchandise', not to refer to SC 'branded' merchandise – i.e. items that display SC's logo – but rather to describe the different costumes, accessories and 'in-world' props that ticket holders are encouraged to purchase in their preparations. The merchandise designer explained their role:

> To make sure that it all felt part of our world and theatrical and it didn't become too merchandise-y, really, for want of a better expression. Because we need to make sure it feels like a costume and it all has an importance in the world, and a reason to wear [it].[81]

The show-specific merchandise has previously been made available in physical pop-up shops that we have described in relating other experiences. The dedicated online stores that are linked to via the microsite are the venues through which ticket purchasers are encouraged to source the necessary items in the lead-up to the event. There are also shops on site where these can be purchased, along with souvenir items and poster prints – these are the only SC 'branded' items that have been made available.

7: Operations

This sector includes the site services who manage the physical buildings infrastructure such as communications and networking, power, rigging, structures and plumbing. Then there are those who manage the flow of people through the site – health and safety, security, first aid – and its day-to-day management including cleaning teams. They also oversee the general amenities such as toilets, the bars and the independent traders, including all food outlets. The operations manager described their function:

> I want to make sure that what they're creating is safe and not in the way of people being able to escape in an emergency. So we can't hang big heavy curtains in front of a fire exit, for example. You know where the creative might not want to see the fire exit – I need to have the fire exit. I like getting involved quite early on to make sure that the creative and production [input] joins with my goal of keeping the venue safe, and to make sure there's enough cleaners, there's enough security hired, that they have the training that they need.[82]

The operations team deploy an expansive in-house CCTV system which is also used by the SM and FoH teams – there is a close liaison between the three departments as they are responsible for managing space, performance, people and audience. As we have described, the performers play a central, dynamic role in populating and animating the spaces, while effectively moving people and crowds through the spaces *in addition to* simultaneously playing a part in negotiating their own safety, the safety of other performers and that of audience members. The increased proximity of large-scale audiences to the performers called for additional health and safety measures, and security and CCTV play a key role in providing this. The safety of the cast is built into the design of the locations; CCTV is a prominent planning and design feature which also subverts and contradicts the idea of freedoms and escapism foregrounded in past SC productions, particularly in *Moulin Rouge!* where outlandish audience behaviours were encouraged. The operations team and the departments that report to them all need to be made familiar with the action sequences so as to discern when appropriate intervention may be required:

> Security actually comes to our fight rehearsals so that they see every single fight sequence in the world and they know how to tell whether something is fiction or reality.[83]

As with all of the different sectors on our diagram, operations have had to adapt to the specific challenges of immersive experiences in order to ensure the safety of *all* those working and playing within these spaces. Entering and participating within these elaborately realised spaces brings with it a level of intensity that mirrors the creative and technological complexity required to create them. Each of the sectors plays a crucial and distinct role in shaping these immersive experiences, and each has evolved significantly over a period of significant creative and technological innovation.

Conclusion

What we have seen in this account of the evolution of Secret Cinema is a clear process of *becoming industrial*, in which previously distinct artistic practices have developed into a collaborative, industrially organised production model that has its own particular qualities. The chapter concludes by summarising the key characteristics that have emerged around workflows, practices and professions that are specific to SC and other immersive productions. These have been framed as iteration, immersion, automation and adaptation.

An iterative process

Iterative principles and practices are applied throughout – from the production design and development, iteration is an idea and a concept that is returned to time and time again in the interview responses, and appears to be a defining feature of the immersive creative process which marks it out from traditional film, television and theatre and has more in common with a game design model. The final experience is tested and refined through preview shows, with content constantly adapting and developing in response to audience testing.

An immersive process

It is an all-encompassing process where lines are blurred between the professionals and the performance. For example, the performance director will be a performer within the experience – this is a unique quality and behaviour that the immersive experience demands. Film directors do not normally move on-camera, nor do theatre directors appear on stage alongside the performers who they are directing; they monitor 'out of shot', on a remote screen or 'in the wings'. Within SC performances, these professionals are required to move in and around the site during the performances. The immersive quality of the creative practice was remarked upon by an SC production designer in relation to the demands of working on a production: 'Clear your diary. Just don't expect any social activities or any other work to go on alongside because it's all-consuming.'[84]

An automated process

We see increasing innovation in the level of automation in video, sound and light processes, cueing systems and stage management. These have all evolved and developed to accommodate the escalating technical complexities of production and the expanding numbers of audience members.

An adaptive process

As we noted at the beginning of this chapter, in 2018 SC clearly stated its ambition to export established productions into new, international territories. Both *Casino Royale* and *Stranger Things* underwent international adaptation. The *Casino Royale* event launched in Shanghai in partnership with SMG Live on 23 November 2019. It was forced to end its planned run early due to COVID. People working on this production observed key differences and distinctions between different international audiences. The transfer of these productions to different geographic locations and into the context of different cultures brought with it some very specific and initially unexpected challenges:

> What we found in London was we had all these games and missions and it was very rare that anyone would complete them, because they come in, they get side-tracked by the bar, they have a bit of food. When we went to China they loved the game and people were completing it within the first half-hour and we're like oh shoot, we need to add more in for these guys to do – they wanted to play, you know, that was their big thing.[85]

An SC video designer explained the adaptation of the gameplay mechanics for the Shanghai audience, and the different narrative premises that were used in order to be culturally appropriate; here, the story mechanism and audience motivation were adapted:

> It was global financiers in *Casino Royale* [in London], which wouldn't translate apparently, so it became assembling the parts to a bomb [in Shanghai]. They were trying to track down where the parts will be manufactured instead of trying to track currency across the globe ... the software was actually the same.[86]

An SC lighting designer explained:

> It caught us by surprise. The audience were so hungry for narrative and information. It's the first one that shifted the experience. *The pre-film was more important than the film.* So we up-scaled the world; we brought James Bond – who was never in London in the pre-film – we brought him into the world, because it was really important. We did much more of the parkour sequences in Madagascar than we did in London. They were much bigger in China because *that was what the audience wanted and so that's what we had to give them*.[87]

It is fitting to conclude this chapter with observations around the centrality of the audience and also the emphasis placed on audience interactions. The binary tension that characterised this most recent period is massification to individualisation, in which events were designed to cater for very large numbers, but opportunities for meaningful individual engagements were enhanced and unique to each audience member. As an SC production designer explained:

> You had your version of a great show and other people have another version of it, and it is great that you don't see everything. That sort of is the point, but we need to make sure that everyone's version of the show is equally great and then when they get together at the end of a night and get to chat about it, then it becomes this even bigger thing.[88]

This sense of the participatory dualism of massification and individualisation revealed is also captured in the new 'tag' line that emerged in this period: participants were invited to 'find yourself in the story'. This is a more passive, but also a more individualised invitation. In the next two chapters of the book, we turn our considerations to the individual audience experience and to the wider audience community that has evolved with and through this process of industrialisation.

Notes

1 Thomas Maller, interviewed by Natalie Wreyford, 6 November 2020.
2 SC props maker, interviewed by Natalie Wreyford, 23 February 2021.

3 Doug Bolton, 'Brief encounters', *The Guardian*, 28 October 2005, available at www.theguardian.com/culture/culturevultureblog/2005/oct/28/briefencounter?CMP=gu_com (accessed 13 June 2022); Support Future Shorts, 'Future Cinema @ SE1 Club London', 28 November 2007, YouTube video, 3:19, available at www.youtube.com/watch?v=nmhZVqSdh3Y (accessed 13 December 2021).
4 Tim Heap, 'Review: Baz Luhrmann's *Romeo + Juliet* gets the Secret Cinema treatment', *Attitude*, 8 October 2018, available at https://attitude.co.uk/article/review-baz-luhrmanns-romeo-juliet-gets-the-secret-cinema-treatment/18778/ (accessed 13 December 2021).
5 SC senior producer, interviewed by Natalie Wreyford, 10 December 2020.
6 SC senior producer, interviewed by Wreyford, 10 December 2020.
7 Maller, interviewed by Wreyford, 6 November 2020.
8 Secret Group Limited, Annual report and financial statements for the year ended 31 December 2019, Companies House, 24 July 2020, 1; available at https://find-and-update.company-information.service.gov.uk/company/05071764/filing-history (accessed 31 August 2021).
9 Matt Hills, *Fan cultures* (London: Routledge, 2002) – *hyperdiegesis* is 'the creation of a vast and detailed narrative space, only a fraction of which is ever directly seen or encountered within the text, but which nonetheless appears to operate according to principles of internal logic and extension' (p. 137).
10 Helen Scarlett O'Neill, interviewed by Wreyford, 9 October 2020 – Toby Stevens is an art director with an impressive list of film and TV credits, working across commercials, music videos, television series and feature films, as well as his work on a number of SC productions. See www.imdb.com/name/nm1005309/?ref_=nv_sr_2 (accessed 13 December 2021).
11 Ollie Tiong, interviewed by author, 20 September 2021.
12 Video animator, interviewed by Natalie Wreyford, 29 October 2020.
13 SC presents *Stranger Things*, SC presents *Casino Royale*, SC presents William Shakespeare's *Romeo + Juliet*, SC presents *Blade Runner: The Final Cut* – a secret live experience, SC presents Baz Luhrmann's *Moulin Rouge!*, which have all been published on www.secretcinema.org/credits (accessed 14 July 2021).
14 Charlotte Bence, interviewed by author, 15 September 2021.
15 Jess Denham, 'Secret Cinema denies using unpaid workers after criticism following *Star Wars* £75 ticket sales', *Independent*, 19 March 2015, available at www.independent.co.uk/arts-entertainment/films/news/secret-cinema-criticised-using-unpaid-workers-star-wars-despite-higher-ticket-price-10118869.html (accessed 13 December 2021).
16 Mark Burrows, 'Million-pound question: why save Secret Cinema while real cinemas are in ruins?' *The Guardian*, 14 October 2020, available at www.theguardian.com/film/2020/oct/14/secret-cinema-bailout-arts-venues (accessed 13 December 2021).
17 SC props maker, interviewed by Natalie Wreyford, 23 February 2021.
18 Moore, interviewed by author, 8 October 2021.
19 Performer, interviewed by author, 27 October 2021.

20 They have raised $23.1m to date from the following sources: Equity Crowdfunding ($6.6m) in 2021; Later Stage VC ($5.4m) in January 2021; later stage VC ($6.55m) in October 2018; later stage VC (Series A) ($4.55m) in January 2015 (Active Partners, Social Capital and Neon Adventures). In total – $23.1m ≡ £16, 796, 610 (based on 1US$ ≡ GB£0.727117, 1 September 2021, XE.com).
21 SC senior producer, interviewed by Wreyford, 10 December 2020.
22 See https://active.partners/company-profile/secret-cinema (accessed 13 December 2021).
23 See https://neon.com/technology/secret-cinema (accessed 13 December 2021).
24 See www.socialcapital.com/portfolio (accessed 13 December 2021).
25 Government grant of £945, 219.38 ≡ $1.3m in October 2020, via Arts Council England as part of the pandemic cultural recovery programme of funding – Arts Council England, Cultural Recovery Fund data, 2 April 2021, available at www.artscouncil.org.uk/publication/culture-recovery-fund-data (accessed 13 December 2021).
26 SC senior producer, interviewed by Wreyford, 10 December 2020.
27 Kulkarni, interviewed by author, 8 September 2021.
28 Dixon, interviewed by author, 24 September 2021.
29 McClean, interviewed by author, 6 September 2021.
30 Charles Gant, 'Secret Cinema chiefs talk global ambitions, management changes and Casino Royale', Screen Daily, 30 January 2019, available at www.screendaily.com/features/secret-cinema-chiefs-talk-global-ambitions-management-changes-and-casino-royale/5136312.article (accessed 13 December 2021).
31 Gant, 'Secret Cinema'.
32 'Slate' essentially means a collection of projects. The word originates in analogue production practices where projects would be written up on an actual black 'slate'. Multiple films are on the SC development slate at any one time.
33 SC senior producer, interviewed by Wreyford, 10 December 2020.
34 According to the annual financial reports posted to Secret Group Limited, Companies House, UK, available at https://find-and-update.company-information.service.gov.uk/company/05071764 (accessed 13 December 2021).
35 See Chapter 4, pages 118 and 120.
36 In the department listings (see Figure 5.2), the prefix 'production' denotes that the role has a project/production-based nature, rather than any specific organisational level (this is consistent with how those working in the film industry are credited.)
37 Ma, email exchange with author, 19 November 2021.
38 Bence, interviewed by author, 15 September 2021.
39 March, interviewed by author, 16 September 2021.
40 O'Neill, interviewed by Wreyford, 9 October 2020.
41 Maller, interviewed by Wreyford, 6 November 2020.
42 Maller, interviewed by Wreyford, 6 November 2020.
43 Dingsdale, interviewed by author, 27 October 2021.
44 Introduced and defined in Chapter 2, page 54.
45 Maller, interviewed by Wreyford, 6 November 2020.
46 SC senior producer, interviewed by Wreyford, 14 October 2020.

47 Barnes, interviewed by Wreyford, 14 October 2020.
48 O'Neill, interviewed by Wreyford, 9 October 2020.
49 Kulkarni, interviewed by author, 8 September 2021.
50 Kulkarni, interviewed by author, 8 September 2021.
51 See Chapter 4, page 142.
52 Simon Gordon, interviewed by Natalie Wreyford, 11 November 2020.
53 SC senior producer, interviewed by Wreyford, 10 December 2020.
54 Maller, interviewed by Wreyford, 6 November 2020.
55 Andy Barnes, interviewed by Wreyford, 14 October 2020.
56 Mika Handley, interviewed by author, 21 September 2021.
57 Tim McQuillen-Wright, interviewed by author, 3 September 2021.
58 McQuillen-Wright, interviewed by author, 3 September 2021.
59 Lead animator, interviewed by Wreyford, 29 October 2020.
60 Handley, interviewed by author, 21 September 2021.
61 Ian William Galloway and Salvador Bettencourt, 'Immersive experiences: Mesmer Studios, a webinar', *Disguise*, 11 August 2021, video, 1:20:48, available at www.disguise.one/en/insights/webinars/immersive-experiences/ (accessed 13 December 2021).
62 Global performance director, interviewed by author, 6 October 2021.
63 Galloway, interviewed by author, 1 October 2021.
64 Galloway, interviewed by author, 1 October 2021.
65 Terry Cook, interviewed by author, 15 September 2021.
66 Secret Cinema, 'Secret Cinema presents *Casino Royale* (2019)', 8 October 2020, Vimeo video, 1:19, available at https://vimeo.com/466193279 (accessed 13 December 2021).
67 Secret Cinema, 'Secret Cinema presents *Stranger Things* (2019–2020)', 1 March 2021, Vimeo video, 1:07, available at https://vimeo.com/518249300 (accessed 13 December 2021).
68 Luke Swaffield, interviewed by author, 22 September 2021.
69 Emmet O'Donnell, interviewed by Wreyford, 4 November 2020.
70 O'Donnell, interviewed by Wreyford, 4 November 2020.
71 See Chapter 4, page 137.
72 Helen Smith, interviewed by author, 7 September 2021.
73 Lorna Adamson, interviewed by author, 12 September 2021.
74 Sophie Cairns, interviewed by author, 17 September 2021.
75 Maller, interviewed by Wreyford, 6 November 2020.
76 Maller, interviewed by Wreyford, 6 November 2020.
77 Smith, interviewed by author, 7 September 2021.
78 SC senior producer, interviewed by Wreyford, 10 December 2020.
79 Victoria Gagliano, interviewed by author, 21 September 2021.
80 Global performance director, interviewed by author, 6 October 2021.
81 Merchandise designer, interviewed by Natalie Wreyford, 11 December 2020.
82 Operations manager, interviewed by author, 9 September 2021.
83 SC senior producer, interviewed by Wreyford, 10 December 2020.
84 McQuillen-Wright, interviewed by author, 3 September 2021.

85 Swaffield, interviewed by author, 22 September 2021.
86 Galloway, interviewed by author, 1 October 2021.
87 Cook, interviewed by author, 15 September 2021. Other immersive experience producers have noted the interest and demand in their experiences from this particular demographic. Punchdrunk's production *Sleep No More* has been running in Shanghai since December 2016. Talking about *Immersive Gatsby*, Brian Hook, co-founder, Hartshorn-Hook Productions stated 'It's pretty common, and I'm talking pre-pandemic, for about 25% of our audience members to be Chinese-speaking, and to the extent where we translated all of the website into Mandarin' (interviewed by author, 28 September 2021).
88 McQuillen-Wright, interviewed by author, 3 September 2021.

6

Secret Cinema as experience community

> One thing about the Secret Cinema audience is that they were non-traditional and they were exploratory, they were romantic, and I think that these are the kinds of people who will be drawn to this.
>
> SC performance designer[1]

In this chapter, we turn our attention to the central facet of the SC experience design and business model – the audience. As our immersive experience production model in figure 5.1 reveals,[2] the audience play a pivotal role in the SC event as it unfolds. Since SC's first screening, its audience has evolved considerably. They have transitioned from a group that we once described as the 'early adopter hipster elite',[3] who played the key role of acting as taste makers, supporting Riggall's cinephilia and the early underground sub-cultural ethos. Colluding in the sense of exclusivity and of being 'in the know' was a key element of the early audience's shared identity. We show how this audience has expanded to engage members of more mainstream fandoms. We also trace the emergence of a community of elite fans of SC who have dubbed themselves the 'Positive People of Secret Cinema' (PPSC) – a group formed from a shared love of SC – who have evolved their own mores, values, rules, tastes and shared cultural practices.[4] We will firstly lay out how the audience has been positioned and articulated through SC's evolution.

SC audience articulated as collaborators and as community

The centrality of the audience has always been evident in public articulations of the founder Fabien Riggall's vision. We have already seen how audiences were repeatedly encouraged into acts of rebellion and pseudo-protest in their construction as activists by SC and here we return to the earliest articulations of audience as community espoused by Riggall. From the outset, his vision of the audience has always been articulated as a community with shared values that he is addressing and helping to realise. This comes across most clearly in his statement below:

> It was not about the vision that I had ... it was about the vision that the audience had about another way of experiencing film ... The way I see it is that you have a format in which you can experience the film, you can live the film.[5]

Here, we see Riggall refer to a 'vision that the audience had'; the vision is externalised to a notional audience that are, in reality, a reflection of Riggall's own tastes and preferences. He goes on to describe the audience as the co-producer of the vision: 'We will keep building this with our audience'.[6] This is the text of a speech given at the Toronto Film Festival, reported in *Screen Daily*, and the emphasis was very much on both the economic and the cultural value of SC to a future film economy and how it was shaping film production and consumption of the future.

As we demonstrated in Chapter 4, Riggall describes himself as a cultural entrepreneur with activist leanings. From the early days of the underground, secret, cult events that we described in Chapter 2, he has courted his audience as cultural intermediaries and as collaborators who can support him in taste making, communicating the cultural value and excitement of SC to a wider potential audience.

In a public statement in 2021 the audience appear as Riggall's key collaborators and co-creators of SC experiences:

> I'd never been to business school – I started the idea, and it grew very quickly ... the audience created SC really, because they're the ones who came, and took part, and as I went along, I made quite a few mistakes ... there wasn't anybody to say 'No' to these ideas, and the ideas that the audience were having, so we were able to build something quite imaginative, with a group of very creative people. We were able to turn SC into something that was quite underground, it was my intention to always keep it underground – but for it to grow a massive underground if that makes sense; but what was interesting [was] that we were able to get it to a certain point, to create the magic of it so it would then be able to become a business, because to be fair, it wasn't really a business.[7]

This notion of audience as collaborator was particularly prevalent in the early days when SC/FC would conduct vox pops at the end of an experience to request suggestions for future events. These were then included in the post-experience promotional video, so would serve to recruit further audience collaborators. There is an interesting, contradictory and yet *revolutionary*, sense of a 'massive' underground here. Notions of collective and community were central to the way in which SC positioned their events and to their direct address to their audience:

> The idea of the internet is really creating this community online that then come together in a social experience at the venue, and the internet for us is hugely positive. Some people say that the internet is killing cinema but for us it's actually creating that community of people who want to get together to watch film.[8]

Here, Riggall described the value of the online context as a means to develop a community. In a further instance, he positioned one of his earlier branches of activity, The Other Cinema,[9] in a similar way: 'The idea ... is to build a network of community local cinemas around the world simply through the internet, through the power of community'.[10] There was a further assertion of the size and the quality of this community:

> SC has become a happening[;] in the old days of happenings, where people would dress up, they would bring props, they helped dress the space, they keep the secret. Over the course of two months, 25,000 people kept the secret and I think that's really a testament to what the audience want is to be part of a community. They want to be part of an experience, and they want to create that experience with the performance.[11]

Here he was referring back, with some nostalgia, to participatory art movements such as Fluxus, the Merry Pranksters and the situationists in this evocation of 'happenings'.

The early adopters (2006–2013)

This early audience, the most ephemeral of all, were formed through their participation in *secret* events which were largely communicated by word of mouth. This group were quite happy to maintain the secrecy of the earlier events and their subjectivity as members of this exclusive, *underground* activity can be understood in relation to the concept of the 'neo-tribe' and 'neo-tribalism'. These terms are introduced into debates around the relationship between sub-cultural identity, activism and consumer culture to comprehend the highly *constructed* nature of these communities of belonging which constellate around particular acts of cultural consumption. The concept of the contemporary neo-tribe also foregrounds the potentially complex affective pull of these sites of temporary belonging.[12] What the SC audience experience design did from quite early on, is offer up both a broad SC community of belonging and then within this also provide ways of creating internal, even tighter structures of affiliation that could be exploited as part of the SC audience engagement strategy. A lead performance designer offered up an account of the process of discovering the power of this element within their design:

> What I really noticed in *Lawrence of Arabia* was we were able to work with the audience in the secret moments before they come into the production and that they would go with us on that journey. We would create entirely new worlds within this bubble of secrecy before we open the show.[13]

What the designer also indicated here is the element of trust that was present within this audience – evidenced here in their willingness to go on 'that journey' with the production:

> We asked the audience, depending where they lived in London, to change their Facebook profile picture to one of three new flags, which we designed for the film. People would change their profile picture and suddenly you would see Facebook going crazy. People you didn't even know that were going to go to SC or had been before, suddenly you saw all these flags popping up and people were going, 'Oh my God. What are you doing? What are these flags about?' ... By experiencing this tribalism in the pre-narrative ... when we brought them together at Alexandra Palace, they were already in character. They had experienced some of those dynamics and then experienced these moments of unity as we all ran up the hill towards the Palace. It was like 5,000 people a night so 5,000 people suddenly meeting in the field and then running up the hill with camels and donkeys.[14]

What is revealed here is the extent to which this evidence of willing involvement in these assignations and allegiances became part of the resource that the creative team could deploy in the design of the event. This is captured very clearly in this statement: 'We knew the audience and how to work with their abilities more intensely than a director, who is used to working with actors'.[15]

Developing an external, 'whole audience', tribe of SC attendees and these internal opportunities for affiliation while maintaining narrative coherence has been an ongoing audience engagement strategy for SC. One such example is being assigned to the house of either the Capulets or the Montagues, and then displaying belonging, at the production of *Romeo + Juliet*. The willingness of the SC audience to participate in activities beyond the event itself has already been evidenced in the various flash mobs that accompanied productions throughout SC's development – for example, *The Red Shoes*, *Bugsy Malone*, *Prometheus* (see Chapter 2), *Brazil*, *Back to the Future* (see Chapter 3) and *Star Wars: The Empire Strikes Back* (see Chapter 4). Through these moments of participation, the audience performed their engagement with the particular SC event but also, *importantly*, promoted further participation in SC events in general.

Established fan communities (2014–2018)

Having already developed a well-understood and highly loyal SC audience of early adopters, the shift to engaging a wider and much larger audience with the *BttF* event in 2014 brought with it some challenging moments.[16] The shift in communication register and reach in to this wider, well-established (and international) fan community inevitably led to tensions between the expectations of the early adopters (those who attended the initial SC screenings and showed the most trust in the creative team) and those of a textually literate, *BttF* fanbase, who had no natural or previous loyalty to or affiliation with SC.

> I didn't know much about 'immersive theatre' but I'd seen occasional posts about SC and thought 'what an interesting idea!' But it was down in London and I'm up in Liverpool. There just wasn't that 'pull' to make me dive in … until they announced *Back to the Future*! … I realised I HAD to try it! I didn't think it would be big or anything, though, just potentially interesting. I was so wrong, it was HUGE. They built the whole town and once I'd heard what they were doing I knew I'd probably be a fan for life![17]

This quote reflects a moment of significant transition when Darren Carnall, who became the founder of the 'PPSC', was sufficiently drawn by his investment in *BttF* to make the journey to London to experience the SC event. In previous publications we have explored the high-profile social media debacle that took place when the opening night was cancelled just hours before it was due to commence.[18] Large numbers of participants who were travelling far from home – without their mobile phones – were, at very short notice, cast adrift in London without an event to attend. Highly textually literate *BttF* fans took to social media to express their extreme disgruntlement. Despite this difficult opening, which momentarily rendered highly visible the clashing fan subjectivities, once the production was under way the audience feedback via social media was largely positive. This was reflected in the responses to our own pre- and post-event questionnaire and the post-experience interviews we carried out, which inform our discussion here and in the discussion of cosplay that follows.[19] As well as massifying this reach in to established fan communities, the *BttF* production also presented audiences with a significantly more extensive set of costuming, adornment and prop requirements. As we shall see, this created a context within which the more ludic practices of cosplay could flourish.

Cosplay

The central requirement for audiences to dress up in costume has been part of the SC experience design since the 2008 production of *A Night at the*

Opera. Like other aspects, this has become increasingly complex and an increasingly commercial aspect of the production. The dress requirement takes two forms depending on whether or not the film's title has been disclosed to the audience: 1) where the title remains unannounced, costume instructions offer guidance about the period and theme and promote further speculation around the title; 2) where the title is known specific references to character subjectivities or tropes within the film are used to establish costume instructions for the participants to follow. As we have seen in previous chapters, online and/or offline opportunities to purchase SC-sourced versions of the costumes accompany these instructions. This dressing up can be understood within the framework of cosplay.

Cosplay refers to the pleasures and aesthetics of dressing up as beloved film, comic, game or musical icons and has been widely studied as a phenomenon within fan sub-cultural practices. It has also been broadly discussed as a specific 'playful' practice, aligning with play forms such as mimicry and make believe. These practices are now routinely referred to as cosplay – a term joining 'costuming' and 'playing' to capture their performative dimensions. As Nicole Lamerichs helpfully describes, 'cosplay can be understood as culture of costuming that occurs beyond the institutional remit of the theatre'.[20] Lamerichs' ethnographically informed research is particularly relevant here as:

> [i]t connects the field of fan studies intimately with performance studies, and shows us that costumes can be anchored social practices outside the traditional theatre space. Within fandom, the costume is not merely an aesthetic dress, worn at a specific performance, but also a material object that fans produce with great skill and dedication. While the costumed performance of fans reproduces famous characters from mass culture, understanding it only as mimicry would be too narrow. Cosplay is a culture of crafting and performing that speaks to our wider imagination.[21]

We will now go on to outline the stages of cosplay as we have seen them emerge from our own participation in and observation of SC events:

1. The first moment of potential 'play' comes at the very early stage after ticket purchase, when engaging with the online questions that determine the allocation of an identity (we mentioned these thematised questionnaires in Chapter 4). The participant can already inflect their responses with an element of play and performance. These questions may ask the ticket holder to align with a performative identity – for example, in *Stranger Things* audiences were offered a choice of rockers, punks, hip hoppers, movers & groovers, New Romantics and pop kids. For *Romeo + Juliet* audiences were assigned to either Montague or Capulet.
2. Pre-event costume construction/assembly: although not all costumes are wholly *made* and many are collected from a range of sources, this is the material practice of costume making that Lamerichs outlines above.

6.1 Audience members capture images of costumes and preparations, to share on social media.

3. Capturing and sharing images of the cosplayer as they prepare, travel to, queue for and enter the event space (see Figures 6.1 and 6.3).
4. Participation in multiple small games, tasks, challenges, play activities and interactions – in character and amongst other cosplayers and cast members.
5. Post-event communication via social media channels, either as cosplay character or as self.

As we have already established, a key element within the main SC format is the assignment of a new, unique, individual identity. Once this has been assigned to the participant, they are invited to both engage with and develop this identity in a number of ways. Attendees have been known to deviate from these to develop costumes that reflect their own fandoms or engagements with the film. As we have noted elsewhere:

Since so many of the *BttF* participants are established devotees and fans of the text, they arrived in their own self-selected identities – many of them choosing to play key central characters from not just the first *BttF* but also the two sequels. These minor acts of disobedience led to a preponderance of Martys, Biffs, Goldies and Docs whose actions and behaviours were easily confused with those of the actual professional actors who shared the landscape. Said one participant: 'I always dress as Doc Brown to fancy dress parties and am a bit of an inventor like him!'[22]

As a SC costume designer revealed: 'For *BttF* there was a guy who had some of the shoes from the film that he was wearing – he was a super fan that had come over from Amsterdam. Obviously ours aren't going to be as good as his because his are real!'[23]

In the SC 'Tell No One' format the possibility of deviating from the costuming directions was not present – thus participants tended to follow the prescriptive instructions more closely and precisely. An example of this was *The Handmaiden*, the audience for which were *not* aware of the film they were going to see (although some may have guessed the title) and arrived in outfits that very much conformed to the instructions, which were: 'Formal attire ... Gentlemen will wear black gloves. Ladies will wear white gloves.'

The development and inhabiting of these 'costumes' is a key element in the participatory framework of the SC experience. As we have seen SC have themselves hosted both online and physical 'pop-up' shops, to which ticket purchasers were directed once they had been through the series of questions that led to their identity being assigned. These shops offered tailored items, to assemble costumes that directly aligned with the range of choices on offer. For *Stranger Things* these reflected the six 1970s and 1980s sub-cultural identities. For *Casino Royale*, the tailoring and accessories all underscored the 'playboy spy' aesthetic of the Bond format and provided the relevant colour options to go with the particular identity allocated (see Figure 6.2).

The physical pop-up shops and those on-site at the event can offer a complementary range of accessories from scarves, to boiler suits, handbags, badges and goggles – all depending on the narrative environment. Such is the significance of SC audience cosplaying activities that totally unrelated sites offer products specifically for a given production. A vendor on eBay offering cyberpunk goggles explicitly referenced SC and the *Blade Runner* production, stating 'Secret Cinema *Blade Runner* costume goggles perfect for your Secret Cinema dress'.

As an extension to these cosplay practices, there may also be explicit instructions about items or equipment to bring. These can play a more or less central role in the experience for in-event mini-games, small tasks, activities, etc. These have included writing a love letter to a stranger for *The*

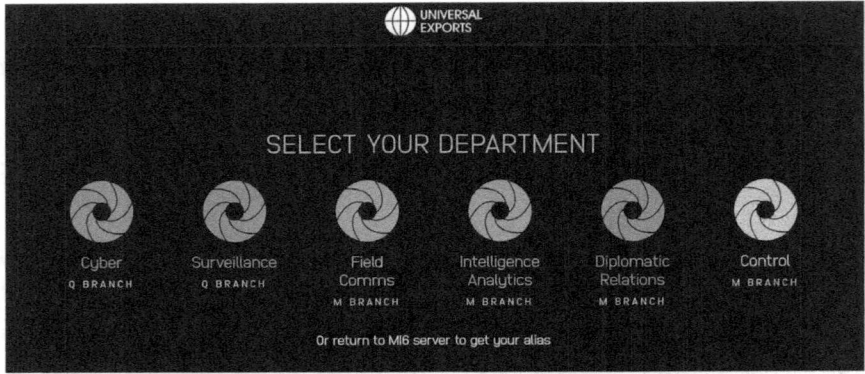

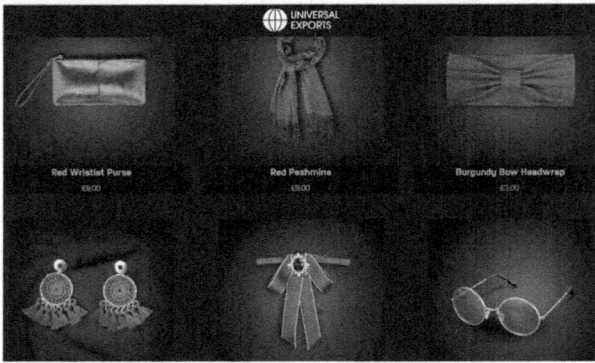

6.2 *Casino Royale* identities and costuming. Audiences were assigned a colour-coded identity for which matching accessories could be bought from the online store.

Handmaiden, and printing and bringing business cards – which, as we saw in Chapter 5, played a central role in the experience design of *Casino Royale*.

Having covered the costume and costuming element, we now move forwards to discuss the play element which emerges through practices of 'performance' that are also aligned with the individual 'identity' construction. Some of this play is quite heavily prescribed by SC through specifically assigned tasks. These have included learning songs, writing letters, articles, travel pieces, new biographies and poems, all to be produced from the perspective of the 'identity' being donned for the purposes of the experience. This process of identity construction can take place over a significant period (from the moment of ticket purchase, which can sometimes be three or more months before the event) and is accompanied by the sharing and displaying of the identity across social media channels and accounts (see Figures 6.1 and 6.3).

These social media posts are frequently accompanied by playful commentary and statements from the audience indicating excitement and anticipation. Some of these will reveal existing knowledge about SC (and therefore indicate repeat participation) or will indicate a thrill regarding the unknown elements of the experience to come. Lamerichs underscores the complexity of the affective dimension of cosplaying:

> I found that affect could be directed at many things, not just the text, but also the community and the costume as an object of fandom and selfhood. In fan studies, affect is often perceived as related to the source text but in cosplay it is actively constructed towards other objects (e.g., sewing machine; fabric) and subjects (e.g., friends, fellow-fans, characters). However, during my interviews and participant-observation, I also found that affect could be directed at different aspects of the text or game.[24]

The pre-event, 'in-character' communications between SC audience members are part of the construction of the overall affective experience of SC – they create a buzz, a sense of exclusivity and in-group belonging.

Capturing cosplay

The principal evidence of participant cosplay and their affective pleasures in these practices is these photographs, which are displayed and shared and make it largely evident. Over time there has evolved a fairly standard set of images that are constructed, captured and shared via social media channels. We have identified these images as predominantly falling into six different types:

1. *An image taken at home:* this is an excitement-building image, usually showing the elaborate costume in a domestic setting. It may feature within a set of 'getting ready' shots. Sometimes it may be accompanied by descriptions of how the costume has been sourced, i.e. 'they're my Grandmother's gloves', 'the feather's from a second-hand shop'.
2. *The journey to the event:* images are captured on public transport and usually stress the humorous incongruity of the costumes amongst normal commuters or travellers. These may also feature descriptions of the complexity of the journey.
3. *Queuing images:* these are another very standard format – usually featuring not only the attendee but contextual background and other participants. These position the costumed participant as part of an anticipatory collective. As with the first two types, these images are often accompanied by text that anchors the affect, capturing a sense of thrill and expectation.
4. *The pre-event staged image:* this is one that has evolved from being participant-led to being facilitated by the organisers. This type of image captures the participant within an element of the set. Lamerichs has underscored the central importance of this image within cosplay practices,

6.3 Secret Cinema audience members as tourists. This is a moment where audience members can take a picture of themselves against an icon of the film, before they surrender their mobile phones. These now obligatory 'photo opportunities' are set up at the entrance to the site. The images proliferate on social media streams with the designated event hashtag and then become an integral part of the social media marketing campaign. Top left: *Back to the Future* in 2014; top right: *Stranger Things* in 2019; bottom left: *Casino Royale* in 2019; bottom right: *Romeo + Juliet* in 2018.

as it features the costumed participant in the context for which the costume was designed.[25] This is the moment at which audience members can take a picture of themselves against the film's iconic imagery, before they surrender their mobile phones. Here the style conforms to a standard 'tourist' image taken at a landmark and is destined to be shared on social media as proof of presence (see Figure 6.3).

These authorised and staged photo opportunities were established to facilitate the creation and dissemination of social media content that celebrated and promoted the event for future participants. This completed

the social media marketing loop: attendees post and promote their experiences, revealing none of the detail but all of the excitement and intrigue – these are then shared, reposted and promoted by SC.
5. *The post-event image:* this is less frequently part of the photographic evidence base – often taken in the same space as the controlled pre-event photograph and quite often posted alongside the first as 'before and after' shots. These images are usually marked by dishevelment that stands in for or connotes the excitement of the event itself.
6. *The 'journey home' image:* sharing the evidence of dishevelment referenced above but now often in another, incongruous setting, to underscore the excitement of the event (as above) but also, once again, to highlight the distinction of participation by marking out the subject's difference from either other people or the context that appears in the background (e.g. period costume on modern public transport).

As can be seen above, these cosplaying images also help the audience's affective and playful engagement with the experience to function as labour in the service of SC. As Meghan O'Hara has argued in relation to Punchdrunk's *Sleep No More* audience,[26] sharing these images on social media platforms gives away any ownership of these images and posting them to official sites (e.g. Secret Cinema's Facebook site) guarantees their exploitation in the service of the SC experience economy. These images also form the evidence of engagement and are a powerful means of demonstrating participation, affective response and showcasing costume construction. They also evidence *expert* engagement with the overall experience – they are particularly important where no images can be captured within the experience itself, beyond the controlled photo opportunities listed at 4 and perhaps 5.

Character play during the experience

As we outlined in Chapter 3, throughout the show, and particularly the pre-screening element of this, the SC participants can engage in a diverse range of games, missions, playful and performative activities that are the key to deeper engagement within the SC experience. Below are four anonymised responses from *BttF* participants in 2014, who all described this performative and playful aspect of the experience:

> I dressed for the part and stayed in character all night. I interacted with many actors, including the man playing Doc Brown, a housewife cheating on her husband, and a staff member at Roy's Comic Book store who interviewed me for a job. I went to the Enchantment under the Sea ball, and found the 1985 zone.

> We even participated in several role-plays where characters asked us to deliver a letter and another asked us to book a holiday for a newlywed couple. My

girlfriend and I certainly felt like we were playing our characters, I got the impression many people felt the same as they were dressed up which really added to the experience. It was a very exciting experience, to be involved in role play.

Other places offered some great possibilities for interaction and role playing, like the *Telegraph*, which set its reporters tasks, or the recording studio, which engaged people in a gameshow for a little while, and at one point the bicycle shop, which had an amusing paint-can lifting competition. When group events of playing or watching like these happened, the sense of community was emboldened.

I took part in Doc Brown's experiment (which was hilarious) and got picked on by bullies twice, which was weirdly the highlight for me.

The play element is present throughout the pre-screening experience as the participants engage in these activities in the spirit or mode of 'as if' that is central to any form of play. It is this shift from inhabiting one's everyday identity to this playful character that is elaborated through not just the costume but also through the game-ful engagement with the myriad mini-tasks and activities that comprise the SC pre-screening experiential design. Many of the productions included opportunities for the participants to engage in more overt acts of performance, including *Moulin Rouge!*, *Dirty Dancing*, *Romeo + Juliet*, *Blade Runner* and *Stranger Things*. These could range from the performance of a poem, skit, song or dance routine created in advance by the audience member, to engaging in activities organised by SC such as a dance class, an aerobics session, an impromptu individual song or dance performance or a collective sing-along.

These more performative elements are accompanied by other game-like opportunities: for example, the *Casino Royale* experience included the development of more than ten different narrative tracks for participants to follow, each with distinct 'mission' opportunities. One of these tracks, an early encounter and exchange of business cards with a character named Madame Woo, led to a complex mini-performance that included playing poker with the character of Le Chiffre then participating in a secret handover of a 'briefcase' and an exchange of information with the villains.[27] These were activities that combine role play with elements of puzzle solving, sometimes acts of collecting and gathering resources, which offered opportunities for deeper engagement with the performers and the set. *Stranger Things* offered a myriad of distinct mission tracks providing opportunities for all levels of involvement – including a secret track that only a few participants would ever access, which led to a very intimate, interactive performance with a Russian scientist. As we demonstrated in Chapters 4 and 5, the detailing and complexity of these missions has significantly increased across the development of SC and they have become a highly celebrated aspect of the experience. As we shall see, deep engagement with these missions, 'leaning in' to the role-play opportunities, are key elements in the formation of the *expert* fan subjectivity discussed below.

The super-fan community I: Positive People of Secret Cinema (2018–2019)

In September 2018 Jane and Darren Carnall set up a new Facebook community which they called the Positive People of Secret Cinema (PPSC).[28] The group was explicitly established as a 'positive' space in which to evince enthusiasm for the SC events. The Carnalls were inspired to establish the group in response to grumblings of negativity (at the time, in response to the cancellation of some of the *Romeo + Juliet* screenings due to bad weather) that (in the view of some fans) spoiled the public SC Facebook site.[29] Darren had already emerged as a prominent SC fan (known as 'Gun Guy' due to the replica guns he created for his *Romeo + Juliet* persona), recognised on the public site, and was urged to set up a separate community through which to discuss costuming plans and to share experiences. Membership is by private arrangement, and specifically monitored by the site administrators to ensure that the group retains its intended purpose. Prospective members must answer three questions before being considered for admission:

1. Have you been to/are planning to go to SC? If you have been before, name one of your favourite events and why.
2. The key tenets of this group are kindness, positivity and friendship. Do you agree to abide by these principles and help us make this a friendly, safe space for all fans of SC?
3. This group is a SPOILER-FREE ZONE. Do you agree to not post any details of active events that could ruin that 'first time magic' for people who have yet to go?[30]

Agreeing to these principles is taken very seriously by the PPSC, and they are embraced and internalised by the community. This is evidenced in moments such as the following:

> I was a little negative on this group yesterday about the ... announcement. Although I don't feel differently today about it, I realised this isn't the place for me being a grump. This group is awesome and apologies for bringing the vibe down.[31]

Members of the group are careful of their tone and negotiate any negative statements or reflections very carefully. This is evident in this interview response from another group member:

> The customer service experience and communication from SC regarding the moving of dates/access to changed dates and refunds, as well as then announcing new shows that were subsequently changed hasn't been great. I know so many people who have issues with their partner company Fever and that has put a negative spin on things for many people. I haven't booked extra dates for some of these events due to the issues I've seen others have and I do feel this will damage SC's brand reputation unless they fix it before the next round of ticket purchases.[32]

The negative sentiment here is shifted on to the intermediary agent handling the bookings for SC – Fever – rather than attached to SC directly. These comments are largely typical of how any negativity is managed by the membership, normally through providing a positive rationale for any SC actions and through identifying an external driver for the negative impact. The guiding principles are also reinforced through a set of eight rules published on the site, which include the following:

1. Be kind and courteous;
2. No hate speech or bullying;
3. No promotions or spam;
4. Respect everyone's privacy;
5. No rivalries with other groups;
6. SC cast/crew are always welcome;
7. Respect the SC cast and crew;
8. No spoilers during an active event.

The articulation of these rules includes further contextual detail that reinforces the values 'welcome' and 'respect', and the rule around hate speech includes explicit reference to protected characteristics. The values of trust and authenticity are also underlined. It is interesting to note that two rules are dedicated to reinforcing a positive relationship and attitude towards the cast and crew, and the cast and crew are also the 'exception' to the 'no promotions' rule, as they are invited to promote other events that they are involved in. This overt assertion of an explicit intention to support the SC creative team has been crucial in the wider recognition of this particular community of dedicated super-fans.[33] The site also functions for this community of fans to visibly evidence their expert participation in the SC experiences while simultaneously upholding the 'Tell no one' instruction; the site does have special 'spoilers allowed' discussion threads where members can exchange detailed guidance on a particular production – this may include members colluding to establish 'dead drops' to share 'found' resources in relation to specific missions.

In understanding the specificities of fan practices and specifically fan community formation in relation to SC it is useful to consider the valuable work that Rebecca Williams has done in augmenting existing cultural studies approaches to fandom through an interrogation of theme park fandom as spatially inflected. This attention to the spatial aspects is particularly relevant to any consideration of these SC fan practices, which specifically revolve around physical participation in spatialised narratives and story 'worlds'.[34]

> Part of the attraction of being physically present within theme park spaces is that it allows the fan to experience the bodily sensations associated with immersion in the theme park environment. In 'theme-park attractions ... The senses now come into play with a greater immediacy that actually takes its toll on the participant's body'.[35]

Williams' account of theme park fandom also points to the role of blogs and other community postings that serve to prepare others for their participation in these spaces, writing that there is a 'pedagogical element to many of these blogs, as they work to "teach" other visitors, especially first-time visitors, how to "properly" plan for and prepare for the trip'.[36] This 'teacherly' aspect is very much part of the PPSC community where 'tips' postings appear fairly regularly in relation to different events, as well as in response to a new member's request for information. 'Tips' postings take the form of members sharing practical suggestions for how to get the most out of the experience.[37] We summarise the general, non-specific tips here:[38]

1. *Costume and accessories:* dressing up, sourcing props, ensuring you have the right colours for any affiliations or identities that will structure the event.
2. *Being equipped/ready for action:* this relates to 1. above but is focussed on being able to be light on your feet and able to move quickly and easily – so travelling light. There is considerable reference to appropriate footwear, particularly amongst women members.
3. *Preparing your body:* there are repeated recommendations to 'eat heartily' before attending and to only have one or two drinks for 'Dutch courage'. These two postings are typical: 'dive straight into the (inter)action' and 'don't get too distracted with getting drinks or food'.
4. *Interaction and exploration:* almost all tips include some version of 'even if you are shy, your character isn't'. PPSC followers are recommended to 'lean in' to the experience and to try everything. 'Look for clues, there's usually a hidden space you can gain access to if you take the right actions! (at *Moulin Rouge!* it was Zidler's office and a stage performance, at *Romeo + Juliet* it was the Capulet mansion party).'
5. *Screening:* differences of opinion emerge here – for some the movie is the time to eat and enjoy both the film and the accompanying live action; for others this is a prime moment to continue their engagement with the live set, and they claim actions/re-enactments and opportunities are still available.
6. *After the experience:* there is a recommendation to share your 'love' on social media but again a reinforcement of the 'no spoilers' rule.

There are also more offbeat recommendations, such as 'flirting' and 'making a spectacle of yourself' that largely reinforce the fourth recommendation to really lean in to the experience. You can see that the tips bring the embodied nature of the experience very much to the fore.

This specific tips 'thread' on the PPSC Facebook site, and the generally regular posting of more event-specific recommendations, are also an opportunity for the members of the community to display (and share) their *cultural capital*. In research on sub-cultural practices, theorists have adapted the work of Bourdieu in order to identify the ways in which the markers of distinction, of expertise, and hierarchies of privilege are established and asserted within these communities of belonging. Bourdieu's concept of cultural capital is central to this work and in what follows we explore how this form of 'capital' is particularly evident in the emergence of the PPSC super-fan community. Here the term is used to signal the specific way in which PPSC members communicate their 'expert' knowledge of *how* to be a good SC participant and the status and rewards that this expert status accrues for them, as this particular insight quoted from Twitter exemplifies:

> So many possibilities, so many things to do and to see, the cast are universally brilliant, and the staff are so friendly and helpful. Seriously, well done everyone! Looking forward to my next trips as tour guide to SC virgins. And thanks to #positivepeopleofsecretcinema for teaching me how to get the most of the experience. I literally could not have done this without you.

The PPSC community frequently offer to take new members to events and to help them maximise their experience. The display of cultural capital here is not solely for self-aggrandisement, it is also both 'teacherly' (as described above) and an act of generosity in seeking to share that expertise amongst a wider community. Acting as 'tour guide' and writing 'tips' entries also serve to translate the expert knowledge or cultural capital of the PPSC member into symbolic capital through which this expertise is recognised and rewarded in the form of status. Later, we shall see how SC also reward this community of experts with special access to productions and or missions.

This PPSC member included an image of themselves in four different *Stranger Things* costumes with the caption '4 visits, 4 personalities, 4 completely different experiences'. This example contains a number of the elements that we have identified as core to the SC audience experience: the element of cosplay that we have already discussed in detail; the element of repeatability – facilitated by the multiple 'tracks' and missions that are built into the experience that lend themselves to this repetition; the sense of an 'experiencing community' that has shared values, that has a pedagogic dimension (where members learn from one another) and that is carried through into fostering a shared experience through this act of passing on the learning to the 'SC virgins'. This social media post also serves to directly communicate the expertise and high status of this PPSC community member – their expert costuming, their achievement accessing the 'many possibilities' and this role as 'guide'. In the 'well done everyone' comment directed at SC, this member also positions themselves as a peer, and also as a reviewer of SC experiences, further underscoring their high status within this community.

The value of participation

The PPSC Facebook group had 2,400 members in December 2021, with a core of around 50 frequent 'posters' who maintain the tone, while also promoting community events, discussion groups and related social opportunities. We were able to reach out to this community, interview fifteen of these most active members and gain permissions to include text and images from past postings from a further thirty participants. From these interviews and from their Facebook community site more generally we have gleaned the following five key values and pleasures that they attach to their participation in these events. These are: pleasure in participating, being inside the film, role play, ludic pleasures and the pleasures and rewards of replay.

The value that is communicated most frequently, unsurprisingly perhaps, is their pleasure in participating in SC events. They variously describe the events as 'awesome', 'absolutely amazing', 'brilliant', 'great'. A particularly vivid account was given by one of the community:

> I find I am much more outgoing and prepared to get involved than I'd expected. They are genuinely some of the best nights of my life ever. They feel almost hallucinatory – the memories are sparkling and extreme – some of them still make me laugh hysterically – they felt hyper. I love experiencing the worlds – I would really like to be able to see more and do more and hate it when the evening is over. I love that you can't take photos so that everyone around you is a part of the world and no one breaks out of character. I was surprised at how much I love watching the films afterwards – the extra scenes they do around the room are fun but I mainly like seeing the details in the film of the world I've just been experiencing myself.[39]

There is considerable affective intensity evidenced here; there are many superlatives and a sense of genuine transportation, of being entirely taken by the experience. This level of intensity is also more widely evidenced in the frequency with which the members of the community will post 'memories' of particular events, which then produce an immediate flurry of shared, remembered pleasures.

Members of the community frequently reflect on the intensity of the experience of being situated within the film, further reflecting the spatialised fandom that Williams described in relation to theme park pleasures. Here, four respondents reflect on the scenography and their sense of being there:

> It's like you are in the world of the movie/TV, you can interact with the characters (cast) the surroundings (sets) are top notch. Also I'm not really a costume dress-up person, but for SC it's the exception, it's fun. Also if you don't, then visually you stand out. So the more people who dress up, the better the atmosphere.

> I just loved the attention to detail, being greeted at the entrance to 'Kellerman's' by Max Kellerman really set the scene for the whole day. I love that everything and everyone are in character, from the themed food and drinks, actors playing out key scenes of the film to security being part of the cast and how intrinsically part of the movie set you really feel.

> The value came from the complexity of the world, the acting, and the staging during the film. I quickly went from, 'What makes this so expensive?' to 'OH! I totally understand the cost and see where the money goes.'

> I was blown away by the authenticity of the set and cast. I just wasn't expecting the quality. I totally believed I was in the film, on the set, in that world. This is true of all the SC events I have attended.

This sense of presence, of being part of the film set, or being in the world of the film is very clearly communicated here and specifically marked out as a distinct feature of SC events which is absent from or not so well achieved in other experiences. This is underscored again here: 'Where comparisons can be made e.g. level of participation, cast expertise and set design I would say that SC is much better for participation and set design'.[40]

Role play/identity play

The sense communicated here, of being liberated from normal habits of behaviour, frequently emerges in their discussions:

> [R]emember that you are in character, in a world that is pure fantasy.

> Stay in character, do something in keeping with the spirit of the event, and do what you can to enhance the experience for others – it can be giddyingly good fun!

> You don't interact as yourself but as a member of the cast/an extra in the film. The character you are is randomly chosen for you by their website but usually falls into different categories, with different roles, styles of dress, even likes and dislikes. In turn, this means you will act differently, and the actors will relate to you in a different way. You will follow a different storyline and may even have access to other areas. Although I usually go with the website suggestions as closely as possible, I sometimes add my own taste. If I go to a SC event more than once, I always go as a different character and category to

vary my experience and so that I feel I am not missing out on a chance to experience something and to have fun with all the possible 'looks'. I spend a long time researching and preparing each outfit and try to find vintage and authentic pieces rather than 'costumes' from a fancy-dress shop, which feels less authentic. This helps me to fully feel like part of the cast.

This stepping outside of oneself into character is a widely celebrated, interactive, participatory and highly immersive element of their experience. This collection of responses captures more of the affective intensity mentioned above.

Ludic pleasures

The specific pleasures engendered by the underpinning game mechanics are also clearly evidenced by our respondents here, as well as being central to the list of 'tips' that we presented above:

> At *Casino Royale*, I proactively interacted with a whole range of characters. I followed possibly 3 or 4 missions across each visit. I used my character and back story to bribe bar staff for info, spoke to Valenka, Le Chiffre's girlfriend, who gave me a mission to pass on a message in return for cash to play poker with. I also followed another character across a range of missions throughout the evening, ending up on the top table in *Casino Royale* just as the finale hit.

The importance given to participation in these *missions* is emphasised throughout the responses; engaging in a number of these over an evening is key to a *successful* event. These detailed descriptions of missions are followed by superlatives such as 'it was awesome' and 'it was brilliant', and these accounts are always advanced when asked to reflect on the *distinct pleasures* of participation in SC experiences.

> My group of friends gathered together for photos and to travel there together. I loved walking through a shopping centre with everyone staring at us then on the tube more and more 'similarly weird' people started to appear!! As soon as I arrived I was approached by one of the SC team who asked me to demo my act – my friends hadn't seen it and were astonished – I would NEVER normally do something like that but I was filled with an incredible excitement and invulnerability. I was directed to the club where I auditioned for the club boss then went to perform at tables round the club. (The respondent is here referring to the 2018 *Blade Runner* production.)

This account is interesting in a number of ways – the sense of abandonment of one's everyday self which is prevalent in pervasive games but also present in the PPSC tips as a direct recommendation to give oneself over to *what the character would do*. The participant above also describes the empowerment that they experienced through this abandonment – this sense of not just 'excitement' but also 'invulnerability'.

> We headed to the airport and Venice – I would've loved to sit and eat pasta listening to opera but we started on our assigned mission to find a contact number. Then I noticed a suspicious-looking character and we decided to follow him instead. This took us into a fast-paced sequence running from country to country – I was involved in setting up a dodgy financial deal, reporting back at a casino, inspecting a body in the urinals, collecting a bag from the airport and handing it over to my contact in the piazza (possibly not in that order). I was involved in dialogue and lots of running! Loved it. Realised at some point that we were the baddies! At the end tried to bribe our way onto the main gambling table but were told we couldn't afford it. Didn't have a moment to myself and was lucky that someone brought me food while I watched the film. I realised afterwards that I still hadn't seen parts of the world. (The respondent is here referring to the 2019 *Casino Royale* production.)

This account of their experience at *Casino Royale* captures the complexity and game-like nature of the 'running about', solving puzzles, role play, improvisation, interesting identity shifts (realising they were the 'baddies') as well as strongly communicating their absolute pleasure in all this frenetic action. This reinforces the testimony of our *BttF* respondents and provides further detail of the pleasures of engaging with these ludic elements.

On the pleasures of replay and new 'adventures'

The multiple tracks, missions and storylines built into an SC production facilitate repeat attendance, and despite the high ticket price, members of the PPSC community frequently attend a production more than once. This includes opportunities to attend as PPSC groups wearing their own badges and occasionally working as a team within a production in order to maximise their experience. These comments illustrate this:

> Aside from the 'big events' with each show that everybody sees, the whole experience was different! You bump into different characters, you might get walked up to by someone who asks you a question and off you go on an adventure. You might realise you didn't talk to someone last time so you deliberately hunt them out so you can interact with them, or sometimes the actors themselves recognise you from your multiple visits and they target you to give you a storyline they know you haven't done yet. You could go ten times and it would be different every time.

> There are special offers towards the end of the run and I like to take advantage of that and go again and again. Sometimes with a group (PPSC) sometimes with friends who may not have been to an SC event before. I went to *Stranger Things* six times.

Both these respondents are repeat attendees, evidencing the extent to which each experience is distinct and individualised, and produced through the interaction between the player/participant and the complex choices available for their engagement. Here the first participant also indicates how repeated participation can be recognised and rewarded by the creatives and performers.

The five values – pleasure in participating, being inside the film, role play, ludic pleasures and the pleasures and rewards of replay – are those most frequently articulated, shared, exemplified, emphasised and repeatedly circulated amongst the PPSC members. This process of developing a shared and collective appreciation of the SC productions has been the foundation of the emergence of a strong *community*.

An experiencing community

We have previously identified the existence of an experience community which is both specific, and characteristic of large-scale immersive experiences, which we have defined as: 'temporally fleeting and shallow gatherings of people brought together in elaborate, highly constructed and crucially commodified narrative environments'.[41] In this analysis of these communities we drew on the work of play and ritual theorist Victor Turner and his useful distinction of consumer-/consumption-oriented ritualised practices, and his useful notion of the liminal and liminality as a means through which to theorise how these practices sit outside everyday behaviours. We also drew on the important concept of *communitas* to describe the communing practices produced through these behaviours and rituals. There is no doubt that the SC brand has evolved their own modern 'ritual' aligned to the clearly delineated format that we outlined in Chapter 3, with behaviours, costumes, values and rhythms that provide the context for affectively intense experiences through which these temporary but nonetheless significant experience communities are established and embodied. We develop these earlier observations through our consideration of the emergent community formed through the norms, behaviours and expectations of the PPSC membership, which are shaped by bonding and belonging practices.[42]

Bonding practices involve sharing and comparing experiences, demonstrating a collective commitment to and pleasure in a key activity. The PPSC Facebook site provides an important space for sharing their collective pleasure in the experiences but also more directly communicating in advance (ahead of the event) and then more and more frequently attending as a group. Figure 6.4 is taken from the PPSC group night at *Casino Royale* which inaugurated a regular practice of collective attendance.

> I think mostly sharing in the excitement and SC love. Not all partners and friends understand the passion that we have for SC and we sometimes feel unable to share in that. In addition, many of us have felt anxious about going

6.4 Positive People of Secret Cinema (PPSC) group night at *Casino Royale*, 2019.

to events alone and this gives us a chance to meet up with others (e.g. Group Nights) so that we can feel confident about attending. Great friendships had already been formed before the COVID-19 pandemic and this proved to be vital for many who were able to interact with PPSC members and participate in PPSC events on-line through very difficult times.

Our respondents also talked about the immense value they received from their participation in the PPSC group:

> You are involved with other, likeminded people who all share a love for not only SC, but other immersive events. We share info on what to expect, we create friendship groups, and through lockdown, have really supported each other by hosting and participating in a whole range of other events which was amazing. As a single person, living alone, this interaction was a lifeline for me … and supported me with, not only a social life, but my mental health. My pandemic experience would have been totally different without the friendships I've created through PPSC.

> … real sense of community, and a new (sub-)group of lifelong friends I have found within PPSC. We would not have necessarily met otherwise, but I treasure the friendships and they were a godsend during lockdown when I was facing redundancy, deciding to end an unhealthy romantic partnership, and would have felt very alone and isolated. That value is impossible to measure.

Whether or not this was the community that Riggall imagined in his earliest visions, that we outlined at the beginning of this chapter, these insights reveal that a highly functioning and supportive grass-roots community has emerged through participation in SC events.

Affiliation and tokens of belonging

A key element of the value ascribed to their participation is also a sense of belonging, of being included and recognised by others with shared tastes:

> I met this crazy bunch of nerds and weirdos in December & I'm proud to say many are my new best friends. I've never known such a welcoming and inclusive group of super fans before and I can't imagine anyone else will ever out do the love and enthusiasm of #positivepeopleofsecretcinema. So happy I found you guys!

As well as establishing a very overt sense of their group identity online, the PPSC community also carry their collective identity into their participation at events; as we have seen in a number of these responses, the members attend as a 'group', adding a further dimension to Williams' 'spatialised fandom'. Darren Carnall has played a key role in providing the group with both public and private *tokens of belonging* – these are also valuable markers through which to achieve symbolic capital since, when they are seen and recognized by the SC artists and creatives, the wearer is frequently accorded special privileges, as further discussed below. The public tokens are badges, which can be either generic PPSC badges or designed specifically in relation to the particular experience. Here we see examples of standard and generic badges and examples of badges themed for *Dirty Dancing* (Figure 6.5). These can be worn at the events and are indeed designed for this purpose. They enable fellow PPSC members to identify one another and more recently these have become an important way in which the creatives at the SC events recognise and reward PPSC members for their loyalty to the SC brand. Car bumper stickers are another public token, that is displayed outside the event. The private tokens take the form of mugs and other such memorabilia. In producing these tokens Darren Carnall participates in what Oliver Carter describes as *fantrepreneurship*.[43] This portmanteau term signals that these acts of production and commercial activity largely express participation in fandom rather than being a significant form of meaningful and gainful employment.

The super-fan community II: Secret Cinema engagement

As we have seen in the responses above, from 2018 onwards the PPSC members began to be recognised by SC creatives and performers during

6.5 PPSC badges designed and created by Darren Carnall.

their events. This has varied from informal recognition, leading to enhanced opportunities and activities in the event – 'during productions, wearing a PPSC badge has given me in-character recognition from actors (they know we get it, and will play along), which is good fun' – to a slightly more formalised PPSC 'mission'[44] – 'in my second visit, [to *Casino Royale*] which was a PPSC meet up night, we were not only participating in missions with the actors (this time I did missions with the characters of Dimitrios and Solange) but we were given a PPSC specific mission to collect as much cash as possible and return it to M' – through to specific consultation with this group of super-fans as an element in SC's formal preview/testing process which, as we saw in Chapter 5, played a significant part in refining the production ready for the official opening:

> SC have used the group to gather insight and feedback on their productions. Some of us were invited to attend the preview of *Stranger Things* and to give feedback in advance of the full launch. They have used us for marketing purposes and even created our own mission at *Casino Royale*. It also connects and engages you with SC further when you feel that your input is valued in this way.

Darren Carnall explained further this formal consultation:

> There were fifty VIP and fifty standard tickets, and their condition was that everybody chosen was a part of the main PPSC group, especially those active members around since the start. So I had to choose which 100 to invite out of a group membership of over 1,100. Not daunting at all!! Thankfully I came up with a way that made this as fair as it could possibly be. In fact it even removed my need to 'choose'. I got Facebook to give me a list of those group members who were the most active on a daily basis over the last month – and then I simply invited that top 100. Completely fair and without favouritism. *Even I could have been left out of it!*

As we shall see, SC's direct engagement with established fan communities to inform the development and iteration of their productions is a practice that goes beyond the PPSC community.

The global community of 'Bond' aficionados

Our online research identified a very rich account of how SC engaged with established fan communities in reviewing and promoting their *Casino Royale* production. Figure 6.6 shows a screengrab from Calvin Dyson's YouTube review of this experience.

What both the review and this image reveal is the specific fan engagement strategy deployed for this production: the use of a professional PR agency (here, Visible PR) was a considerable step change from the earlier use of

6.6 James Bond influencers: Calvin Dyson is to the left of the image and Joe Lamb, the representative from SC promotions partner Visible PR, appears to the right.

'word of mouth' strategies via social media. Here the Visible PR strategy was to bring together well-known, *international* James Bond YouTubers and influencers who have significant reach out to distinct fan communities. David Zaritsky for instance is based in the USA, has 43,000 followers and his reviews and Bond-related postings can receive over 100,000 views. Others in the image are from India, Brazil and the Netherlands. The group includes Joseph Darlington, who has been running a podcast on James Bond for fifteen years, and the author Mark O'Connell who has written a humorous novel on being a Bond fan entitled *Catching Bullets*. The group were brought together for a day that included an opportunity to hear from two representatives from the SC production team and they were then given access to a preview staging of the production. These individual super-fans or representatives of specific fan communities then played a key role in creating the social media visibility for the event, thus playing a vital part in the promotion for the production.[45] This promotional labour is not the only way in which the audience form part of the overall production.

Audience labour in SC productions

As we have previously observed:

> [i]n SC audience members are simultaneously inculcated in to a narrative of fictional secrecy whilst also being recruited as extras to the production of the secret event itself. Audience members are simultaneously invoked as performer

and spectator as they enter the set, and through this process complete and cohere the experience both for themselves and for others.[46]

The ambiguous space created by the dual role these participants play – both performers and *spectacle* – coupled with the extraordinary affective intensity evidenced by our respondents and wider audiences via social media, can be considered a form of modern carnival – an interpretation that is reinforced in Chapter 1. We have already identified a range of affective labours in which the SC audience engage as part of their experience. Here we bring these different elements together, to consider how these play an absolutely central role in the success of these productions, returning to the notion of the audience as co-creators of the experience that Riggall asserted. As we indicate here, all participants in SC events play a key role in providing the animation, spectacle and participation that secures the success of the pre-screening entertainment. It is the attention to detail in costumes, props and behaviours that completes the scenographic elements of the event. Participant costumes and engagements lend authenticity and periodicity – without these participants, these sets would make very little sense except as a curiosity or a sideshow, such as visiting an animated film lot.

In the further spatial and temporal phases of labour set out below we complete our analysis of the *workers* within the immersive experience production model presented in Chapter 5, Figure 5.1. Here we fully delineate the affective and creative labours of the audience.

Promotional speculation
SC generate audience interest and engagement through teasers and obscure trailers ahead of the event that hint at their potential next experience. These 'hints' and 'teasers' stimulate *potential* participants into acts of speculation across social media; this speculation creates a buzz around the production and leads to an increase in the circulation and visibility of SC's official promotional materials.

Post-ticket purchase/pre-event
Participant labour before the event can be categorised as 'unpaid advertising' (see also O'Hara, 2017 for discussion of the social media labour of Punchdrunk *Sleep No More* fans).[47] This labour is often in response to specific instructions to prepare for the experience on offer. As we have seen, the website functions to dictate and direct forms of audience interaction and audience behaviours and activities. As they follow these instructions they create materials, images, texts that then circulate via social media using the publicised hashtags. The audience quickly adopt whatever rhetoric, thematic or linguistic style that SC has established for the event. The audience's affective

anticipatory and *preparatory* engagement with the event is commodified in the picking up and redistribution of these new artefacts as SC objects.

The audience productivity and creativity also complete an important element of consumer marketing and audience development by instantiating a 'collective' that is 'in the know'. SC audience members then quickly exchange images, texts and other immaterial artefacts that inaugurate their affiliation with the 'secret' community of SC participants. This pre-event labour is very important in establishing and reinforcing the organisational identity of SC and in securing their framing as skilled creators of exclusive and immersive 'experiences'. This anticipatory labour has to be carefully managed to balance the contradictions and paradoxes between notions of exclusivity and secrecy, and the drive towards wider audience engagement.

During the show

Whilst the actors, vendors, guides and security already offer a not insignificant population for the space it is only once the audience arrives that the 'event' can take place. During the event the participants form a vast resource of extras. Through their compliance in dressing up and prop collection they not only populate but, crucially, animate the static, simulated scenography that has been re-created in such detail. The costume instructions are shaped through close, collaborative conversations between the costuming and merchandising departments (see Chapter 5, page 151). Complying with the instructions is what provides SC with the final element required to complete these experiences and their subsequent documentation through the post-experience promotional videos. The 'extras' play three critical roles related to 'completing' or enhancing the 'authenticity' of the experience:

Periodicity. Participants' costumes complement and significantly augment the simulated film sets/spatialised narrative of the experience. A good example of this would be *BttF* where the 1950s period was recreated. Another example would be the *Moulin Rouge!* production where the nineteenth-century bohemian and neo-burlesque aesthetic proposed by the costume instructions was critical in completing the simulated environment of Montmartre.

Visual storytelling. Costumes can play an important role in visualising elements of the story. A particularly good example of this would be *Romeo + Juliet* where the costumes reflected and made visible the 'two factions' through the distinct colours red and blue. Participants appropriately dressed formed part of the spatialisation of the conflict that lies at the centre of the narrative. They gave a key dynamic to the narrative – a clear visual aesthetic – that was legible both to other participants and (importantly) to the performers within the space.

Simulated plot points. Audience engagement activities can also help to drive forward elements of the spatialised narrative. This can be groups of audience members completing a scene – such as a simulated dance class in the *Dirty Dancing* production – or more small-scale or individual acts which are instrumental in *triggering* the tracks that drive the narrative forward. Examples include the localised 'Action for Truth' protest sequence in *Stranger Things*; the Hill Valley parade in *BttF*; and the VIPs playing members of the LAPD in the climactic raid on the snake-pit bar in *Blade Runner*.

There has been one specific deviation from this norm in the design of a situation/categorisation of extra/participant – the Creatures of the Underworld ticket holders for *Moulin Rouge!*, who were required to fully complete the experience for the other participants during the screening. Their role as participant and 'extra' extended beyond the complex interleaving of *flaneurie*, voyeurism and role playing enabled and structured through the improvised set and interactive spaces of the pre-film entertainment. It was the ecstatic, affective engagement of the 'Creatures' during the film, made visible through their, guided and instructed, audible participation in singing and their visible participation in dancing scenes, that formed a critical, additional and essential part of the scenographic augmentation that surrounded the duration of the film screening. Their live singing, dancing and shouting were a critical element of the spectacle. They filled 'the pit' in front of the stage and screen and it was they who provided the interaction for the live actors' performance in tandem with the film.

Post-event promotion

During this stage the post-event photographs and exclamatory statements via social media operate to reinforce the marketing and promotion message that they may well have contributed to before the event. Here the labour is not only promotional but also functions to endorse 'critical acclaim' that may have been established through the limited press review evenings or events.

Conclusion

The many forms of labour described here are critical to the way in which these SC productions are realised. As our immersive experience production model shows, the audience complete the production, they finalise, instantiate and bring to fruition the process of logistical, artistic and technical labour that is involved in the design of the experience.

In this chapter, we have seen the shift in audience subjectivity from the early adopters, through mainstream fandoms and fan practices to the development of super-fan communities. In the next, final chapter we shall see a further development of this audience, in which they not only laboured for SC but were fully commodified by SC in the organisation's progress towards greater commercialisation. In an interesting turn, we will see the affective intensity, the trust and the loyalty of the SC audience that we have evidenced within this chapter become an asset to be sold to investors, who were themselves hailed as members of the secret community – being invited to invest in their own commodified pleasures, in a product that they themselves had created.

Notes

1. Helen Scarlett O'Neill, interviewed by Natalie Wreyford, 9 October 2020.
2. See Chapter 5, page 166.
3. Atkinson and Kennedy, 'Where we're going'.
4. In an interview on 6 December 2021, SC CEO Max Alexander told the authors it was clear that these three audience 'types' were well understood within the organisation. What Alexander also indicated was a sense that the early audience were now disgruntled by the move to attract more mainstream audiences.
5. *Screen Daily*, 'Secret Cinema founder Fabien Riggall on future of cinema', 19 September 2014, available at www.screendaily.com/comment/secret-cinema-founder-on-future-of-cinema/5077742.article (accessed 13 December 2021).
6. *Screen Daily*, 'Secret Cinema founder'.
7. Riggall, interview by Mishcon de Reya, *Jazz Shapers*.
8. 'Secret Cinema on Sky Movies'.
9. See Chapter 2, page 57.
10. Future of StoryTelling, 'Bringing film to life: Fabien Riggall (Future of StoryTelling 2013)', 3 October 2013, YouTube video, 4:01, available at www.youtube.com/watch?v=rK78mBx52sM (accessed 13 December 2021).
11. Cheshire, 'The screen saver'.
12. See for instance: Andy Bennett, 'Subcultures or neo-tribes: rethinking the relationship between youth, style and musical taste', *Sociology* (1999) 33, 599–614; Elizabeth Rata, *A political economy of neotribal capitalism* (Lanham, MD: Lexington Books, 2000); Ivana Rihova, Dimitrios Buhalis, Miguel Moital and Mary-Beth Gouthro, 'Social constructions of value: marketing considerations for the context of event and festival visitation', *Ideological, social and cultural aspects of events* (2015), 74–85.
13. O'Neill, interviewed by Wreyford, 9 October 2020.
14. O'Neill, interviewed by Wreyford, 9 October 2020.
15. O'Neill, interviewed by Wreyford, 9 October 2020.
16. See Emma Pett, *Experiencing cinema: participatory film cultures, immersive media and the experience economy* (New York: Bloomsbury, 2021). In this work, Pett also points to this period as a turning point where the audience were 'reconfigured' (53).

17 Darren Carnall, founder of Positive People of Secret Cinema, interviewed by author, 23 September 2021.
18 Atkinson and Kennedy, 'Where we're going'; and see Chapter 3, page 100.
19 Carried out for Atkinson and Kennedy, 'Where we're going'.
20 Nicolle Lamerichs, 'Costuming as subculture: the multiple bodies of cosplay', *Scene* (2014) 2(1–2), 123.
21 Lamerichs, 'Costuming as subculture', 123.
22 Atkinson and Kennedy 'Tell no one'.
23 Susan Kulkarni, interviewed by author, 8 September 2021.
24 Nicolle Lamerichs, 'Cosplay: the affective mediation of fictional bodies', *Fan studies: Research popular audiences* (2014), 128.
25 Lamerichs' ethnographic research has demonstrated how this is always a critical stage in the pleasure of cosplay design and construction. Lamerichs, 'Cosplay: the affective mediation', 123–31.
26 Meghan O'Hara, 'Experience economies: immersion, disposability, and Punchdrunk Theatre', *Contemporary Theatre Review* (2017) 27(4), 481–96.
27 This was our own direct experience during our attendance at *Casino Royale* in July 2019.
28 Available at www.facebook.com/groups/PositivePeopleofSecretCinema/ (accessed 13 December 2021). There was an earlier 'Positive People of Hill Valley' (see www.facebook.com/groups/ThePPHV, accessed 13 December 2021) that was formed in 2014. This is another private group with a membership of less than 500. It appears to be a more 'text'-specific fan site (in this instance, the text is *Back to the Future*) than the wider PPSC site, which has very much become a Secret Cinema fan community.
29 This is www.facebook.com/SecretCinema/ (accessed 13 December 2021).
30 See www.facebook.com/groups/PositivePeopleofSecretCinema/ (accessed 13 December 2021) and Darren Carnall, interviewed by authors, 24 September 2021.
31 Available at www.facebook.com/groups/PositivePeopleofSecretCinema/, reproduced here with the permission of the community member (accessed 13 December 2021).
32 AD, anonymised PPSC member, interviewed by author, 14 October 2021.
33 Matt Hills, 'From fan culture/community to the fan world: possible pathways and ways of having done fandom', *Palabra Clave* (2017) 20(4), 856–83; Will Brooker, *Using the Force: creativity, community and Star Wars fans* (London: Bloomsbury, 2002).
34 Rebecca Williams, *Theme park fandom: spatial transmedia, materiality and participatory cultures* (Amsterdam: Amsterdam University Press, 2020).
35 Williams, *Theme park fandom*, 12, citing Angela Ndalianis, *The horror sensorium: media and the senses* (Jefferson, NC: McFarland, 2012), 72.
36 Williams, *Theme park fandom*, 12.
37 Other individuals have established themselves as SC experts through video blogs and YouTube experience guide videos; these are also carefully marked as 'spoiler-free'. They will normally feature a 'getting ready' section that shows the blogger preparing and/or assembling their costuming and then will

cut to an after-show video where they review the experience and share their excitement, with further tips on how to maximise your experience. Here are three, but there are many more: Alan Simmons, 'Secret Cinema's *The Empire Strikes Back*: tips and spoiler-free walkthrough', 14 June 2015, available at www.liveforfilm.com/2015/06/14/secret-cinemas-the-empire-strikes-back-tips-and-spoiler-free-walkthrough/ (accessed 13 December 2021); SandyMakesSense, 'My Secret Cinema experience – *Blade Runner*! London vlog', 7 June 2018, YouTube video, 7:28, available at www.youtube.com/watch?v=Zu4gM7PDmA0&t=309s (accessed 13 December 2021); Taylor Fuller, 'Secret Cinema … is it worth it?', 11 August 2019, YouTube video, 4:06, available at www.youtube.com/watch?v=drYry5SiiLQ&t=138s (accessed 13 December 2021).
38 These are drawn from across the PPSC Facebook group postings between 2018 and 2019.
39 CM, anonymised PPSC member, interviewed by author 12 October 2021.
40 TR, anonymised PPSC member, interviewed by author 20 October 2021.
41 Atkinson and Kennedy, *Live cinema*, 10.
42 Ilja Simons, 'Events and online interaction: the construction of hybrid event communities', *Leisure Studies* (2019) 38(2), 145–59.
43 Oliver Carter, 'A labour of love: fantrepreneurship in home video media distribution', in Jonathan Wroot and Andy Willis (eds), *DVD, Blu-ray and Beyond* (Cham: Palgrave Macmillan, 2017), 197–213.
44 After initial publication, it emerged through consultation with PPSC founder Darren Carnall that this was not in fact an SC authorised bespoke experience but the result of a very enthusiastic member of the PPSC community liaising directly with some SC employees. SC management and the majority of the staff at the event had no awareness of this activity.
45 Figure 6.6 is taken from Dyson Calvin, 'Secret Cinema *Casino Royale* experience and review', 17 July 2019, YouTube video, 13:39, available at www.youtube.com/watch?v=YSKqXiCZjAM&t=3s (accessed 13 December 2021). All those pictured in the photograph produced reviews of the experience, mainly on YouTube. Two of these are: James Bond Netherland, 'Secret Cinema presents *Casino Royale* | the Bond experience', 3 July 2019, YouTube video, 1:33, available at www.youtube.com/watch?v=dlraItQEhLM (accessed 13 December 2021); David Zaritsky, 'How to do Secret Cinema *Casino Royale*: a review', 14 July 2019, YouTube video, 21:21, available at www.youtube.com/watch?v=Pju28kcXllM (accessed 13 December 2021). This also features a 'how to get the most out of the experience segment.
46 Atkinson and Kennedy, 'From conflict to revolution'.
47 O'Hara, 'Experience economies'.

7

Secret Cinema, 2020–2021: pivoting, pipelines and poaching

> Disneyland is the pinnacle of immersive theatre and I think everyone's just trying to get back to Disneyland, because that's all they want.
>
> *Video projection designer*[1]

> We're building a short-term theme park, but you don't make your money from building a short-term theme park. You make your money from building Disney World.
>
> *Senior producer*[2]

As we have demonstrated, up to 2019, over its fifteen-year evolution and seventy-five productions, Secret Cinema's multiple and fractured identities, branding, titles and creative experimentation were stripped back, synthesised and unified into a formulaic brand and format. SC achieved industrial-scale immersion, while offering individual and stratified experiences in which audience engagement could range from compliantly passive to intensely participatory.

In this concluding chapter, we re-contextualise SC within the wider immersive experience industry of 2021, reaffirming and building on the 'immersive experience industry ecosystem' model that we established in Chapter 1. Here we present the rich, overlapping experiences and collaborations within the immersive experience industry of 2021 against the backdrop of the major transitions precipitated by the totalising convergence of the creative production of film, theatre, games and screen media. The use of digital technologies in the production of creative outputs accelerated significantly and innovative new applications were developed in response to the challenges wrought by the COVID-19 pandemic in 2020. As physical productions began to return towards the end of 2021, these creative advances and collaborations continued apace and the same technologies, tools and software used to produce screen-based media were brought together with established stage craft and emerging immersive performance talents and techniques. The industrialisation of immersive experience that we have tracked through this book means that our ecosystem model of interconnecting organisations is more hybridised than ever – characterised by the emergence of super-hybrid experiences that were increasingly influenced by gaming and new technologies. The picture of 2019 that we painted in Chapter 1, with mass-immersive-scale events at their zenith, looked very different in 2021, following this period of rapid change, adaptation and evolution during and after the lockdowns engendered by the global pandemic.

What we will set forth in this concluding chapter is SC's sustained and resounding influence upon the techniques, professional practices and audience engagement strategies of immersive experiences throughout this period, re-instantiating their leading position at the epicentre of the emergent immersive experience industry.

SC and the immersive sector during COVID (2020)

> We were supercharged and we had real wind in our sails ... and obviously the pandemic stripped all the momentum out of the business.
> *Senior leader at Secret Cinema*[3]

During the period while SC's production of *Casino Royale* in Shanghai was developed in late 2019 – which was 'a huge, ambitious show to mount within fifteen weeks ... a build of a three-storeyed building, with sixty cast' (SC performance director)[4] – troubling news of a threatening new virus was intensifying in China. The show closed in January 2020 when local lockdown restrictions were introduced and, as the performance director lamented, 'we opened a £10m show for five weeks, which was not ideal'.[5] During the same period, SC announced a landmark deal with Disney which would have led to a number of new productions in 2020,[6] but as their *Stranger Things* experience in London concluded a month later, a UK national lockdown was enforced and cinemas and theatres were ordered to close on 20 March 2020. The outlook for the film, theatre and immersive industries, with their business models based on mass, intimate gatherings of people, looked exceptionally bleak.

Just one month later, in early April 2020, the 'AFT' (Action for Truth), a fictional resistance group devised for the *Stranger Things* experience, hosted a Zoom-based lockdown party – a 'bitchin' 80s reunion'.[7] The event repurposed the *Stranger Things* narrative themes around a party in Hopper's cottage in the woods; participants could download spooky woodland backgrounds and were encouraged to dress in their *Stranger Things* outfits. Playing hits from the 1980s, interspersed with tasks and games, it was infused with the secret excitement of an underground rave. The party culminated in an out-of-sync, cacophonous rendition of 'Electric Dreams'. A further two parties ran on 23 and 25 April using exactly the same content and format with the added augmentation of a secret 'Zoom room' that audience members could use for a smaller, secret activity – mirroring the on-site experience of SC productions with hidden rooms and secret spaces. Moreover, we saw the experiential iteration that has been typical of SC productions, this time using online digital technologies.

SC's 'Secret Sofa' initiative was then launched at the end of April 2020, sponsored by Häagen-Dazs ice-cream. The initiative had its own website and social media campaign. Spanning eight weeks, Secret Sofa involved the screening of eight titles, starting with *The Grand Budapest Hotel* on 17 April, then *Groundhog Day*, *Moulin Rouge!*, *Casino Royale*, *Romeo + Juliet*, *The Shawshank Redemption*, *Dead Poets Society*, concluding with *Ghostbusters* on 5 June. All but one of these had previously been SC experiences, so not only did they have nostalgic appeal for the established SC experience community, there was previously developed content, characters and storylines that could be repurposed for these events. In the days leading up to the screening, audience members were given costume suggestions and themed activities to engage in that were related to the film, along with an invitation to share images of these engagements on social media. For *The Grand Budapest Hotel* pre-screening activities included the complex construction of a 'Courtesan au Chocolat'; for *Groundhog Day* audience members were instructed to post video clips of themselves presenting the news broadcast for that day on social media. The screenings themselves were essentially synchronised 'watch parties'[8] in which audience members were instructed to find the film from the source of their choice (their own DVD; via a streaming service) and to be poised to press 'play' at exactly the same time. An online 'after-show party' was also created using the same format as the Zoom lockdown parties, with up to 1,000 people in virtual attendance.[9] The global performance director described the preparation that went into the Secret Sofa events:

> I would spend Monday to Wednesday writing scripts and making sure the cast were ready. And then Thursday, Friday we'd rehearse it on Zoom and then Friday night we go live. So it was a very quick turn-around. But the great thing was that we would use a lot of the skills that we already had from theatre but then apply them online, where you can also use new tricks.[10]

The director expresses three interesting points here – firstly that the work was intense, with compressed timeframes, secondly that theatre skills were adaptable to these spaces and thirdly that this was seen as a valuable creative space for experimentation. Aside from the option to pay a small ticket price to participate in the after-show Zoom party,[11] and the commercial sponsorship provided, there was no other financial exchange between audience and SC. Secret Sofa essentially kept SC's established audience engaged, and kept the

SC brand alive and *revered* through the lockdowns – it was awarded the Best Virtual Film Club at the 'Time In' Awards of 2020.[12] What emerged was another sandbox space for experimentation with digital performance techniques and virtual audience interaction design. This was not a space that was unique to SC – numerous ground-breaking and critically acclaimed online theatrical performances were devised during this year including Chekhov's *The Seagull* on Zoom in May,[13] and a new, online Zoom mystery *Plymouth Point* by Swamp Motel in June. *Plymouth Point* was branded as 'an Alternate Reality Game event for teams of up to six players', which later evolved into a trilogy – the rights for which have since been bought by a major television company.[14] These experimentations emerged out of necessity, but they laid the ground for the virtual and hybrid performances that have followed. Swamp Motel described the technology that they innovated as part of their process:

> It's an automated theatre stack on the back end and a video conferencing platform on the front end, that we now deliver all the games and experiences through. It is a completely new piece of technology that was built by somebody who was within our network who was a lighting designer by trade. He learned to code going into the pandemic because he realised that there wasn't going to be a huge demand for lighting design in the next three to what turned out to be eighteen months.[15]

At a similar time, Darkfield, an immersive theatre company known for their site-specific work, launched Darkfield Radio, a smartphone app delivering 360° immersive audio experiences to audiences in their homes. There are numerous instances of what came to be referred to as 'pivots' during these years, a term which belies the extraordinary privilege in terms of resource and access required to achieve the kind of shift in business model, creative output and audience engagement that is being described. Another instance of 'pivot' came for SC in June: following news in early May of the postponement of *Dirty Dancing*, the SC UK drive-in was announced on 18 June. This was part of a much wider renaissance of the drive-in model as a socially distanced, relatively low-cost, alternative to a traditional cinema visit.[16] SC curated a programme of back-catalogue and cult titles which were screened at the Goodwood Racecourse in West Sussex. The Häagen-Dazs sponsorship continued, along with new media partners JBL, who provided the high-quality audio speakers for the cars. Entertainment was provided by Johnny and Frankie Starlight, who had hosted the SC Zoom parties, and played music and initiated activities such as 'glove-box bingo' and a car-based version of Twister. Attendees were invited to join 'Zoom rooms', so that they could communicate with the hosts and have their images projected onto the big cinema screen. The hosts traversed the site in a golf buggy – their interactions with audience members projected onto the big screen. The production 'invested £750,000 in the event making a £330 total profit, which they are splitting with Goodwood'.[17] Again, although this initiative did little in the way of turning a profit for the organisation, it served to sustain awareness of the SC brand, maintained a connection with their audience and enabled further experimentations with hybrid modes of spectatorship and participation. This experimentation – particularly car-based cinematic experiences – presumably informed the *Stranger Things* 'drive-into' experience which was subsequently announced later that year, in August 2020. This was a partnership with Netflix and Fever;[18] the experience lasted one hour and was based in a disused LA car park. Running from October 2020 it was described as:

> a selection of the Netflix series' scenes will be played out around groups of 24 cars and the event will take place in a multi-level space. The journey will take fans on a 60+ minute tour through Starcourt Mall, Russian labs and the Upside Down. Guests will be guided where to drive and park-up to watch each 'chapter' in the story play out, and they will encounter *Stranger Things* characters surrounding their convoy. The production will include 'sensory surprises' and the sights and sounds of 1980s Hawkins, Indiana.[19]

The LA-based production precipitated new models of online collaboration where a number of the key SC creatives developed and designed the experience at-a-distance, since they were unable to travel to the production's location.

A further televisual and immersive theatre collaboration of the same year was Punchdrunk's partnership with Sky Studios and Plan B Media in the production *The Third Day*. The show was created by Dennis Kelly and Felix Barrett as an experiment in immersive television; six episodes were broadcast via Sky Atlantic, Now TV and HBO in September followed by a live broadcast of one continuous take over twelve hours (from 9.30am to 9.30pm) on the island of Osea, UK on 3 October. 'Original plans were to invite fans to visit the island themselves, with trained performers, functioning sets, and live musical acts all working together to create a lived-in version of Osea music festival. (HBO actually created a similar event for *Westworld* at the 2018 SxSW Festival.)'[20] With a live festival originally planned for 10,000 attendees, the creative team had to respond very quickly to the restrictions imposed by lockdown. The twelve-hour live show went on to receive the best live event award from the Royal Television Society in 2021 and was nominated for a BAFTA in the same year.

Then, in October 2020, the UK government announced that SC were to receive Cultural Recovery funding (worth £977,000). A social media backlash ensued with a range of criticisms regarding their validity as a cultural institution being levelled at SC. This provoked the following response:

> As with most event producers, 2020 has been an extremely difficult year for Secret Cinema, from rescheduling shows, cancelling projects and taking the heart-breaking decision to make a third of our talented colleagues redundant. Some questions have arisen on social media about our eligibility; mainly out of confusion about what we are and what we do. We aren't a cinema and it seems that we have been a little too secret. So we'd like to lift the veil of secrecy and be transparent.[21]

This profound change in SC's communication strategy was a major turning point for the organisation (and indeed for our own research). From this point on, we see a markedly different approach in how information is shared about SC productions – from the publication of their credit listings, to the release of planning application documentation, to more detailed financial reporting submitted to Companies House, and to more information and insight provided by a range of individuals from their organisation in press interviews.

The funding would have provided a much-needed lifeline for SC's finances – their revenue dropped in 2020,[22] from £15.8m in 2019 to £6.2m, a fall of £9.6m, leading to a loss of £2.1m (after taxation). Following this government investment SC also increased administrative staff numbers, from 40 in 2019 to 45 in 2020.[23]

SC and immersive sector post-lockdown (2021)

As the *Stranger Things* drive-into experience continued through early 2021 in the USA, the UK entered a second wave of COVID-19 infections and enforced lockdown. Other online immersive shows emerged as theatre companies continued in their pivot to other digital formats. This included Les Enfants Terribles' production of *Sherlock Holmes: An Online Adventure* which launched in January 2021.[24]

In May 2021, as the UK emerged from the latest lockdown, SC launched a 'Crowd Cube' crowdfund campaign in an email addressed directly to its audience:[25]

> For over a decade you have been the beating heart of our Secret Worlds. You've already taken centre stage at our experiences, now is your chance to play a key part in our next chapter. We're excited to open up our story even further and invite you to become a shareholder in Secret Cinema by investing in Secret Shares – in our upcoming crowdfunding round.[26]

The campaign video features both Fabien Riggall and Max Alexander. Entitled 'Secret Cinema, secret shares: be part of the story', it adapted a tag line used previously – 'Find yourself in the story' – to position future investors as agents central in the evolution of the organisation. In Riggall's address to the viewers, he stated: 'This is a really exciting time for Secret Cinema, as we enter the next chapter. I would like to invite you, as our *secret community*, to become shareholders'. Here, we see a significant turning point in the evolution of the audience as the 'secret' community, previously personified by Riggall as rebels, anarchists and activists but here directly addressed by him as he seeks to mobilise them to become investors. Alexander's address seemingly shifted to address those 'outside' the existing SC community, i.e. venture capitalists; he centralised and commodified the audience a key 'asset' of the company:

> It's the loyalty, it's the enthusiasm, sometimes even the tolerance of our fans that allows us to push boundaries and gives us permission to take risks. But when we get it right, when it really works, we're rewarded with extraordinary advocacy and loyalty, our fans come back to the next show.

Alexander then went on to underscore the value of what SC offer from an audience perspective – 'Now more than ever, we are convinced of the need for *live, present and congregational storytelling*' – and from a business perspective – 'we have a *pipeline* that twelve months ago we couldn't have dreamed of'.

There are two interesting points to note here – firstly, the increasing acknowledgement of the audiences, and the 'fan' base, as a key asset; and secondly this notion of a pipeline – which further solidifies the conceptualisation of their work as a set of industrial practices. Another point of note in this statement by Alexander is the interesting description of their offering as 'congregational storytelling', evoking a sense of communion and devotion on the part of the audience. By the end of the campaign on 30 June 2021, SC had raised over £4,782,205 from 5,616 investors against an original target of £1m.

As the prospect of theatres in the UK opening came closer,[27] SC released news of their next in-person show: the first mention on Twitter, Facebook and Instagram came on 20 June: 'The wait has been endless, but the time has finally come. Another Secret World is near, can you work out which? 3 days. 3 clues.' Here we see two notable shifts – communication timeframes were shorter and their frequency, style and content changed. The identity of the event was announced very soon after, on 24 June; tickets went on sale on 5 July; and levels of highly specific detail about the event increased:

> Step into the delightful yet scandalous world of the Netflix original series *Bridgerton*. As guests at this anticipated soirée you will get a taste of the luscious life of the highest echelons of 1813 England. Whilst the main attraction of the evening is, naturally, the dance floor, there is plenty more to discover. From duelling practice with the gentlemen to games of chance with the married

ladies of the Ton, etiquette lessons in the drawing room to secret encounters in forbidden parts of the grounds. All to the sound of re-imagined pop classics by our string quartet.[28]

Here the SC format and guidelines were clearly and unequivocally laid out. However, citing the production challenges compounded by COVID-19, SC had to delay the show's planned opening in November 2021 by fourteen weeks. This, they stated, 'has the benefit of lining up with the launch of Season 2 of *Bridgerton* on Netflix'.[29] At the same time, other experiences were starting to open up within the immersive sector including the long-running *Immersive Gatsby* production alongside brand-new experiences such as *Monopoly Lifesized* in August 2021.

The immersive experience industry ecosystem model 2021

In updating our immersive experience industry ecosystem model of 2019 to include the new experiences and companies that emerged in 2020 and 2021 (see Figure 7.1),[30] we can see some very clear trends start to emerge, not least the fact that the sector has experienced significant growth. As the co-producer Brian Hook confirmed:

> It's certainly grown from our position. We've just secured funding for the next three big shows that we're doing – all of a similar scale to *Doctor Who*.[31]

An SC professional flagged why this may be the case for immersive performance where traditional theatres have continued to struggle:

> I think the immersive sector is slightly better place to deal with social distancing than other sectors of live entertainment, just by virtue of the fact that you can control the flow of people, whilst you're going to have a massive amount of problems for smaller, mid-sized theatre spaces ... getting enough people in to fill seats but also keeping them in a captive space for two to three hours.[32]

Amongst other new immersive developments – a DC Comics Universe restaurant opened in London in autumn 2021, called Park Row after the area of Gotham City in which Batman's enemies live, and an immersive version of *Cabaret* opened in November 2021. In September 2021 Punchdrunk announced their 2022 production *Burnt City* (in a purpose-built building in new premises in Woolwich),[33] and they re-opened *Sleep No More* in Shanghai in November 2021.

The circles in the ecosystem diagram represent a mix of organisations and specific experiences since the latter are staged by a number of collaborating and partnered organisations – we will provide examples of some of those in a moment. Within all of these examples, theatre remains the one common

pivoting, pipelines and poaching 213

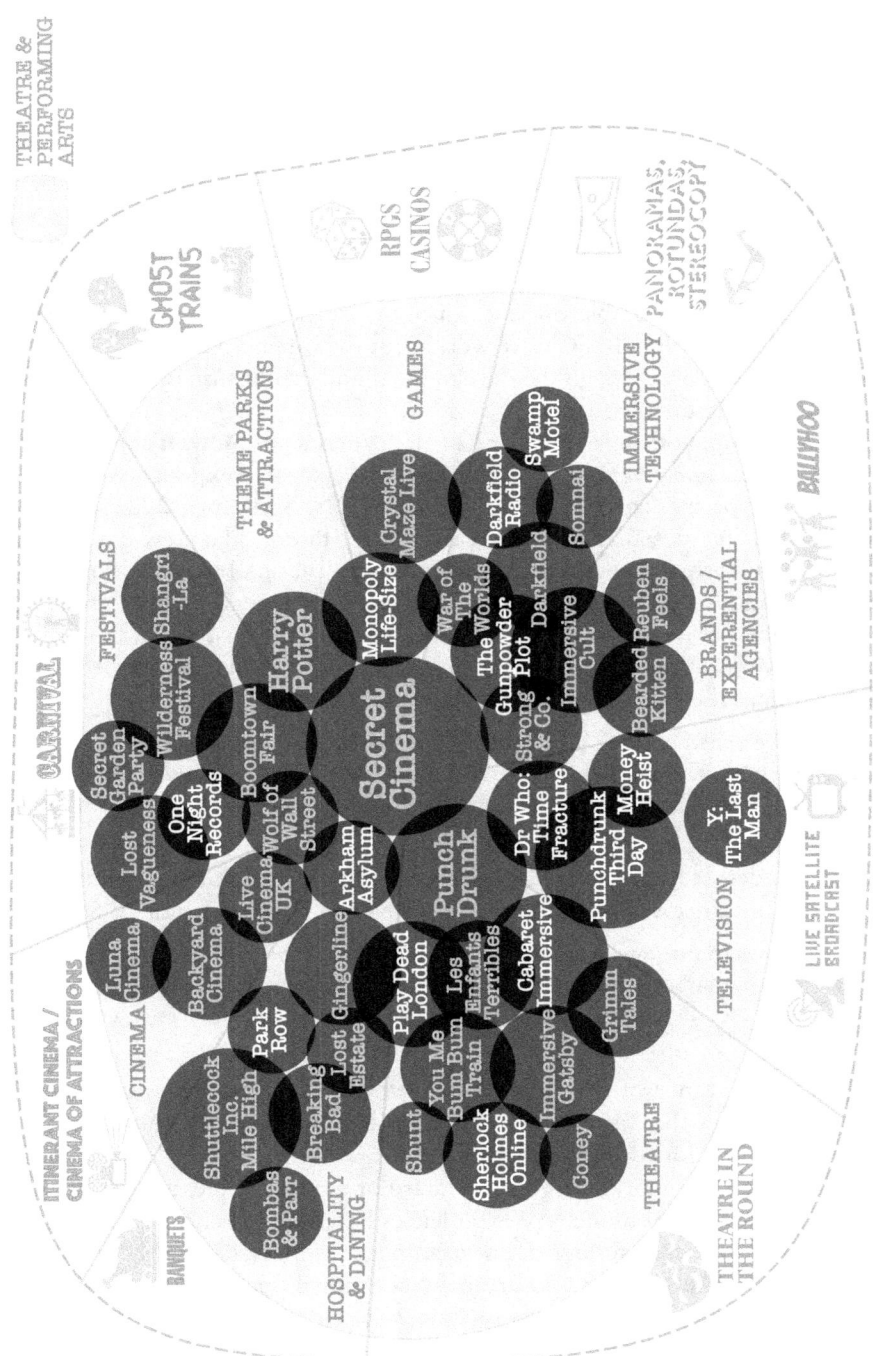

7.1 The immersive experience industry ecosystem model 2021.

factor that unites all of the experiences. Many of the new experiences are technologically driven, hybridised and/or game-based. We see the increasing presence of televisual and gaming properties alongside film and cinema IP. These build on the commercial success of escape rooms and include *Money Heist*, *Monopoly Lifesized* and SC's *Arcane*. This close affinity between games and many of the principles of immersive theatre emerged in Chapters 4 and 5, and will be discussed again shortly.

What remained consistent across both the 2019 and 2021 models is SC's central position and influence. We argue that this remains the case for two reasons: firstly, the notable presence of SC workforce and expertise in all new experiences; secondly, SC were working at the vanguard of new developments, most notably through the development and production of hybridised physical and digital experiences.

A key example of the significance of the expertise of SC workforce was the *Dr Who: Time Fracture (DWTF)* immersive theatre experience which opened in a permanent venue – Immersive LDN – in April 2021 under social distancing measures.[34] With a cast of forty-three and a crew of thirty-seven, *DWTF* brought together creative expertise that had been networked, developed and honed within SC. The production managers, sound, lighting, performance, set designers, stage management and the cast all had credits within previous SC experiences. One of the producers explained the benefits of developing the *DWTF* experience during lockdown:

> I think we ended up with a cast that you otherwise couldn't get. The cast is an amalgamation of Punchdrunk, Les Enfants, Secret Cinema. They're absolutely incredible and they've done it all. They've seen it all. There's nothing you can't throw at them.[35]

There is widespread acknowledgement within the professional community of SC's significance within the sector. As a past SC producer noted, SC is:

> ... a gateway into immersive for a lot of people ... The people that I have seen start out at Secret Cinema have gone on to do huge things. And people who have met at Secret Cinema have set up festivals and immersive event companies.[36]

In a further instance of this influence, *Arkham Asylum*, a new immersive experience set in the Batman universe and due to open in autumn 2022, was led and developed by SC alumni.[37]

Secondly, SC are working at the vanguard of innovation, leading the way in the development of immersive experiences based on television properties where others have then followed. For example, a *Money Heist: 2021* experience based on the popular and critically acclaimed Spanish Netflix series *La casa de papel* was announced in June 2021. It was located in multiple cities across the world including Paris, Miami, Mexico City, London and

New York, with each experience adapted for the specific region and the city's venue. The London experience, which launched in November 2021, was sited at the former Christie's auction house in South Kensington. This experience was a collaboration between a triumvirate powerhouse: Netflix (as the IP owners), Fever (as the ticket sales and experience aggregation platform) and media partners Social Media Network (as the promoters and influencers).

We see an increased format hybridity of experience elsewhere: for example, in July 2021 Play Dead London, an immersive murder mystery production company, claimed to launch the world's first hybrid immersive theatre experience. Titled *The Case of the Clown in the Woods*, the experience incorporated elements of the Choose Your Own Adventure format and was 'Part Knightmare, part Treasure Hunt'. For this production, half of the cast were active in a real-life, physical location and half were active on Zoom.[38] A third, 'layered reality' experience was announced in November 2021 – *The Gunpowder Plot* – created by the Ellipsis Entertainment Group. This followed from their two previous immersive experiences which blended virtual reality with live performance – *Somnai* and *War of the Worlds* – and exemplified an increasing trend of this VR/real-world mix within other smaller-scale experiences launched during this period.[39] The use of technologies within production experience design has also advanced apace – the use of virtual production techniques and a games engine to prototype sets for immersive productions has been flagged as a key development. The UK-based research and innovation investment in this area has further stimulated and supported experimentation;[40] in November 2021 *Lost Origin* – which was developed within the UKRI 'Audience of the Future' scheme and promoted as 'a mixed reality experience' – was launched in London for a limited release. This was another cross-sector collaboration, between experienced immersive pioneers Factory 42, Almeida Theatre and Sky.[41] Clockwork Dog also emerged as an important organisation making bespoke 'show control' for immersive experiences,[42] particularly those based on games and escape rooms; they designed and built the system for *Monopoly Lifesized*, for example.

SC's *Ghostbusters: The Gates of Gozer* virtual event was announced in October 2021. Upon its launch, a very clear articulation of the offer was provided by SC:

> Travel back to the '80s and experience never-before-seen storylines based on the original film in this live virtual adventure. Get ready for the jaw-dropping detail of any Secret Cinema event, brought to you online and to a whole other level! Team up with the Ghostbusters to investigate paranormal activity, explore the infamous 550 Central Park West and uncover spine-chilling secrets from other dimensions. The world needs saving and you're the one for the job! Immersive theatre. 3D binaural sound. Real ghostbusting.[43]

Key to this outline is the introduction of 'never-before-seen storylines' and the 'live virtual adventure'. Having already staged two *Ghostbusters* events (in 2008 and 2013), as well as the Secret Sofa event, SC were able to build, iterate and adapt this version to new levels of depth and detail within a fully virtual environment.

Once again, a social media backlash ensued, citing the lack of an in-person experience, prompting a swift email response which sought to underscore the quality of the experience and the level of work and creative investment that had been put into the show:

> It has taken a little under a year to develop the bespoke technology. It will include live performances and interactions, real sets and special effects, alongside interactive games, motion-triggered filters, 3D binaural sound design, and more. It is a new interactive virtual format that COVID-19 forced us to dream up. With a lower price-point, lower age restriction and no geographical barriers, we hope this virtual product will be an easily accessible format for our audience. However, it's not meant to be a substitute for the physical shows, with two on sale at the moment and plenty more planned for 2022.[44]

Prior to the launch, one of the creative team had already highlighted the imperative for providing behind-the-scenes insight:

> They're building the biggest online theatre show anyone has ever done with a bespoke platform and software, with fifteen soundproof, live-TV studios, with green screens and live visual effects elements, full costume, full cast. There's almost a behind the scenes as part of the publicity because people have to know it's not just a Zoom show.[45]

The production followed the previously established strategic alignment of SC event launches with new franchise film release dates, creating synergistic marketing opportunities for the studio and SC (such as that seen with *The Empire Strikes Back*, and most recently with *Bridgerton*). On this occasion: 'Secret Cinema has teamed up with Sony for an at-home virtual *Ghostbusters* experience to celebrate the release of the latest film in the franchise, *Ghostbusters: Afterlife,* which comes out on 19 November'.[46]

In a unique turn of events, the post-experience promotional video – the evolution of which we have tracked through this book – now appeared as a preview video which shows audiences already engaging in the experience. The video also clearly defined the prequel narrative set-up, which would previously have been hidden within the microsite. The SC experience is set one year after the Ghostbusters' victory at the 'Ivo Shandor building', which is introduced in the 1984 film. The film revealed that Ivo was the designer of 550 Central Park West – also known as 'Spook Central' – where the cult leader of Gozer and other worshippers would perform rituals on the building's rooftop. Ivo was the main villain of *Ghostbusters: The Video Game*. The premise of the SC experience was that audience members enrol at the new Ghostbusters school, The Paranormal Institute. This retroactive worldbuilding approach has been honed throughout SC's evolution, but this was a watershed moment where the event was given a subtitle – which introduced and foregrounded their unique IP – making clear that this was not just a replaying of the original film. What we see emerging here is an 'interstitial IP' – the creation of new IP that exists in the spaces *in between* the films (we saw this with *Blade Runner* in Chapter 4). Alexander explained how what he described as 'new canon' relates to the original IP:

> The IP is always derived and so it always reverts back to the IP owner but that isn't really the whole story, which is there's no sense in which I think our studio partners would want to reactivate that IP without us. We retain an interest and a joint control of the IP for a period ... they want their live experiences, particularly for their tent-pole productions. They can't just be echoes of the movie ... increasingly, they want their experiences to be dramatically rich.[47]

With lower-priced tickets and a limited capacity (which was due to the performance demands upon the fifteen cast members rather than any limitation imposed by the online platform), Alexander revealed the commercial incentive behind the *Ghostbusters* online show both as a shop window and as a promotional gateway for the more lucrative model of large-scale in-person experiences:

> A lot of people can't make it to our shows. But if you can do a $10 or $20 experience, which is really great fun, you might get to love us ... And then once you've got to love us and know us, maybe that's the time that you want to really dress up like a lunatic and go and run around a warehouse in South London.[48]

SC's next in-person experience was *Arcane: Enter the Undercity*, in Los Angeles – a collaboration with Riot Games which ran in November and December 2021. Again, we note the use of a subtitle to denote the creation of specific IP – this experience was based on the global game property *The League of Legends*, and was launched to coincide with the release of the second season of a Netflix series based on the same narrative universe. The SC experience was said to be:

> .... focused much more heavily on the 'gamification' of the guests' experience than in previous mission-based Secret Cinema events ... This experience differs from our more traditional format ... Secret Cinema Presents *Arcane* is a two-hour intensive experience with a more intimate audience combining the best of immersive entertainment, escape room games and theatre. It is built upon layers of different games with some audiences competing against each other and others working together.[49]

The increasing alignment of performance experience and games design that was brought to the fore in Chapter 5 was here underscored by SC's Max Alexander:

> I've been wanting to do a game for ages because people who design games have quite a similar starting point. They come into their creative journey as we do, which is how do you create conditions where grown-ups are prepared to invest? ... you have to invest your avatar with some degree of importance. His survival is your survival and his success is your success and you have to emote alongside him. We always start whenever we think about the creative design of our shows. The first thing we think about is the audience vessel.[50]

What became abundantly clear in these two productions is the adaptation of IP, which increasingly builds on already extended narrative universe properties, and both productions signalled an interesting shift away from a film screening being central – a move away from SC's 'more traditional format'; whether this is a permanent move on the part of SC has yet to be seen. Alexander hinted at different 'scales' of experience in the future where audiences could choose the elements to engage with.[51]

What this period also demonstrated is that, while many organisations had no alternative but to close their doors, SC were able to shape-shift, diversify and experiment, playing with formats and techniques, advancing the form using digital formats, increasingly blending both the aesthetics and creative processes of game design with immersive experience. Throughout this process of experimentation, SC maintained the visibility of their brand while moving ever further from the original artistic vision of their experiences as an *escape* from an increasingly online world.

Further avenues

We suggest that three areas should be the next focus for future research and industry development: people, practices and place.

People

A majority of immersive production companies work under the principles of a project-based organisation, common across the creative industries. Because of this, the same issues of job insecurity and precarity remain. From an individual perspective:

> We are freelance. There isn't any stability within anyone working at any level in that sector and if that sector is so important to the uniqueness of our cultural offer as a country then they need to understand that.[52]

As much research already undertaken has shown, issues of precarity and insecurity impact upon minority groups, care-givers and those least represented in the creative industry sectors,[53] and these existing issues have been further compounded by the pandemic.[54]

From an organisational perspective there is more work to be done as the industry matures. For example, more discussions around the suitability of contracts are called for when working on immersive productions. A number of our interviewees called for new standards and guidelines; an SC senior producer expressed the 'difficulty' of 'navigating traditional industry bodies and structures':

> An example is our relationship with Equity. We hold conversations with Equity for every show, they sign off our contract. But actually what we do doesn't fit within their standard theatre agreement: our theatre managers do totally different hours and totally different work from traditional theatre managers. They're on the floor running after actors who might be stuck in conversations, talking about where R2D2 has gone. It's a different role, it's a different dynamic. It comes with different health risks and different professional responsibilities.[55]

This points to a characteristic that is specific to immersive: the different nature of the performances, the varying expectations of the performers, the increasing blurring of the difference between audience and performer and also the increasing expectations of different parts of the company to 'perform', as we saw with the front of house team in Chapter 5.

Based on the rich information provided by our interviewees, we have devised a model to communicate the wide continuum of performance demands and audience expectations (see Figure 7.2).

The continuum spans the highly controlled, explicitly rule-bound productions (on the left) to the most free-form, sandbox play performances on the right. Common to many of the experiences on the left is the requirement for performers to engage in repeated, 'looped' performances – the nature of which have been called 'punishing' and 'gruelling' by many of our interviewees:

> One of the most common problems that we deal with from a performer welfare perspective is the question of repetition on performers and what that does to people's mental and physical health ... We've got a performer on their own in a room doing the same three- or four-minute track over and over and over again, night after night, and that can be really, really punishing on people's mental health.[56]

These challenges are likely to be exacerbated within online experiences since clearly these offer peak efficiency within a business model based on repetition. Producers are already attempting to mitigate the effects of this, as Alexander confirmed above – audience sizes were limited with the SC *Ghostbusters* experience to reduce the pressure on performers. Hartshorn-Hook are the

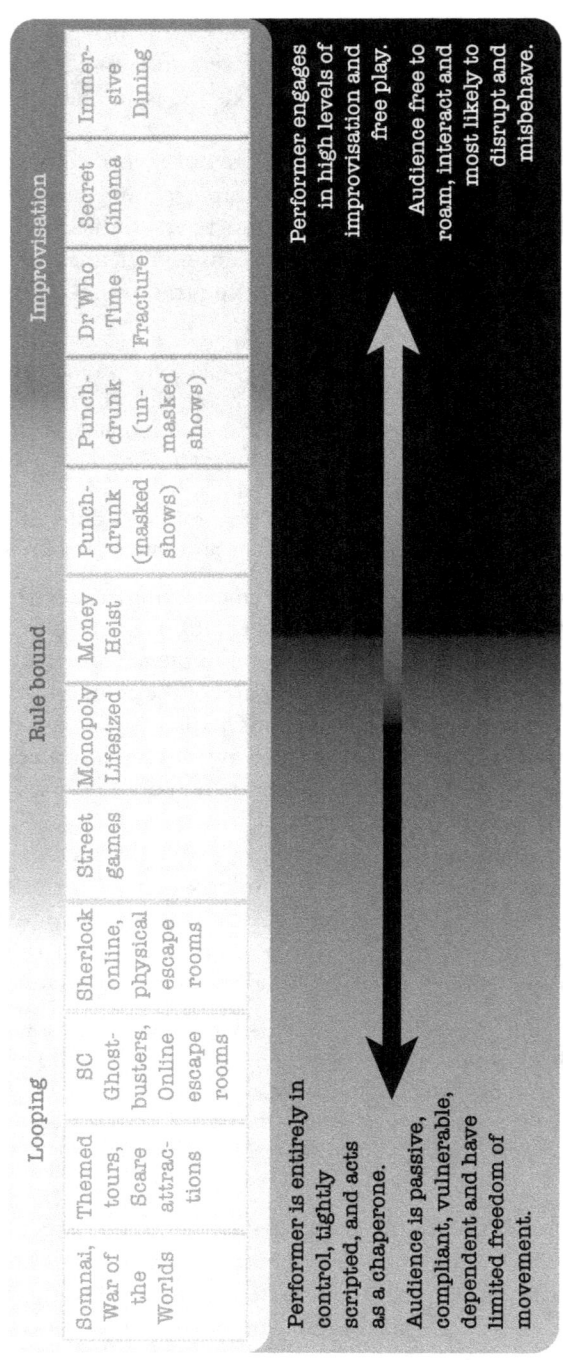

7.2 Immersive performance continuum.

first company known to have employed a safeguarding officer and, within their *DWTF* experience, they addressed the pressures of looped performances through regular character and scene changes. We would suggest that our model could be the starting point in focussing attention on development and training needs within the diverse employment contexts and demands of immersive experience performance practice.

Practices

There are clear calls for standardisation and support within the sector; a senior producer stressed the need for:

> ... an industry body specific to immersive entertainment ... which encompasses loads of different things from the small dining experience of the vaults all the way up to events for 5,000 people, that comes up with a set of industry regulations and standards in terms of fees, contracts, working hours, all of these things.[57]

There are already drives towards formalisation and support within the sector through the recently established Immersive Entertainment Network,[58] as one of the Network's founders explained:

> it's a hub that brings people together and nurtures new work and also can provide more of a guiding voice for people outside of the immersive industry, to say these are all of the possibilities and all of the options and all of the people taking risk and making new work.[59]

This is a very positive, ground-up initiative, led by key advocates within the sector. However, there needs to be more structural support, access to funding and policy engagement in order for this formalisation and support to be recognised and upheld across the many diverse spaces of production, particularly as the sector continues to advance and evolve.

Place

This is a critical piece of the puzzle for large-scale immersive experiences, as Eddy Hackett, creative director of Lost Estate, a company that designs and stages immersive theatre, music and dining experiences, put it: 'the single most challenging thing for any immersive company is to find that space that you perform in'.[60]

An SC location manager explained the nature of this challenge:

> In order to make money we need a space big enough to do the thing – how much is the rent? can we partner up with a developer or council on an empty site and get it rent-free in exchange for the cultural value we are bringing to the area?[61]

This highlights a key point of contention which has shaped some of the mainstream press responses to SC – the impact of their presence upon an area is very often foregrounded as problematic, and critiqued by local authorities and community representatives. For example, their attempt to restage *Dirty Dancing* in Waltham Forest was met with resistance by local residents.[62] This has led to complex PR challenges – one such response to these was SC's commissioning of a consulting report to track and report positively upon the impacts of an SC residency.[63] Whatever the realities of these situations and disputes, there need to be further understandings developed around the extent and potentials of immersive-led regeneration, particularly since a number of our interviewees noted key impacts of their organisation's work. For example, Maxine Doyle, a director from Punchdrunk, told us:

> It was interesting in New York. I think that's really where we could see the most obvious effect – in the street where we moved in, there was a strip club over the road and nothing else and then within four to five years there were more hotels and then more restaurants. And I'm not saying that was just because of us, but we were definitely part of a boom and actually all of our shows – I think I can say honestly they were all installed in less developed areas and they all have quite a positive impact on the areas surrounding them.[64]

And here Tom Beynon, a development producer from *Monopoly Lifesized*:

> There's a lot of space out there and the pandemic has only really helped that for experiential stuff, especially in central city locations. City of London were quite excited about the idea, and the location is actually perfect for them as it's not really got an attraction or anything, so it's drawing people from Oxford Street up to that side of the road. They recognize that having *Monopoly* there is probably going to increase the value of the real estate around it.[65]

With Punchdrunk already establishing a fixed UK site for their productions,[66] this seems like a critical next step in the process of the ongoing industrialisation of this sector – with organisations simultaneously seeking both a permanent venue and the development of productions that can effectively tour nationally and internationally. As the sound director for *Monopoly Lifesized* stated:

> *Monopoly [Lifesized]* have nailed it because that is very much just a black box. We could build that, pick it up, put it anywhere, but certainly like *Dr Who* and all the SC stuff we build to suit the venue. So whenever we go anywhere, it's a different venue, it's a different gig – we have to redesign the production for a new space.[67]

Throughout this book, we have documented how SC have moved from a hyper-temporal mode – their earlier, shorter-term, 'event-led' distribution and promotional model has transformed into long-running experiences with increasing timeframes. Some of the SC creative team expressed similar ambitions:

> ... to move into more permanent locations. It would be something that transforms the economics of our shows. Imagine every single time you put on a show, going into these buildings and investing millions of pounds into the infrastructure just to make them safe ... it's all expenses that we could just put into the production. We have grown because of our nomadic nature, but I think as we become a much more established force in the creative industry, people will forgive us not changing the location as often; as long as we keep the content engaging and we absolutely transform and blow their minds when they walk inside.[68]

Moving into permanent spaces offers many positive outcomes, including cost efficiency and the reduction of significant waste. This has become an urgent issue for the sector and an organisation called Isla was established in September 2020, founded by event professionals and industry specifically to address the sustainability of future events. Whether or not this attention to matters of sustainability will create meaningful and positive change for the sector remains to be seen. What is clear is that further research, advocacy and leadership is needed to support and evaluate the impact of these initiatives.

Copying the copiers

We opened this chapter with two quotations which drew a direct comparison between SC and Disney – of course there is now a direct connection between Disney and SC through their formalised partnership and indeed the next production SC announced would be with Disney (in 2022). These quotations were used to illuminate many of the theme park alignments that have been expressed by our interviewees and we could have quoted others such as 'it did seem to be leaning towards being more of a theme park ride than a bespoke experience'.[69] We saw this inter-relation in Chapter 4 through the direct influence that SC's production of *The Empire Strikes Back* appears to have had upon the Disney *Galaxy's Edge* experience. While SC *may* be moving towards the model of an immersive theme park, there is evidence to suggest Disney's ongoing co-option of immersive theatre practice that has been developed and honed by the UK immersive sector. Another SC creative who has experience of working in theme parks in the USA made the following observation about the Marvel Avengers campus at the Disneyland Resort which opened in June 2021:

> There's a lot of actors playing film characters that can talk to guests, which is a huge deal – that has never happened before. You would have costumed

characters walking around a park that have masks on that can't speak, whether it's a Mickey Mouse or a Hulk or a Batman. Very rarely are they allowed to have what they call 'face characters', where they can talk ... now they've got all these Marvel characters walking around and kids can come up to them and ask them specific things.[70]

When asked about SC's apparent creative influence in these domains, Alexander acknowledged that:

the fertilisation happens in both directions and it's a very warm and privileged relationship. Any one of them could roll over one day and crush us, right? We're a little company, but actually we find the relations with the studios benign and respectful in both directions.[71]

There was an interesting moment of reincarnation in September 2021 when Disney+ announced an immersive experience re-creating a 'post-apocalyptic world' inspired by the new show *Y: The Last Man* in the Vaults, Waterloo Station, London. This evoked memories of early SC productions, sited under the very similar railway arches of London Bridge – in particular *Watchmen* in 2009, which had strikingly similar themes, being another comic book adaptation.[72] The press description stated that the *Y: The Last Man* experience '... draws on key themes from the show represented in five main experiential rooms ... The immersive walkthrough experience concludes with a screening of the new drama.'[73] This sounds *exactly* like the established SC experience. As the mega-brand Disney corporation co-opt the underground practices by using these gritty, temporary locations and seek the brand association and integrity that this now brings, others will surely continue to imitate and copy. The specific 'format' that we have outlined in this book is no longer unique to SC; it is now established as replicable and has already been taken forwards by other organisations, which are now increasingly significant across the immersive experience sector more generally in both the UK and beyond.[74] For example, explicit replication was evident through a US-based Netflix *Bridgerton* experience in September 2021 – *The Queen's Ball: A Bridgerton experience*. This was a collaboration between Netflix, Shondaland and Fever in Los Angeles, Chicago, Montreal and Washington, DC. The location was specified as 'a secret ballroom in Los Angeles',[75] and despite this familiar SC trope, the experience had nothing to do with SC. At the same time, a partnership between Netflix and Fever launched a *Stranger Things* immersive experience to take place in May 2022 in both New York and San Francisco, again in a 'secret location' with participants invited to 'step inside the world of *Stranger Things* for a one-of-a-kind immersive adventure'. Again, an experience that uses the language of SC promotions and sounds uncannily like the SC experience staged in the UK in 2019 and 2020, but there was no direct involvement with SC.[76] Alexander did not express any concern about these developments:

> There's so much IP in the world and we are so good at what we do. I celebrate the fact that there are more participants in the marketplace and more things for people to do.[77]

As an organisation, SC have constantly divided opinion, attracting both extremes – lavish praise and vociferous criticism. Love them or hate them, SC's influence is now visible in many aspects of contemporary popular culture. Throughout their history, they have demonstrated an uncanny ability to capture, ride, exploit and shape the *Zeitgeist* for others to follow. As a corporate entity, in 2021 they had yet to declare a profit; a conservative projection is that the business will break even between 2022 and 2023.[78] Despite this, we see their commercialisation continue apace; in October of 2021 Michael Lynton from Sony Pictures and Joshua Berger from Warner Bros UK joined the SC board,[79] bringing with them the expertise and networks that shape the world's screen industries. Along with their partnership with Disney, this puts SC in a position of considerable influence and visibility among three of the five major global film studios. We have already seen how SC experience aesthetics have been co-opted by Disney and by others, evidencing the wider commercial value of the sites of innovation we have mapped in our ecosystem model.

Whatever the specific future for Secret Cinema, in this book we have evidenced and analysed their profound impact upon screen spectatorship practices, screen marketing techniques and film exhibition approaches. They have also influenced branding strategies far beyond film, and – as we would argue – transformed the *entire* immersive entertainment system. Thus, the incontrovertible legacy of the extraordinary creative collaborations that SC have nurtured and sustained is the flourishing immersive sector that has now evolved in their wake.

Notes

1 Duncan McClean, interviewed by author, 6 September 2021.
2 Harry Ross, interviewed by Natalie Wreyford, 7 October 2020.
3 Max Alexander, interviewed by author, 6 December 2021.
4 Thomas Maller, interviewed by Wreyford, 6 November 2020.
5 Maller, interviewed by Wreyford, 6 November 2020.
6 Sarah Atkinson and Helen. W. Kennedy, 'Disney teams up with Secret Cinema – watching movies will never be the same again', *The Conversation*, 28 February 2020.

7   Tickets were £5 with all proceeds donated to the Trussell Trust food bank charity. The party took on Sunday 12 April 2020, 9pm–12am with tickets limited to 1,000 places.
8   The growth of online 'watch parties' was precipitated by the lockdown – these had previously emerged from Netflix Party – a Google Chrome extension launched in March 2020, which synchronises video playback via Netflix with group chat. It is now called Teleparty. Many ran throughout the lockdown, including Live Cinema's initiative with Haiku Salut live-scoring *Spirited Away* in June 2020; see Gemma Barkerwood, '*Spirited Away* watch party with Haiku Salut soundtrack', Haiku Salut (blog), 4 June 2020, available at www.haikusalut.com/blog/2020/6/4/spirited-away-watch-party-with-haiku-salut-soundtrack (accessed 13 December 2021).
9   According to the global performance director, interviewed by author, 6 October 2021.
10 Global performance director, interviewed by author, 6 October 2021.
11 Tickets were £10, with profits (after production costs and service charges) donated to the Trussell Trust.
12 Time Out Editors, 'Time In Awards: the winners', *Time Out*, 8 July 2020, available at www.timeout.com/london/things-to-do/time-in-awards-the-winners (accessed 13 December 2021).
13 Auckland Theatre Company, 'Chekhov's *The Seagull*', Auckland Theatre Company, 8 May 2020, available at www.atc.co.nz/auckland-theatre-company/2020/chekhovs-the-seagull/ (accessed 13 December 2021).
14 Miriam Attwood, 'Swamp Motel's original mystery thriller IP, *The Isklander Trilogy* optioned by Gaumont UK', *Storytelling PR*, 17 August 2021, available at https://storytellingpr.com/swamp-motel-isklander-trilogy-optioned-by-gaumont-uk/ (accessed 13 December 2021).
15 Daniel Hemsley, managing director of Swamp Motel, in an interview by author, 7 September 2021.
16 These included Luna Cinema, Brighton Big Screen, Adventure Drive-in and travelling cinemas, all showing back-catalogue titles.
17 K.J. Yossman, 'As Secret Cinema launches crowdfunding initiative, is its business model working?', *Variety*, 7 June 2021, available at https://variety.com/2021/tv/news/secret-cinema-crowdfunding-business-model-1234987811/ (accessed 13 December 2021).
18 Founded in 2011, 'Fever is the global leader in the digitization of the Experience Economy, helping over 40 million people every month to discover the best experiences in their cities. Through its platform, Fever inspires users to enjoy the best local experiences, from gigs to theater, live music, immersive experiences, and pop-ups, while empowering event organizers to create new original content.' See https://feverup.com (accessed 13 December 2021).
19 The *Stranger Things* 'Drive Into' experience in LA was later launched, presented by Netflix and Fever, with Secret Cinema priced at $59 for 2 people in one car. Fayola Douglas, 'Secret Cinema takes cars to Upside Down for *Stranger Things* "drive-into" experience', *Campaign*, 21 August 2020, available at

pivoting, pipelines and poaching 227

www.campaignlive.co.uk/article/secret-cinema-takes-cars-upside-down-stranger-things-drive-into-experience/1692414 (accessed 13 December 2021).
20 Ben Travers, '*Westworld* comes to life at S×SW: photos of Sweetwater, Samurai, and more from the HBO experience', IndieWire, 9 March 2018, available at www.indiewire.com/gallery/westworld-sxsw-photos-hbo-town-sweetwater/ (accessed 13 December 2021).
21 Max Alexander, 'A note about our Arts Council Funding', *Secret Cinema*, October 2020, available at www.secretcinema.org/a-note-about-our-arts-council-funding (accessed 13 December 2021).
22 Secret Group Limited, Annual report and financial statements for the year ended 31 December 2020, Companies House, available at https://find-and-update.company-information.service.gov.uk/company/05071764/filing-history (accessed 31 August 2021).
23 Secret Group Limited, Annual report 2020, p. 18.
24 From 27 January to 4 April 2021, available at www.sherlockimmersive.com/creative-team (accessed 13 December 2021).
25 Sent on 24 May 2021.
26 Shares were priced at £20.78 each.
27 At the end of July 2020.
28 In an email circulated to the Secret Cinema mailing list, 24 June 2021.
29 In an email from SC on 26 August 2020.
30 See Figure 1.1, page 7.
31 Brian Hook, co-founder, Hartshorn-Hook Productions, interviewed by author, 28 September 2021.
32 Lead animator, interviewed by Wreyford, 29 October 2020.
33 Royal Borough of Greenwich, 'Woolwich as a major cultural destination', Royal Borough of Greenwich, 2021, available at www.royalgreenwich.gov.uk/info/200224/arts_and_culture/1912/woolwich_works (accessed 13 December 2021).
34 This also houses the *Immersive Gatsby* experience. *DWTF* was forced to close shortly after, in July 2021, due to flooding, but reopened again in November 2021.
35 Brian Hook, interviewed by author, 28 September 2021.
36 Sophie Kendrick, interviewed by Natalie Wreyford, 5 March 2021.
37 See www.deptstudios.com/ (accessed 13 December 2021).
38 What's On Stage, 'Play Dead London: *The Case of the Clown in the Woods*', What's On Stage, 4 July 2021, available at www.whatsonstage.com/shows/internet-theatre/play-dead-london-the-case-of-the-clown-in-the-woods_249607 (accessed 13 December 2021).
39 Including *Tempest* (https://tenderclaws.com/tempest, accessed 13 December 2021), an interactive VR show.
40 The UK's Research and Innovation 'Audience of the Future' fund 'has invested £39.3 million in the development of new immersive technologies such as virtual, augmented and mixed reality': UK Research and Innovation, 'Audience of the future challenge', UKRI, 24 May 2021, available at www.ukri.org/our-work/

41. *Theatre Weekly*, 'Factory 42 with Almeida Theatre & Sky present *Lost Origin*[,] a unique, immersive & interactive adventure', *Theatre Weekly*, 20 October 2021, available at https://theatreweekly.com/factory-42-with-almeida-theatre-sky-present-lost-origin-a-unique-immersive-interactive-adventure/ (accessed 13 December 2021).
42. See https://clockwork.dog (accessed 13 December 2021).
43. See https://tickets.secretcinema.org/ghostbusters-gates-of-gozer/?v=b (accessed 13 December 2021).
44. Sent on 28 October 2021.
45. Ian William Galloway, interviewed by author, 1 October 2021.
46. Business Fast, 'Secret Cinema partners Sony for at-home *Ghostbusters* experience', 26 October 2021, available at www.businessfast.co.uk/secret-cinema-partners-sony-for-at-home-ghostbusters-experience/ (accessed 13 December 2021).
47. Alexander, interviewed by author, 6 December 2021.
48. Yossman, 'As Secret Cinema…'.
49. Nicola Blackford, quoted in James Batchelor, 'Bringing *League of Legends* to life: Secret Cinema's first games experience', *Games Industry Biz*, 9 November 2021, available at www.gamesindustry.biz/articles/2021-11-09-bringing-league-of-legends-to-life-secret-cinemas-first-games-experience (accessed 13 December 2021).
50. Alexander, interviewed by author, 6 December 2021.
51. Alexander, interviewed by author, 6 December 2021.
52. Helen Scarlett O'Neill, interviewed by Wreyford, 9 October 2020.
53. Natalie Wreyford et al., *Creative majority* (London: A report for the All Party Parliamentary Group for Creative Diversity, 2021).
54. Natalie Wreyford, Helen Kennedy, Jack Newsinger and Rowan Aust, 'Locked down and locked out: the impact of the COVID-19 pandemic on mothers working in the UK television industry' (Nottingham: University of Nottingham, 2021); Raising Films, 'How we work now: learning from the impact of COVID-19 to build an industry that works for parents and carers' (London: Raising Films, 2021).
55. SC senior producer, interviewed by Wreyford, 10 December 2020.
56. Charlotte Bence, interviewed by author, 15 September 2021.
57. SC senior producer, interviewed by Wreyford, 10 December 2020.
58. See www.immersiveentertainment.net (accessed 13 December 2021) – on which is listed the forms of entertainment that they include: ARGs; escape rooms; experiential art; immersive audio; live-action role play (LARP); live experiences incorporating VR or AR; scare attractions; immersive interactive theatre; themed attractions; and transmedia and virtual experiences. This has since evolved into the Immersive Experience Network – https://immersiveexperience.network – established by Andy Barnes, Joanna Bucknell, Owen Kingston and Sheena Patel.
59. SC associate creative director, interviewed by Natalie Wreyford, 14 October 2020.

60 Eddy Hackett, interviewed by author, 16 September 2021.
61 Ma, email exchange with author, 19 November 2021.
62 Lanre Bakare, 'Secret Cinema defends plans for London event despite complaints', *The Guardian*, 22 January 2021, available at www.theguardian.com/film/2021/jan/22/secret-cinema-london-event-green-space-dirty-dancing-walthamstow-residents (accessed 13 December 2021).
63 Homfray, Douglas and Dedman, 'Changing the scene'.
64 Maxine Doyle, director, Punchdrunk Theatre, interviewed by author, 16 November 2021.
65 Tom Beynon, development producer, *Monopoly Lifesized*, interviewed by author, 23 September 2021.
66 Royal Borough of Greenwich, 'Woolwich'.
67 Luke Swaffield, interviewed by author, 22 September 2021.
68 SC senior producer, interviewed by Wreyford, 10 December 2020.
69 Ma, email exchange with author, 19 November 2021.
70 Gavin Fox, an SC web designer and pre-narrative designer, 2012–2014, interviewed by author, 31 August 2021.
71 Alexander, interviewed by author, 6 December 2021.
72 See Chapter 2, page 39.
73 Fayola Douglas, 'Disney+ creates post-apocalyptic world inspired by new show *Y: The Last Man*', *Campaign*, 16 September 2021, available at www.campaignlive.co.uk/article/disney+-creates-post-apocalyptic-world-inspired-new-show-y-last-man/1727532 (accessed 13 December 2021).
74 See Chapter 1, note 1.
75 See https://bridgertonexperience.com (accessed 13 December 2021).
76 See https://strangerthings-experience.com/ (accessed 13 December 2021).
77 Alexander, interviewed by author, 6 December 2021.
78 Yossman, 'As Secret Cinema …'.
79 Nancy Tartaglione, 'Michael Lynton and Josh Berger join Secret Cinema board', Deadline, 20 October 2021, available at https://deadline.com/2021/10/josh-berger-michael-lynton-secret-cinema-board-1234858856/ (accessed 13 December 2021).

Appendix 1

Secret Cinema productions

Production number	Film title	Dates	Organisation branding & subtitle(s)[1]	Location	Ticket pricing, Audience size, Box office[2]
Chapter 2					
1	*Dreams That Money Can Buy* (1947, Dir: Hans Richter)	2005	Launched Future Cinema in 2005 as 'live cinema'	London Bridge tunnel	
2	*The Big Lebowski* (1998, Dir: Joel Coen and Ethan Coen)	7 February 2006	Future Cinema	Bloomsbury bowling lanes, London	
3	Future Cinema tour, *Nosferatu* (1922, Dir: F.W. Murnau)	1 June 2006 9 June 2006 23 August 2006	Future Shorts and Stella Artois presents Future Cinema 2006 UK Tour	'SE1' (or 'seOne') Club in London Ashton Court Mansion, Bristol Edinburgh	
4, 5	Future Cinema Village: *Kill Bill: Vol 1* (2003, Dir: Quentin Tarantino), *Ferris Bueller's Day Off* (1986, Dir: John Hughes)	22 and 23 July 2006	Future Shorts and Stella Artois presents Future Cinema at Greenwich	Greenwich Park, London	

6	*The Matrix* (1999, Dir: Lana and Lilly Wachowski)	16 November 2006	Future Cinema presents …	Mansion House, Dublin, Ireland	
7	*Metropolis* (1927, Dir: Fritz Lang)	23 November 2007	Future Shorts, Future Cinema and Stella Artois present; 'Future Cinema' logo with the tag line 'The Cinematic Event Company'	Fabric nightclub, London	*Audience size:* 400
8	*Paranoid Park* (2007, Dir: Gus Van Sant)	16 December 2007	Secret Cinema launch: *Paranoid Park* hosted by Future Shorts	Shipwright Yard, London Bridge	
9	*Funny Face* (1957, Dir: Stanley Donen)	13 February 2008	Secret Cinema	Royal Academy of the Arts, London	
10	*If…* (1968, Dir: Lindsay Anderson)	29 May 2008	Secret Cinema presents	Dulwich College, London	*Audience size:* 1,000
11	*Eraserhead* (1977, Dir: David Lynch)	18 July 2008	Future Cinema presents, featuring Guillemots	Latitude Festival, Suffolk	*Ticket pricing:* £55 day ticket, £130 weekend festival ticket
12	*RockNRrolla* (2008, Dir: Guy Ritchie)	27 August 2008	Future Cinema '*RockNRolla* – The Live Event'	seOne club, London	*Audience size:* 3,000 capacity
13	*A Night at the Opera* (1935, Dir: Sam Wood and Edmund Goulding)	3 October 2008	Secret Cinema (in association with Nokia Connecting People)	Hackney Empire, London	*Ticket pricing:* £10 (Plebeians), £13.50 (Partisans)

Production number	Film title	Dates	Organisation branding & subtitle(s)[1]	Location	Ticket pricing, Audience size, Box office[2]
14	*Ghostbusters* (1984, Dir: Ivan Reitman)	28 November 2008	Secret Cinema (in association with Nokia Connecting People)	Royal Horticultural Hall, Lawrence Hall, both in London; Brighton Corn Exchange	
15	*Anvil! The Story of Anvil* (2008, Dir: Sacha Gervasi)	15 February 2009	Secret Cinema (in association with Nokia Connecting People)	Shepherd's Bush Empire, London	*Ticket pricing:* Estimated £17.50
16	*Watchmen* (2009, Dir: Zack Snyder)	5 March 2009	Future Cinema In association with Nokia Connecting People, Smirnoff Original Nights (end credits) Future Cinema presents an exclusive preview event (poster)	seOne club, London	*Ticket pricing:* Estimated £17.50 *Audience size:* 3,000 capacity
17	*Sounds Like Teen Spirit?* (2008, Dir: Jamie Jay Johnson)	2 May 2009	From Future Cinema, the creators of Secret Cinema, Secret Screenings – A new monthly film club Secret Screenings 001 present …	London, DoYs, Brighton and Cameo, Edinburgh	*Ticket pricing:* £9 Picturehouse members, £11 standard

List of SC productions

18	*The Harder They Come* (1972, Dir: Perry Henzell)	20 June 2009	Secret Cinema	Coronet Cinema at Elephant and Castle, London	*Ticket pricing:* Estimated £17.50
19	*All Tomorrow's Parties* (2009, Dir: Jonathan Caouette)	24 June 2009	Future Cinema presents	Picturehouse, Edinburgh	
20	*Black Cat, White Cat* (1998, Dir: Emir Kusturica)	19 July 2009	Future Cinema presents	Latitude Festival	*Ticket pricing:* £135 weekend festival ticket
21	*The Warriors* (1979, Dir: Walter Hill)	6 September 2009	Secret Cinema sponsored by Absolut Vodka	London Fields, London	*Ticket pricing:* £18 standard *Audience size:* 2,500+
22	*Alien* (1979, Dir: Ridley Scott)	31 October 2009	Secret Cinema in partnership with Windows Phone	Disused warehouse, Shoreditch, London	*Audience size:* 1000+
23	*Bugsy Malone* (1976, Dir: Alan Parker)	27, 28 November 2009	Secret Cinema in partnership with Windows Phone	The Troxy, Limehouse, London	
24	*Precious* (2009, Dir: Lee Daniels)	29 January 2010	Future Cinema presents	Rio Cinema, Dalston, London	
25	*Wings of Desire* (1987, Dir: Wim Wenders)	27, 28 February 2010	Secret Cinema in partnership with Windows Phone	Pavilion, London	
26	*Blade Runner* (1982, Dir: Ridley Scott)	15–20 June 2010	Secret Cinema in association with Windows Phone (and Red Bull feature as sponsors)	Canary Wharf, London	*Audience size:* 7,000+ total *Box office:* £136,000

Production number	Film title	Dates	Organisation branding & subtitle(s)[1]	Location	Ticket pricing, Audience size, Box office[2]
27	*Blow-Up* (1966, Dir: Michelangelo Antonioni)	30 June 2010	Future Cinema	Shangri La Studios, Brooklyn, New York	
28	*The Blues Brothers* (1980, Dir: John Landis)	15 July 2010	Future Cinema presents	Latitude Festival, Suffolk	*Ticket pricing:* £65 day ticket, £155 weekend
29	*Blue Velvet* (1986, Dir: David Lynch)	31 July 2010	Future Cinema presents a tribute to the life and work of the late, great Dennis Hopper	The Troxy, Limehouse, London	
30	*Laurence of Arabia* (1962, Dir: David Lean)	3–5 September 2010	Secret Cinema in partnership with Windows Phone	Alexandra Palace, London	*Ticket pricing:* £27.50 standard, £22.75 concessions *Audience size:* 14,000 (3,000 per night)
31	*One Flew Over the Cuckoo's Nest* (1975, Dir: Milos Forman)	11–21 November 2010	Secret Cinema in collaboration with the mental health charity, Mind (in partnership with Windows Phone.)	Princess Louise Hospital, Kensington, London	*Ticket pricing:* £27.50 standard, £22.75 concessions *Audience size:* 6,000 (600 per night)

List of SC productions 235

32	*Alien* (1979, Dir: Ridley Scott)	December 2010	Future Cinema in partnership with Windows Phone; launches in Berlin	Umspannwerk Voltaire, Berlin, Germany	
33	*The Red Shoes* (1948, Dir: Michael Powell and Emeric Pressburger)	11–27 February 2011	Secret Cinema	Tobacco Docks, London	*Ticket pricing:* £27.50 standard, £22.75 concessions[3] *Audience size:* 14,000+ (1,000 per night)
34	*Diva* (1981, Dir: Jean-Jacques Beineix)	28 February 2011	Future Cinema in partnership with English National Opera	London Coliseum	*Ticket pricing:* £20 standard *Audience size:* 2,000+
35	*The Battle of Algiers* (1966, Dir: Gillo Pontecorvo)	15 April–8 May 2011	Secret Cinema	Old Vic Tunnels under Waterloo Station, London	*Ticket pricing:* £35 standard *Audience size:* 14,000+
36	*The Lost Boys* (1987, Dir: Joel Schumacher)	3 September 2011	Future Cinema in partnership with California Presents … California Dreams Future Cinema. Pioneers of Live Cinema (Vimeo Video subtitle)	Canary Wharf, London	*Ticket pricing:* £24.50 standard, £21.50 concessions *Audience size:* 4,000+

Production number	Film title	Dates	Organisation branding & subtitle(s)[1]	Location	Ticket pricing, Audience size, Box office[2]
37	Top Gun (1986, Dir: Tony Scott)	4 September 2011	Future Cinema in partnership with California Presents ... California Dreams (Join us)	Canary Wharf, London	*Ticket pricing:* £24.50 standard, £21.50 concessions *Audience size:* 4,000+
38	The Third Man (1949, Dir: Carol Reed)	7 December 2011 to 22 January 2012	Secret Cinema	Farmiloe Building, Farringdon, London	*Ticket pricing:* £35 standard + £28.50 for 3-course meal *Audience size:* 19,000+ *Box office:* £600,000
39	Brief Encounter (1945, Dir: David Lean)	14–18 February 2012	The Other Cinema presents on one poster and Future Cinema presents the official launch of the Other Cinema	The Troxy, Limehouse, London; also in Edinburgh, Leeds, Birmingham and Norwich	*Ticket pricing:* £20 standard, £15 concessions *Audience size:* 1,600+
40	Bugsy Malone (1976, Dir: Alan Parker)	16 March–14 April 2012	Future Cinema the creators of Secret Cinema present ... A live cinema experience of *Bugsy Malone*	The Troxy, Limehouse, London	*Ticket pricing:* £25 standard, £17.50 concessions, £10 children

41	*La Haine* (1995, Dir: Mathieu Kassovitz)	2–5 May 2012	The Other Cinema Featuring a live score by Asian Dub Foundation	Broadwater Farm Community Centre, Tottenham, London; the Troxy, Limehouse, London; Trianon, Paris; Bournemouth, Brighton, Warwick, Oswestry and York in the UK; Kabul, Afghanistan; Tallinn, Estonia.	*Audience size:* 400+ at Broadwater Farm
42	*Prometheus* (2012, Dir: Ridley Scott)	1–28 June 2012	Future Cinema (although this event has laterally been rebranded as Secret Cinema in post-promotional materials)	20,000 m² office complex on Hampstead Road in London	*Ticket pricing:* £35 standard *Audience size:* 25,000 (900 capacity per screening) *Box office:* £720,000
43	*Searching for Sugar Man* (2012, Dir: Malik Bendjelloul)	4 July 2012	Future Cinema the creators of Secret Cinema present a Secret Screening	The Troxy, Limehouse, London	*Audience size:* 1,000+
44, 45	Wilderness Festival: *Bugsy Malone* and *La Haine*	10–12 August 2012	Future Cinema at Wilderness Festival, Cinematic takeover	Cornbury Park, Oxfordshire	

Production number	Film title	Dates	Organisation branding & subtitle(s)[1]	Location	Ticket pricing, Audience size, Box office[2]
46	*The Imposter* (2012, Dir: Bart Layton)	14 August 2012	Secret Screenings present …	Conway Hall, London	*Audience size*: 400 capacity
47	*Grease* (1978, Dir: Randal Kleiser)	7–9 September 2012	From the creators of Secret Cinema, Future Cinema presents … an all singing and all dancing live cinema experience	Barnes Common, London	*Ticket pricing*: £35 standard, £25 concessions *Audience size*: 9,000+
48	*La Haine* (1995, Dir: Mathieu Kassovitz)	27 September 2012	Future Cinema	Sound Central Music Festival, Kabul, Afghanistan	
49	*The Shawshank Redemption* (1994, Dir: Frank Darabont)	12 December 2012–11 January 2013	Secret Cinema presents … *The Shawshank Redemption* A Live Cinema Experience Tell No One appears at the end of the video for the first time	Bethnal Green Library and Cardinal Pole School, Hackney, London.	*Ticket pricing*: £50 standard, £100 VIP, £30 extra for secret hotel stay *Audience size*: 13,500+ *Box office*: £1.7m
50	*Casablanca* (1942, Dir: Michael Curtiz)	14 February and 23 March 2013	Future Cinema presents *Casablanca* A Live Cinema Experience at the astonishing Troxy	The Troxy, Limehouse, London	*Ticket pricing*: £25 *Audience size*: 800 per night

List of SC productions   239

Chapter 3					
51	*Footloose* (1984, Dir: Herbert Ross)	27 April 2013	Secret Screenings Presents …	The Troxy, Limehouse, London	*Ticket pricing*: Complimentary for those affected by cancellations of *Brazil*
52	*Brazil* (1985, Dir: Terry Gilliam)	2 May–9 June 2013	Secret Cinema presents	BT Building, Croydon, London.	*Ticket pricing*: £45 standard *Audience size*: 25,000+
53	Laura Marling, *Once I Was an Eagle*	13–21, 22–23, 25–30 June 2013	Secret Cinema presents (secretmusic.org)	Cardinal Pole School, Hackney, London	*Audience size*: 300 per night
54	*Saturday Night Fever* (1977, Director John Badham)	15 June 2013–7 July 2013	Future Cinema presents *Saturday Night Fever* A Live Cinema Experience at the Troxy	The Troxy, Limehouse, London	*Ticket pricing*: £25 standard, £20 concessions
55	*Dirty Dancing* (1987, Dir: Emile Ardolino)	30 August–1 September 2013	Future Cinema presents *Dirty Dancing*: the Live Cinema Experience	Hackney Downs, London	*Ticket pricing*: £35 standard, £27.50 concessions *Audience size*: 12,000+

Appendix 1

Production number	Film title	Dates	Organisation branding & subtitle(s)[1]	Location	Ticket pricing, Audience size, Box office[2]
56	*Ghostbusters* (1984, Dir: Ivan Reitman)	October–December 2013	Future Cinema presents *Ghostbusters*: A Live Cinema Experience at the Troxy	The Troxy, Limehouse, London	*Ticket pricing:* £35 standard, £28.50 concessions, £15 children *Audience size:* 14,000+
57	*Who Framed Roger Rabbit?* (1988, Dir: Robert Zemeckis, Richard Williams)	14–23 February 2014	Future Cinema presents *Who Framed Roger Rabbit*: A Live Cinema Experience at the Ink and Paint club	The Troxy, Limehouse, London	*Ticket pricing:* £43.50 standard, £31.50 concessions, £15 children
58	*The Grand Budapest Hotel* (2014, Dir: Wes Anderson)	27 February–30 March 2014	Secret Cinema presents …	Farmiloe Building, Farringdon, London	*Ticket pricing:* £53.50 *Audience size:* 21,000+ (350 each night) *Box office:* £1.1m
59	*Miller's Crossing* (1991, Dir: Joel Coen, Ethan Coen)	20 March–25 May 2014	Secret Cinema (Tell No One) presents … (branded as the '21st Tell no one')	Hornsey Town Hall, London	*Ticket pricing:* £50 *Audience size:* 16,000+ (450 each night)

60	*Back to the Future* (1985, Dir: Robert Zemeckis)	24 July–31 August 2014	Secret Cinema presents … A Live Cinema Experience	Olympic Park, Stratford, London	*Ticket pricing:* £53.50 evening, £140 family *Audience size:* 45,000+ *Box office:* £3.5m
61	*Dead Poets Society* (1989, Dir: Peter Weir)	15–16 August 2014	Secret Cinema presents … *Dead Poets Society*, a tribute to Robin Williams	The Troxy, Limehouse, London; Matthew's Yard, London; Flying Duck, Glasgow; Leaf, Liverpool; Victoria Warehouse, Manchester; The Strand, Belfast; Cinema Society, Teesside; the Grid, Prague; South Street Seaport, New York; Basilica Hudson, upstate New York	*Ticket pricing:* £25 standard *Audience size:* 3,000 attendees, with £24,000+ raised for Mind.
62	*The Great Dictator* (1940, Dir: Charles Chaplin)	21 December 2014	Secret Cinema presents …	Videology and Spectrum in New York; the Troxy, Limehouse, London; Teatro Centrale, Rome; Great Star Theatre, San Francisco; CineFamily, Los Angeles	*Ticket pricing:* £25 standard *Audience size:* 2,000+ attendees across five cities *Box office:* £11,500+

Production number	Film title	Dates	Organisation branding & subtitle(s)[1]	Location	Ticket pricing, Audience size, Box office[2]
63	*Amy* (2015, Dir: Asif Kapadia)	28–29 June 2015	Launch of Secret Cinema X in Association with MAC UK	Koko, Camden, London	*Audience size: 300*
Chapter 4					
64	*Star Wars: The Empire Strikes Back* (1980, Dir: Irvin Kershner)	4 June–27 September 2015	Secret Cinema presents ...	Harmsworth Quays, London	*Ticket pricing: £75 standard* *Audience size: 100,000 Box office: £6.45m*
65	*Dr Strangelove or: How I Learned to Stop Worrying and Love the Bomb* (1964, Dir: Stanley Kubrick)	17–21, 24–28 February and 2–6, 9–13, 17–20 March 2016	Secret Cinema Tell No One	Harmsworth Quays, London	*Ticket pricing: £64.50 evening, £55 matinee, £129 VIP, £40 concessions* *Audience size: 20,000 Box office: £1.24m*
66	*Victoria* (2015, Dir: Sebastian Schipper)	26 March 2016	Secret Cinema X	Ministry of Sound, London	*Ticket pricing: £28* *Audience size: 500 Box office: £12,740*

67	28 Days Later (2002, Dir: Danny Boyle)	14 April–29 May 2016	Secret Cinema presents ...	Harmsworth Quays, London	Ticket pricing: £64.50 evening, £55 matinee, £129 VIP, £40 concessions Audience size: 22,000+ Box office: £1.33m
68	Dirty Dancing (1987, Dir: Emile Ardolino)	15–17, 22–24 July 2016	Secret Cinema presents ...	Leyton Jubilee Gardens, London	Ticket pricing: £65 evening, £129 VIP, £38.50 concessions Audience size: 30,000+ Box office: £1.9m
69	Moulin Rouge! (2001, Dir: Baz Luhrmann)	14 February–30 April 2017 (extended to 11 June)	Secret Cinema presents ...	Canning Town, London	Ticket pricing: Creatures of the Underworld (standing £49), Children of the Revolution (seated £59), Aristocrats (added value £130) Audience size: 70,000 Box office: £4.48m

List of SC productions   243

Production number	Film title	Dates	Organisation branding & subtitle(s)[1]	Location	Ticket pricing, Audience size, Box office[2]
70	*The Handmaiden* (2016, Dir: Chan-wook Park)	9–14 April 2017	Secret Cinema X Tell No One …	The Troxy, Limehouse, London	*Ticket pricing:* Gallery (standard seating) £26.50, Salon (table seating) £30 and Library (sofa Seating for two) – £80 + booking fee. *Audience size:* 5,500 *Box office:* £159,295
71	*I, Daniel Blake* (2016, Dir: Ken Loach, Laura Obiols)	6–8 June 2017	Secret Cinema, Special screenings, a secret youth initiative	The Troxy, Limehouse, London; Blackfriars Ouseburn Cinema, Newcastle	
72	*Blade Runner* (1982, Dir: Ridley Scott)	21 March–10 June 2018 (extended to 8 July)	Secret Cinema presents *Blade Runner – The Final Cut:* A Secret Live Experience	Canning Town, London	*Ticket pricing:* Orion (regular) £45, Phoenix (advanced) £59, Black Galaxy (VIP) £115 *Audience size:* 70,000 *Box office:* £4.8m

List of SC productions — 245

73	*Romeo + Juliet* (1996, Dir: Baz Luhrmann)	9–19 August 2018	Secret Cinema presents…	Acton, West London	*Ticket pricing:* Young Hearts & Rogues £49–£64, Nobles & Underbosses £85 *Audience size:* 60,000 (5,000 per night) *Box office:* £3m

Chapter 5

74	*Casino Royale* (2006, Dir: Martin Campbell)	15 May–6 October 2019	Secret Cinema presents…	Dagenham East, London	*Ticket pricing:* £49 standard, £175 VIP *Audience size:* 120,000 (1,500 per night) *Box office:* £8m
75	*Stranger Things* (TV series, 2016–, creators: Matt and Ross Duffer)	13 November 2019–23 February 2020	Secret Cinema presents…	Canning Town, London	*Ticket pricing:* £49 matinee and evening standard, £79 VIP (Media Hot Shots), £99–£139 *Audience size:* 110, 000

Chapter 7

Appendix 1

Production number	Film title	Dates	Organisation branding & subtitle(s)[1]	Location	Ticket pricing, Audience size, Box office[2]
76	Secret Cinema Drive-in (various titles)	5 July–August 2020	Häagen-Dazs presents The Drive-In from Secret Cinema & Goodwood	Goodwood Motor Circuit, Chichester, West Sussex	*Ticket pricing:* £50 per car
77	*Stranger Things: The Drive-into Experience* (TV series, 2016–, creators: Matt and Ross Duffer)	October 2020–June 2021	Secret Cinema presents Presented by Netflix and Fever	ROW DTLA, Los Angeles	*Ticket pricing:* from $69 (standard for two people in one car), from $135 (VIP)
78	*Arcane: League of Legends Enter the Undercity*: An Immersive Live Experience (TV series, 2021–, creators: Christian Linke and Alex Yee)	21 November–19 December 2021	Secret Cinema presents	Los Angeles	*Ticket pricing:* $70 general admission, $140 premium admission

List of SC productions 247

79	*Ghostbusters: The Gates of Gozer* (Sony/Secret Cinema)	1 December 2021–16 January 2022	Secret Cinema presents	Online: In both GMT and EST time zones	*Ticket pricing:* Public Teams (up to six players) from £21.50/$27.50, Buy-out team (six players) from £17.20/$22
80	*Bridgerton* (TV series, 2020–, creator: Chris Van Dusen)	16 February –27 March 2022	Secret Cinema with Fever present (Shondaland and Netflix)	Wembley, London	*Ticket pricing:* £49 standard, £99 VIP
81	*Dirty Dancing* (1987, Dir: Emile Ardolino)	13–31 July 2022	Secret Cinema presents	Walthamstow, London	*Ticket pricing:* £49 standard, £89 VIP

1 As provided on the post-experience promotional video and/or the accompanying flyer/website.
2 Where available.
3 'Concessions' usually means entitled to social security benefits and/or holding a current National Union of Students card. All other price ranges indicate the difference between week nights and premium weekend nights.

Appendix 2

Secret Cinema post-experience promotional videos

These are listed in production date order, although not all productions had a related video.[1]

Film title	Video details
Nosferatu	Support Future Shorts, 'Future Cinema @ SE1 Club London', 28 November 2007. YouTube video, 3:19, available at www.youtube.com/watch?v= nmhZVqSdh3Y[2]
Kill Bill: Vol. I, Ferris Bueller's Day Off	Support Future Shorts, 'Future Cinema – Village @ Studio Artois', 28 November 2007. YouTube video, 2:00, available at www.youtube.com/ watch?v=peoSfkHYIBA
Metropolis	Support Future Shorts, 'Future Cinema – *Metropolis* @ Fabric London', 28 November 2007. YouTube video, 2:01, available at www.youtube.com/ watch?v=yPR_4unMohM
Paranoid Park	Secret Cinema, 'New Secret Cinema launch video – *Paranoid Park*', 18 January 2008. YouTube video, 1:27, available at www.youtube.com/ watch?v=1Ffzlm2LGG4
Funny Face	Secret Cinema, 'Secret Cinema – *Funny Face*', 21 February 2008. YouTube video, 1:36, available at www.youtube.com/watch?v=uQts0qRPWuM
If …	Secret Cinema, 'Secret Cinema – *If …*', 18 June 2008. YouTube video, 1:44, available at www.youtube.com/ watch?v=K3UXsVsYXAM&t=1s
RockNRolla	Future, '*RockNRolla*, Future Cinema', 12 September 2008. YouTube video, 1:54, available at www.youtube.com/watch?v=xqhQG4QJBfo
A Night at the Opera	Secret Cinema, 'Secret Cinema – *A Night at the Opera*', 18 November 2008. YouTube video, 3:29, available at www.youtube.com/watch?v=BMIDUScs-J8

Film title	Video details
Ghostbusters	Secret Cinema, 'Secret Cinema – *Ghostbusters* at Lawrence Hall', 5 December 2008. YouTube video, 2:31, available at www.youtube.com/watch?v=a3-5q_NgCWQ
Anvil! The Story of Anvil	Secret Cinema, 'Secret Cinema – *Anvil! The Story of Anvil*', 12 March 2009. YouTube video, 2:23, available at www.youtube.com/watch?v=mF96GDBAi44
Watchmen	Future, '*Watchmen*, Future Cinema', 24 March 2009. YouTube video, 2:44, available at www.youtube.com/watch?v=I_v1HpTNG44
Sounds like Teen Spirit	Support Future Shorts, 'Secret Screenings – *Sounds like Teen Spirit*', 16 June 2009. YouTube video, 1:21, available at www.youtube.com/watch?v=nqCjew7zTE8
The Harder They Come	Secret Cinema, 'Secret Cinema – *The Harder They Come*', 26 June 2009. YouTube video, 1:39, available at www.youtube.com/watch?v=MEDwA4W5Z9Y
Black Cat, White Cat	Support Future Shorts, 'Future Cinema – *Black Cat, White Cat*', 4 August 2009. YouTube video, 1:36, available at www.youtube.com/watch?v=3i5bmm_YNNc
The Warriors	Future, '*The Warriors*, Secret Cinema', 21 September 2009. YouTube video, 1:38, available at www.youtube.com/watch?v=GRQ2lKOtis4
Alien	Secret Cinema, 'http://www.secretcinema.org/ Presents *Alien*. October 2009. Somewhere in London', 11 November 2009. YouTube video, 1:39, available at www.youtube.com/watch?v=BJWtFtdQJDM
Bugsy Malone	Secret Cinema, 'Secret Cinema presents *Bugsy Malone*', 17 December 2009. YouTube video, 2:28, available at www.youtube.com/watch?v=SOnswf7XaOE&t=15s
Wings of Desire	Secret Cinema, 'Secret Cinema – *Wings of Desire*', 26 March 2010. YouTube video, 2:13, available at www.youtube.com/watch?v=XDN0YitShiE
Blow-Up	Support Future Shorts, 'Future Cinema presents *Blow-Up*. New York pre-launch event', 2 August 2010. YouTube video, 1:30, available at www.youtube.com/watch?v=qvq6vlLu184
The Blues Brothers	Secret Cinema Presents, 'Future Cinema – *The Blues Brothers*', 13 June 2011. Vimeo video, 1:58, available at https://vimeo.com/25021385

Film title	Video details
Lawrence of Arabia	Secret Cinema, 'Secret Cinema presents *Lawrence of Arabia*', 28 September 2010. YouTube video, 3:50, available at www.youtube.com/watch?v=uB3YnVX3bFU
One Flew Over the Cuckoo's Nest	Secret Cinema, 'Secret Cinema presents *One Flew Over the Cuckoo's Nest*', 10 December 2010. YouTube video, 2:44, available at www.youtube.com/watch?v=-nHZAZZqOqM
Alien	Secret Cinema Presents, 'Future Cinema launches in Berlin – *Alien*', 13 June 2011. Vimeo video, 4:27, available at https://vimeo.com/25022602
The Red Shoes	Future, '*The Red Shoes*, Secret Cinema', 17 March 2011. YouTube video, 2:22, available at www.youtube.com/watch?v=d2CffTu0LH0
Diva	Support Future Shorts, 'Future Cinema in partnership with the ENO presents *DIVA*', 1 April 2011. YouTube video, 1:15, available at www.youtube.com/watch?v=EBcdz4NnTBk
The Battle of Algiers	Secret Cinema, 'Secret Cinema presents *The Battle of Algiers*', 11 May 2011. YouTube video, 3:32, available at www.youtube.com/watch?v=YRep76w-ads
The Lost Boys	Support Future Shorts, 'Future Cinema presents *The Lost Boys*', 7 November 2011. YouTube video, 1:34, available at www.youtube.com/watch?v=rBnC4JEOLbM
Top Gun	Support Future Shorts, 'Future Cinema presents *Top Gun*', 2 November 2011. YouTube video, 2:18, available at www.youtube.com/watch?v=UgO12OxIUAw&t=4s
The Third Man	Secret Cinema, 'Secret Cinema presents – *The Third Man*', 24 January 2012. YouTube video, 3:18, available at www.youtube.com/watch?v=zz89LUWfHko
Brief Encounter	Secret Cinema Presents, 'The Other Cinema – *Brief Encounter*', 27 February 2013. Vimeo video, 1:13, available at https://vimeo.com/60670981
Bugsy Malone	Support Future Shorts, 'Future Cinema presents *Bugsy Malone* – APRIL 2012', 29 March 2012. YouTube video, 2:11, available at www.youtube.com/watch?v=av9e0ulXtkw
La Haine	Future, '*LA HAINE*	The Other Cinema', 25 May 2012. YouTube video, 3:16, available at www.youtube.com/watch?v=btYJ3f8l81Q&t=2s

Film title	Video details
Prometheus	Secret Cinema Presents, 'We live as we dream. Alone', 28 March 2012. Vimeo video, 1:35, available at https://vimeo.com/39343761
Searching for Sugar Man	Future, '*Searching for Sugar Man* | Future Shorts', 2 August 2012. YouTube video, 2:52, available at www.youtube.com/watch?v=oviVWSi7ga4
Bugsy Malone, La Haine	Future, 'Future Cinema at Wilderness Festival', 6 September 2012. YouTube video, 3:26, available at www.youtube.com/watch?v=_7kdVNz–fE
The Imposter	Support Future Shorts, 'Secret Screenings presents *The Imposter*', 14 February 2013. YouTube video, 00:58, available at www.youtube.com/watch?v=mJxhc17uM6M
Grease	Secret Cinema Presents, 'Future Cinema presents *Grease*', 22 July 2012. Vimeo video, 1:36, available at https://vimeo.com/46200867 [pre-experience, not post-experience]
La Haine	Secret Cinema Presents, 'Future Cinema head for Afghanistan', 28 August 2012. Vimeo video, 0:48, available at https://vimeo.com/48359113
The Shawshank Redemption	Future, '*The Shawshank Redemption* | Secret Cinema', 5 December 2012. YouTube video, 3:13, available at www.youtube.com/watch?v=J4rJ3Y6P4h0
Casablanca	Future, '*Casablanca* | Secret Cinema', 3 April 2013. YouTube video, 2:13, available at www.youtube.com/watch?v=xSY7ON0raAs
Footloose	Future, 'Secret Screenings presents *Footloose*', 1 June 2013. YouTube video, 1:02, available at www.youtube.com/channel/UCbwxgH3QRM1CAdMqBJ-oh4w/videos
Brazil	Future, 'Terry Gilliam's *Brazil* | Secret Cinema', 23 June 2013. YouTube video, 3:31, available at www.youtube.com/watch?v=MS4cX-lAC6k&t=8s
Laura Marling, *Once I Was an Eagle*	Future, 'Laura Marling | Secret Music', 3 February 2014. YouTube video, 3:49, available at www.youtube.com/watch?v=obtTfZL2UZY
Saturday Night Fever	Support Future Shorts, 'Future Cinema presents *Saturday Night Fever*', 5 September 2013. YouTube video, 2:56, available at www.youtube.com/watch?v=Qgql23rh5Ys&t=25s
Dirty Dancing	Secret Cinema Presents, 'Future Cinema presents *Dirty Dancing*', 30 September 2013. Vimeo video, 3:24, available at https://vimeo.com/75802027

Film title	Video details
Ghostbusters	Secret Cinema Presents, 'Future Cinema presents *Ghostbusters*', 11 February 2014. Vimeo video, 1:52, available at https://vimeo.com/86396811
Who Framed Roger Rabbit?	Future, '*Who Framed Roger Rabbit*	Secret Cinema', 16 February 2014. YouTube video, 1:14, available at www.youtube.com/watch?v=9ekMl3V1ff0
The Grand Budapest Hotel	Future, '*The Grand Budapest Hotel*	Secret Cinema', 13 May 2014. YouTube video, 2:33, available at www.youtube.com/watch?v=IB2PXPo4rjU&t=38s
Miller's Crossing	Future, 'Secret Cinema presents *Miller's Crossing*', 15 July 2014. YouTube video, 3:16, available at www.youtube.com/watch?v=gcOSt7LyMnw
Back to the Future	Secret Cinema Presents, 'Secret Cinema presents *Back to the Future*', 18 November 2014. Vimeo video, 3:15, available at https://vimeo.com/112151676
Dead Poets Society	Future, '*Dead Poets Society* – a tribute to Robin Williams	Secret Cinema', 2 September 2014. YouTube video, 1:32, available at www.youtube.com/watch?v=pcC-ggDEgb8
The Great Dictator	Secret Cinema Presents, 'Secret Cinema presents *The Great Dictator*', 22 December 2014. Vimeo video, 2:01, available at https://vimeo.com/115166459
Amy	Secret Cinema Presents, 'Secret Cinema presents *AMY*', 28 August 2015. Vimeo video, 2:13, available at https://vimeo.com/137619271
Star Wars: The Empire Strikes Back	Secret Cinema Presents, 'Secret Cinema presents *Star Wars: The Empire Strikes Back*', 17 December 2015. Vimeo video, 2:45, available at https://vimeo.com/149302612
Dr Strangelove or: How I Learned to Stop Worrying and Love the Bomb	Future Shorts, 'Secret Cinema presents *Dr Strangelove*', 10 June 2016. YouTube video, 2:29, available at www.youtube.com/c/futureshorts
28 Days Later	Secret Cinema Presents, 'Secret Cinema presents *28 Days Later*', 17 August 2016. Vimeo video, 3:04, available at https://vimeo.com/179181953
Dirty Dancing	Secret Cinema Presents, 'Secret Cinema presents *Dirty Dancing*', 24 July 2016. Vimeo video, 1:41, available at https://vimeo.com/176063142
Moulin Rouge!	Secret Cinema Presents, 'Secret Cinema presents Baz Luhrmann's *Moulin Rouge!* – trailer', 20 December 2017. Vimeo video, 3:08, available at https://vimeo.com/248180966

Film title	Video details
The Handmaiden	Secret Cinema Presents, 'Secret Cinema X presents Park Chan-wook's *The Handmaiden*', 14 April 2017. Vimeo video, 00:54, available at https://vimeo.com/213272145
I, Daniel Blake	Secret Cinema Presents, 'Secret Cinema presents special screenings of Ken Loach's *I, Daniel Blake*', 7 July 2017. Vimeo video, 2:08, available at https://vimeo.com/224629486
Blade Runner	Pascale Neuschäfer, 'Secret Cinema presents *Blade Runner – The Final Cut* a secret live experience (2018)', 9 January 2019, Vimeo video, 2:53, available at https://vimeo.com/310372174
Romeo + Juliet	Secret Cinema, 'Secret Cinema presents William Shakespeare's *Romeo + Juliet*', 9 December 2019. Vimeo video, 0:30, available at https://vimeo.com/378328807
Casino Royale	Secret Cinema, 'Secret Cinema presents *Casino Royale* (2019)', 8 October 2020. Vimeo video, 1:19, available at https://vimeo.com/466193279
Stranger Things	Secret Cinema, 'Secret Cinema presents *Stranger Things* (2019–2020)', 1 March 2021. Vimeo video, 1:07, available at https://vimeo.com/518249300

Notes

1 Those missing from the seventy-five productions (2006–2020) listed in Appendix 1 are: *Dreams That Money Can Buy* (2005), *The Big Lebowski* (2006), *The Matrix* (2006), *Eraserhead* (2008), *All Tomorrow's Parties* (2009), *Precious* (2010), *Blade Runner* (2010), *Blue Velvet* (2010) and *Victoria* (2016).
2 All URLs listed here were accessed 13 December 2021.

Filmography

Alien (1979, dir. Ridley Scott)
All Tomorrow's Parties (2009, dir. Jonathan Caouette)
Amy (2015, dir. Asif Kapadia)
Anvil! The Story of Anvil (2008, dir. Sacha Gervasi)
Arcane: League of Legends (TV series, 2021–, creators: Christian Linke and Alex Yee)
Back to the Future (1985, dir. Robert Zemeckis)
Back to the Future II (1989, dir. Robert Zemeckis)
Back to the Future III (1990, dir. Robert Zemeckis)
Battle of Algiers, The (1966, dir. Gillo Pontecorvo)
Big Lebowski, The (1998, dirs Joel Coen and Ethan Coen)
Black Cat, White Cat (1998, dir. Emir Kusturica)
Blade Runner (1982, dir. Ridley Scott)
Blade Runner: Black Out 2022 (2017, dir. Shinichirō Watanabe)
Blade Runner 2049 (2017, dir. Denis Villeneuve)
Blow Up (1966, dir. Michelangelo Antonioni)
Blue Velvet (1986, dir. David Lynch)
Blues Brothers, The (1980, dir. John Landis)
Brazil (1985, dir. Terry Gilliam)
Bridgerton (TV series, 2020–, creator: Chris Van Dusen)
Brief Encounter (1945, dir. David Lean)
Bugsy Malone (1976, dir. Alan Parker)
Casablanca (1942, dir. Michael Curtiz)
Casino Royale (2006, dir. Martin Campbell)
Dead Poets Society (1989, dir. Peter Weir)
Dirty Dancing (1987, dir. Emile Ardolino)
Diva (1981, dir. Jean-Jacques Beineix)
Dr Strangelove or: How I Learned to Stop Worrying and Love the Bomb (1964, dir. Stanley Kubrick)

Dreams That Money Can Buy (1947, dir. Hans Richter)
The Empire Strikes Back (1980, dir. Irvin Kershner)
Eraserhead (1977, dir. David Lynch)
Ferris Bueller's Day Off (1986, dir. John Hughes)
Footloose (1984, dir. Herbert Ross)
Funny Face (1957, dir. Stanley Donen)
Ghostbusters (1984, dir. Ivan Reitman)
Grand Budapest Hotel, The (2014, dir. Wes Anderson)
Grease (1978, dir. Randal Kleiser)
Great Dictator, The (1940, dir. Charles Chaplin)
Harder They Come, The (1972, dir. Perry Henzell)
I, Daniel Blake (2016, dirs Ken Loach and Laura Obiols)
If (1968, dir. Lindsay Anderson)
Imposter, The (2012, dir. Bart Layton)
Interview, The (2014, dirs Evan Goldberg and Seth Rogen)
Kill Bill: Vol. 1 (2003, dir. Quentin Tarantino)
La Haine (1995, dir. Mathieu Kassovitz)
Lawrence of Arabia (1962, dir. David Lean)
Lost Boys, The (1987, dir. Joel Schumacher)
Lost in Vagueness (2017, dir. Sofia Olins)
The Matrix (1999, dirs Lana Wachowski and Lilly Wachowski)
Metropolis (1927, dir. Fritz Lang)
Miller's Crossing (1991, dirs Joel Coen and Ethan Coen)
Moulin Rouge! (2001, dir. Baz Luhrmann)
Night at the Opera, A (1935, dirs Sam Wood and Edmund Goulding)
Nosferatu (1922, dir. F.W. Murnau)
One Flew Over the Cuckoo's Nest (1975, dir. Milos Forman)
Paranoid Park (2007, dir. Gus Van Sant)
Precious (2009, dir. Lee Daniels)
Prometheus (2012, dir. Ridley Scott).
Red Shoes, The (1948, dirs Michael Powell and Emeric Pressburger)
RocknRolla (2008, dir. Guy Ritchie)
Romeo + Juliet (1996, dir. Baz Luhrmann)
Saturday Night Fever (1977, dir. John Badham)
Searching for Sugar Man (2012, dir. Malik Bendjelloul)
Shawshank Redemption, The (1994, dir. Frank Darabont)
Sounds like Teen Spirit? (2008, dir. Jamie Jay Johnson)
Stranger Things (TV series, 2016–, creators: Matt Duffer and Ross Duffer)
Third Man, The (1949, dir. Carol Reed)
Top Gun (1986, dir. Tony Scott)
28 Days Later (2002, dir. Danny Boyle)
Victoria (2015, dir. Sebastian Schipper)

Warriors, The (1979, dir. Walter Hill)
Watchmen (2009, dir. Zack Snyder)
Who Framed Roger Rabbit? (1988, dirs Robert Zemeckis and Richard Williams)
Wings of Desire (1987, dir. Wim Wenders)

Bibliography

All in London, 'Dream of elephants', All in London, 1 September 2006, available at www.allinlondon.co.uk/whats-on/event-9433-dream-of-elephants.

All in London, 'Join the new Milk Tray Man on his first official mission', All in London, 5 October 2016, available at www.allinlondon.co.uk/whats-on/event-188616-join-the-new-milk-tray-man-on-his-first-official-mission.

Aftab, Kaleem, 'Secret Cinema's Fabien Riggall on *Star Wars*, cancellations, and building galaxies', *The Independent*, 2 June 2015, available at www.independent.co.uk/arts-entertainment/films/features/secret-cinema-s-fabien-riggall-star-wars-cancellations-and-building-galaxies-10292798.html.

Alston, Adam, *Beyond immersive theatre* (London: Palgrave Macmillan, 2016).

Antus, Madison, 'Secret Cinema X review: *Amy*', *Screen Daily*, 29 June 2015, available at www.screendaily.com/secret-cinema-x-review-amy/5089915.article.

Arabian Business, 'Global giant keen to swoop if Saudi Arabia lifts cinema ban', *Arabian Business*, 16 November 2017, available at www.arabianbusiness.com/saudi-arabia/culture-society/383726-global-giant-keen-to-swoop-if-saudi-arabia-lifts-cinema-ban.

Arrigo, Yasmin, 'Secret Cinema's Fabien Riggall on a decade of creating new worlds', *Campaign*, 26 March 2018, available at www.campaignlive.co.uk/article/secret-cinemas-fabien-riggall-decade-creating-new-worlds/1460405.

Arts Council England, 'Cultural Recovery Fund: data', 19 November 2021, available at www.artscouncil.org.uk/publication/culture-recovery-fund-data.

Atkinson, Sarah, *Beyond the screen: emerging cinema and engaging audiences* (New York: Bloomsbury, 2014).

Atkinson, Sarah, 'Hangmen rehanged – fusing event cinema, live cinema and sensory cinema in the evolution of site and screen responsive theatre', in *Live cinema: cultures, economies, aesthetics*, eds Sarah Atkinson and H. W. Kennedy (New York: Bloomsbury, 2017), 243–64.

Atkinson, Sarah, *From film practice to data process: production aesthetics and representational practices of a film industry in transition* (Edinburgh: Edinburgh University Press, 2018).

Atkinson, Sarah, 'Synchronic simulacinematics: the live performance of film production', in *Image action space: situating the screen in visual practice*, eds Luisa Feiersinger, K. Friedrich and M. Queisner (Berlin: De Gruyter, 2018), 191–202.

Atkinson, Sarah, 'Cinema remixed 4.0 – the rescoring, remixing and live performance of film soundtracks', in *The Routledge handbook of remix studies and digital humanities*, eds E. Eduardo Navas, O. Gallagher and X. Burrough (London: Routledge, 2021), 443–55.

Atkinson, Sarah and Helen W. Kennedy (2015a), 'Tell no one: cinema as game-space – audience participation, performance and play', *G|A|M|E: The Italian Journal of Game Studies* (2015) 5, 49–61.

Atkinson, Sarah and Helen W. Kennedy (2015b), '"Where we're going, we don't need an effective online audience engagement strategy": the case of the Secret Cinema viral backlash', *Frames Cinema Journal* (2015), 1–24.

Atkinson, Sarah and Helen W. Kennedy, 'Introduction – inside-the-scenes: the rise of experiential cinema', *Participations: Journal of Audience and Reception Studies* (2016) 13(1), 139–51.

Atkinson, Sarah and Helen W. Kennedy, 'From conflict to revolution: the secret aesthetic, narrative spatialisation and audience experience in immersive cinema design', *Participations: Journal of Audience and Reception Studies* (2016) 13(1), 252–79.

Atkinson, Sarah and Helen. W. Kennedy, 'Disney teams up with Secret Cinema – watching movies will never be the same again', *The Conversation*, 28 February 2020.

Atkinson, Sarah and Helen W. Kennedy, 'The immersive cinema experience economy: the UK film industry's third sector', in *The Routledge companion to media industries*, ed. Paul McDonald (London: Routledge, 2022), 392–403.

Attwood, Miriam, 'Swamp Motel's original mystery thriller IP, *The Isklander Trilogy* optioned by Gaumont UK', *Storytelling PR*, 17 August 2021, available at https://storytellingpr.com/swamp-motel-isklander-trilogy-optioned-by-gaumont-uk/.

Auckland Theatre Company, 'Chekhov's *The Seagull*', Auckland Theatre Company, 8 May 2020, available at www.atc.co.nz/auckland-theatre-company/2020/chekhovs-the-seagull/.

Austin, Bruce A., 'Portrait of a cult film audience: *The Rocky Horror Picture Show*', *Journal of Communication* (1981) 31(2), 43–54.

Austin, Emma, 'Zombie culture: dissent, celebration and the carnivalesque in social spaces', in *The zombie renaissance in popular culture*, eds Laura Hubner, Marcus Leaning and Paul Manning (London: Palgrave Macmillan, 2015), 174–90.

Bartholomew, Emma, 'Future Cinema offers out Hackney space used for Secret Cinema concept as a pop-up community centre', *Hackney Gazette*, 20 March 2013, available at www.hackneygazette.co.uk/news/future-cinema-offers-out-hackney-space-used-for-secret-cinema-3441438.

Batchelor, James, 'Bringing League of Legends to life: Secret Cinema's first games experience', *Games Industry Biz*, 9 November 2021, available at www.gamesindustry.biz/articles/2021-11-09-bringing-league-of-legends-to-life-secret-cinemas-first-games-experience.

Bennett, Andy, 'Subcultures or neo-tribes: rethinking the relationship between youth, style and musical taste', *Sociology* (1999) 33, 599–614.

Bille, Trine and Mark Lorenzen, *Den Danske Plevelsesøkonomi: Afgrænsning, Økonomisk Betydning og Vækstmuligheder* (Copenhagen: Forlaget Samfundslitteratur, 2008).

BWW News Desk, '*Miller's Crossing* completes run at Crouch End with Secret Cinema's *Tell No One*', *Broadway World*, 28 May 2014, available at www.broadwayworld.com/uk-regional/article/MILLERS-CROSSING-Completes-Run-at-Crouch-End-with-Secret-Cinemas-TELL-NO-ONE-20140528.

Brigante, Ricky, *Interactive, intimate, experiential: the impact of immersive design*, ed. Noah Nelson, with additional contributions by Kathryn Yu and Rachel Stoll (San Francisco: Immersive Design Summit, 2019).

Brigante, Ricky and Sarah A.S. Elger, *New adventures: the strength of immersive entertainment. 2020 immersive entertainment industry annual report*, ed. Noah Nelson (Los Angeles: HERE Institute, 2020).

Brooker, Will, *Using the force: creativity, community and Star Wars fans* (London: Bloomsbury Publishing, 2002).

Brooks, Lucy, 'Postponed: *Thunderbirds: beyond the horizon*, The Buzz at Mercato Metropolitano', *Culture Whisper*, 27 September 2018, available at www.culturewhisper.com/r/theatre/thunderbirds_beyond_the_horizon_the_buzz_at_mercato_metropolitano/11514.

Brown, Ally, 'Future Cinema presents: *All Tomorrow's Parties* premiere', *The Skinny*, 29 June 2009, available at www.theskinny.co.uk/music/live-music/reviews/future-cinema-presents-all-tomorrows-parties-premiere.

Burrows, Mark, 'Million-pound question: why save Secret Cinema while real cinemas are in ruins?' *The Guardian*, 14 October 2020, available at www.theguardian.com/film/2020/oct/14/secret-cinema-bailout-arts-venues.

Business Fast, 'Secret Cinema partners Sony for at-home *Ghostbusters* experience', *Business Fast*, 26 October 2021, available at www.businessfast.co.uk/secret-cinema-partners-sony-for-at-home-ghostbusters-experience/.

Carter, Oliver, 'A labour of love: fantrepreneurship in home video media distribution', in *DVD, Blu-ray and beyond*, eds Jonathan Wroot and Andy Willis (Cham: Palgrave Macmillan, 2017), 197–213.

Chapman, Catherine, 'Kubrick's *Dr Strangelove* meets immersive theater in London. Or: "How I learned to stop worrying and love the Secret Cinema"', *Vice*, 21 March 2016, available at www.vice.com/en/article/4xqpmm/dr-strangelove-secret-cinema-london.

Cheshire, Tom, 'The screen saver: Secret Cinema's mission to save the movies', *Wired*, 4 June 2013, available at www.wired.co.uk/article/the-screen-saver.

Clayton, Richard, 'Laura Marling, Secret Cinema, London – review', *Financial Times*, 19 June 2013, available at www.ft.com/content/f54ebc90-d8c5-11e2-84fa-00144feab7de.

Collage Arts, 'Wonder Works interview', *Collage Arts*, 11 July 2016, available at www.collage-arts.org/wonder-works-interview/.

Convenience Store, 'Asahi hosts "Remastered by Japan" campaign', *Convenience Store*, 30 April 2018, available at www.conveniencestore.co.uk/products/asahi-hosts-remastered-by-japan-campaign/566411.article.

Denham, Jess, 'Secret Cinema denies using unpaid workers after criticism following *Star Wars* £75 ticket sales', *The Independent*, 19 March 2015, available at www.independent.co.uk/arts-entertainment/films/news/secret-cinema-criticised-using-unpaid-workers-star-wars-despite-higher-ticket-price-10118869.html.

Dick, Philip K., *Do androids dream of electric sheep?* (New York: Doubleday, 1968).
Douglas, Fayola, 'Secret Cinema takes cars to Upside Down for *Stranger Things* "drive-into" experience', *Campaign*, 21 August 2020, available at www.campaignlive.co.uk/article/secret-cinema-takes-cars-upside-down-stranger-things-drive-into-experience/1692414.
Dyson, Calvin, 'Secret Cinema *Casino Royale* experience and review', 17 July 2019, Youtube video, 13:39, available at www.youtube.com/watch?v=YSKqXiCZjAM&t=3s.
Electronic Beats, 'We saw Jeff Mills score the sci-fi classic *Metropolis*', *Electronic Beats*, 25 August 2017, available at www.electronicbeats.net/the-feed/saw-jeff-mills-score-sci-fi-classic-metropolis/.
Farmer, Lucy, 'Secret Cinema has fun in the dark, a creative concept that has people buying tickets to an undisclosed film in an undisclosed location', *The Economist 1843 Magazine*, 11 May 2011, available at www.1843magazine.com/content/arts/lucy-farmer/fun-dark.
Future of StoryTelling, 'Bringing film to life: Fabien Riggall (Future of Storytelling 2013)', 3 October 2013, YouTube video, 4:01, available at www.youtube.com/watch?v=rK78mBx52sM.
Future Shorts, 'Fyfe Dangerfield, lead singer of Guillemots and creator of Secret Cinema Fabien Riggall talk about the Future Cinema live rescore event of David Lynch's *Eraserhead* back in 2007', 21 April 2020, YouTube video, 4:46, available at www.youtube.com/watch?v=JmA16lYt0ms.
Galloway, Ian and Salvador Bettencourt Ávila, 'Immersive experiences: Mesmer Studios, a webinar', *Disguise*, 11 August 2021, video, 1:20:48, available at www.disguise.one/en/insights/webinars/immersive-experiences/.
Gant, Charles, 'Secret Cinema chiefs talk global ambitions, management changes and *Casino Royale*', *Screen Daily*, 30 January 2019, available at www.screendaily.com/features/secret-cinema-chiefs-talk-global-ambitions-management-changes-and-casino-royale/5136312.article.
Giddings, Seth and Helen Kennedy, 'Little Jesuses and*@#?-off robots: on cybernetics, aesthetics, and not being very good at Lego *Star Wars*', in *The pleasures of computer gaming: essays on cultural history, theory and aesthetics*, eds Melanie Swalwell and Jason Wilson (Jefferson, NC: McFarland, 2008), 13–32.
Goldstone, Eli, 'Q&A: SC founder Fabien Riggall talks cultural activism', Run Riot, 29 August 2016, available at www.run-riot.com/articles/blogs/qa-secret-cinema-founder-fabien-riggall-talks-cultural-activism.
Grainge, Paul, 'A song and dance: branded entertainment and mobile promotion', *International Journal of Cultural Studies* (2012) 15(2), 165–80.
Green, Tim, 'Stella Artois film festival, 22–3 July 2006 – Greenwich Park London', *Contact Music*, 17 July 2006, available at www.contactmusic.com/music/stellaartoisfilmfestivalx17x07x06.
Gunning, Tom, 'The cinema of attraction[s]: early film, its spectator and the avant-garde', *The Animation Studies Reader* (1986): 17–27.
Hancock, Alice, 'Secret Cinema partners with Netflix for first US screening', *Financial Times*, 26 August 2020, available at www.ft.com/content/5790f238-15a4-4f72-858f-b44eb9d97ef8.

Harris, Ella, 'Navigating pop-up geographies: urban space–times of flexibility, interstitiality and immersion', *Geography Compass* (2015) 9(11), 592–603.

Harris, Ella, *Rebranding precarity: pop-up culture as the seductive new normal* (New York: Bloomsbury, 2020).

Hastings, Rob, 'Secret Cinema gets the MI6 treatment with James Bond experience in *Casino Royale*', *i news*, 14 June 2019, available at https://inews.co.uk/culture/film/secret-cinema-casino-royale-james-bond-302049.

Heap, Tim, 'Review: Baz Luhrmann's *Romeo + Juliet* gets the Secret Cinema treatment', *Attitude*, 8 October 2018, available at https://attitude.co.uk/article/review-baz-luhrmanns-romeo-juliet-gets-the-secret-cinema-treatment/18778/.

Heritage, Stuart, '*28 Days Later* at Secret Cinema: a bloodthirsty attack on the wallet', *The Guardian*, 15 April 2016, available at www.theguardian.com/film/filmblog/2016/apr/15/28-days-later-secret-cinema-bloodthirsty-attack-wallet.

Hills, Matt, *Fan cultures* (London: Routledge, 2002).

Hills, Matt, 'From fan culture/community to the fan world: possible pathways and ways of having done fandom', *Palabra Clave* (2017) 20(4), 856–83.

Homfray, Alex, Douglas Lonie and Joshua Dedman, *Changing the scene: the impact of a Secret Cinema residency* (London: BOP Consulting, 2017).

Horkheimer, Max and Theodor W. Adorno, 'The culture industry: enlightenment as mass deception', in Horkheimer and Adorno, *Dialectic of enlightenment* (Palo Alto, CA: Stanford University Press, 2020), 94–136.

Immerse UK and Digital Catapult, *The immersive economy in the UK report 2019: the growth of the virtual, augmented and mixed reality technologies ecosystem* (London: Immerse UK/Digital Catapult, 2019), available at www.immerseuk.org/wp-content/uploads/2019/11/The-Immersive-Economy-in-the-UK-Report-2019.pdf.

Kennedy, Helen W. 'Funfear attractions: the playful affects of carefully managed terror in immersive *28 Days Later* live experiences', in *Live cinema cultures, economies, aesthetics*, eds Sarah Atkinson and Helen W. Kennedy (New York: Bloomsbury, 2017), 167–84.

Kennedy, Helen W. '"Join a cast of 1000s, to sing and dance in the Revolution": the Secret Cinema "Activist" brand and the commodification of affect within experience communities', *Participations* (2017) 14(2), 682–96.

Klinger, Barbara, 'Once is not enough: the functions and pleasures of repeat viewings', in Klinger, *Beyond the multiplex: cinema, new technologies, and the home* (Berkeley and Los Angeles: University of California Press, 2006), pp. 135–190.

Klinger, Barbara, 'Say it again, Sam: movie quotation, performance, and masculinity', *Participations* (2008) 5(2).

Klinger, Barbara, 'Re-enactment: fans performing movie scenes from the stage to YouTube', in *Ephemeral media: Transitory screen culture from television to YouTube*, ed. Paul Grainge (New York: Bloomsbury Publishing, 2017), 195–213.

Kofler, Andreas, '*The Grand Budapest Hotel* poster and props', *Fonts in Use*, 22 June 2014, available at https://fontsinuse.com/uses/7035/the-grand-budapest-hotel-poster-and-props.

Lamerichs, Nicolle, 'Costuming as subculture: the multiple bodies of cosplay', *Scene* (2014) 2(1–2), 123.

Lee, Benjamin, 'Secret Cinema: *The Empire Strikes Back* review – the force is weak with this one', *The Guardian*, 12 June 2015, available at www.theguardian.com/film/2015/jun/12/secret-cinema-the-empire-strikes-back-review-the-force-is-weak-with-this-one.

London City Nights, 'Ghetts at the Barbican Centre, Secret Cinema's secret gig', *London City Nights*, 9 March 2014, available at www.londoncitynights.com/2014/03/ghetts-at-barbican-centre-secret.html.

Londonist, 'Secret Cinema's *28 Days Later* lacks bite', *Londonist*, 20 April 2016, available at https://londonist.com/2016/04/secret-cinema-s-28-days-later-lacks-bite.

Machon, Josephine, *Immersive theatres: intimacy and immediacy in contemporary performance* (London, Macmillan, 2013).

Machon, Josephine and Stephen Dobbie, *The Punchdrunk encyclopaedia* (London: Routledge, 2018).

Mansell, Robin and W.E. Steinmueller, 'Denaturalizing digital platforms: is mass individualization here to stay?' *International Journal of Communication*, 2022. ISSN 1932–8036. In press; available at http://eprints.lse.ac.uk/105619/.

McGonigal, Jane, 'SuperGaming: ubiquitous play and performance for massively scaled community', *Modern Drama* (2005) 48(3), 471–91.

McRuvie, Sarah, 'Future Cinema present *Saturday Night Fever*', *Clash*, 14 June 2013, available at www.clashmusic.com/live/future-cinema-present-saturday-night-fever.

Moorman, Christine, 'Commentary: brand activism in a political world', *Journal of Public Policy & Marketing* (2020) 39(4), 388–92.

Moreton, Cole, 'The future of Britain's best gig: the lost spirit of Glastonbury', *The Independent*, 3 February 2008, available at www.independent.co.uk/arts-entertainment/music/features/the-future-of-britain-s-best-gig-the-lost-spirit-of-glastonbury-777547.html.

New Musical Express, 'Lost Vagueness organiser leaves Glastonbury festival: popular field set for revamp in 2008', *NME*, 4 February 2008, available at www.nme.com/news/music/glastonbury-239-1331769.

Nissim, Mayer, 'Secret Cinema teases special "expeditions" on new website: recruits are urged to attend for physical condition and training', *Digital Spy*, 23 May 2012, available at www.digitalspy.com/movies/a383140/secret-cinema-teases-special-expeditions-on-new-website/.

Ndalianis, Angela, *The horror sensorium: media and the senses* (Jefferson, NC: McFarland, 2012).

O'Hara, Meghan, 'Experience economies: immersion, disposability, and Punchdrunk theatre', *Contemporary Theatre Review* (2017) 27(4), 481–96.

O'Neill, Shane, 'First Windows Phone 7 ad: a revolution in the desert?' *CIO*, 7 September 2010, available at www.cio.com/article/2372522/first-windows-phone-7-ad--a-revolution-in-the-desert-.html.

Pearce, Celia, 'Narrative environments', *Space Time Play* (2007), 200–205.

Pett, Emma, *Experiencing cinema: participatory film cultures, immersive media and the experience economy* (New York: Bloomsbury Publishing, 2021).

Pine, B. Joseph and James Gilmore, 'Welcome to the experience economy', *Harvard Business Review* (1998) July-August, 98–105.

Pollock, David, 'Secret Cinema in Calais: "We can offer a break from the constant reality of living in tents"', *The Guardian*, 11 September 2015, available at www.theguardian.com/film/2015/sep/11/secret-cinema-in-calais-jungle-fabien-riggal-secretprotest.

Potton, Ed, 'The true spirits of cinema are kept secret', *The Times*, 17 January 2009, available at www.thetimes.co.uk/article/the-true-spirits-of-cinema-are-kept-secret-9q0vrg3ltm6.

Rabinovitz, Lauren, 'More than the movies: a history of somatic visual culture through Hale's Tours, IMAX, and motion simulation rides', in *Memory bytes: history, technology, and digital culture*, eds Lauren Rabinovitz and Abraham Geil (Durham, NC: Duke University Press, 2004), 99–125.

Raising Films, *How we work now: learning from the impact of COVID-19 to build an industry that works for parents and carers* (London: Raising Films, 2021).

Rata, Elizabeth, *A political economy of neotribal capitalism* (Lanham, MD: Lexington Books, 2000).

Riggall, Fabien, 'TedxYouth@Bath 2012: Fabien Riggall secretyouth', Tedxyouthbath, 16 December 2012, YouTube video, 14:53, available at www.youtube.com/watch?v=Xyn65QXhZ-U.

Riggall, Fabien, 'Beauty in the making (the senses)', It's Nice That, 29 July 2015, YouTube video, 24:39, available at www.youtube.com/watch?v=AsozWGEZXlI.

Riggall, Fabien, 'Pioneering Secret Cinema's chief creative officer & founder Fabien Riggall', interview by Mishcon de Reya, *Jazz Shapers*, 15 May 2021, audio, 24:34, available at https://planetradio.co.uk/podcasts/jazz-shapers/listen/2044931/.

Riggall, Fabien, 'Fabien Riggall and Secret Cinema', interview by Etan Ilfeld, The Etan Ilfeld Podcast, 14 July 2021, audio, 49:11, available at https://anchor.fm/etan-ilfeld/episodes/Fabien-Riggall-and-Secret-Cinema-e14cit3.

Rihova, Ivana, Dimitrios Buhalis, Miguel Moital and Mary-Beth Gouthro, 'Social constructions of value: marketing considerations for the context of event and festival visitation', *Ideological, social and cultural aspects of events* (2015), 74–85.

Rosser, Michael, 'Secret Cinema: *The Empire Strikes Back* review', *Screen Daily*, 12 June 2015, available at www.screendaily.com/news/secret-cinema-the-empire-strikes-back-review/5089352.article.

Screen Daily, 'Secret Cinema founder Fabien Riggall on future of cinema', 19 September 2014, available at www.screendaily.com/comment/secret-cinema-founder-on-future-of-cinema/5077742.article.

Secret Cinema, 'On the road to Kabul part II – Asian Dub Foundation', Secret Cinema presents, 4 September 2012, Vimeo video, 1:28, available at https://vimeo.com/48791234.

Secret Cinema, 'Secret Cinema on Sky Movies', 17 March 2008, YouTube video, 5:24, available at www.youtube.com/watch?v=QPaLhQAHGZ4&t=133s.

Secret Cinema, 'Secret Cinema – highlights reel of Secret's history and our future plans', Crowdcube, 24 May 2021, video, 5:11, available at www.crowdcube.com/companies/secret-cinema/pitches/qD0gEq.

Selavy, Virginie, 'Making cinema magical again: SC launch', 9 January 2008, available at www.electricsheepmagazine.co.uk/2008/01/09/making-cinema-magical-again-secret-cinema-launch/.

Simons, Ilja, 'Events and online interaction: the construction of hybrid event communities', *Leisure Studies* (2019) 38(2), 145–59.
Theatre Weekly, 'Factory 42 with Almeida Theatre & Sky present *Lost Origin* a unique, immersive & interactive adventure', *Theatre Weekly*, 20 October 2021, available at https://theatreweekly.com/factory-42-with-almeida-theatre-sky-present-lost-origin-a-unique-immersive-interactive-adventure/.
Time Out Editors, 'Time In Awards: the winners', *Time Out*, 8 July 2020, available at www.timeout.com/london/things-to-do/time-in-awards-the-winners.
Times, The, 'Win tickets to UK's first outdoor film festival', *The Times*, 10 July 2006, available at www.thetimes.co.uk/article/win-tickets-to-uks-first-outdoor-film-festival-fmmrfjq50w3.
Toulmin, Vanessa, 'Telling the tale. The story of the fairground bioscope shows and the showmen who operated them', *Film History* (1994) 6(2), 219–37.
Travers, Ben, '*Westworld* comes to life at SXSW: photos of Sweetwater, Samurai, and more from the HBO experience', IndieWire, 9 March 2018, available at www.indiewire.com/gallery/westworld-sxsw-photos-hbo-town-sweetwater/.
UK Research and Innovation, 'Audience of the future challenge', *UKRI*, 24 May 2021, available at www.ukri.org/our-work/our-main-funds/industrial-strategy-challenge-fund/artificial-intelligence-and-data-economy/audience-of-the-future-challenge/.
Vélez-Serna, Maria, *Ephemeral cinema spaces* (Amsterdam: Amsterdam University Press, 2020).
Walters, Ben, 'Hopper mad: *Blue Velvet* screening prompts Lynchian tributes to Dennis', *The Guardian*, 4 August 2010, available at www.theguardian.com/film/filmblog/2010/aug/04/dennis-hopper-blue-velvet-screening.
Wasko, Janet, Mark Phillips and Chris Purdie, 'Hollywood meets Madison Avenue: the commercialization of US films', *Media, Culture & Society* (1993) 15(2), 271–93.
Westall, Mark, 'Secret Cinema presents a secret cultural protest', *Fad Magazine*, 8 September 2015, available at https://fadmagazine.com/2015/09/08/secret-cinema-presents-a-secret-cultural-protest-loverefugees-to-stand-in-solidarity-with-refugees-worldwide/.
Westling, Carina. E. *Immersion and participation in Punchdrunk's theatrical worlds* (New York: Bloomsbury Publishing, 2020).
Williams, Rebecca, *Theme park fandom: spatial transmedia, materiality and participatory cultures* (Amsterdam: Amsterdam University Press, 2020).
Wilson, Dougal, 'Dougal Wilson reports on Secret Cinema's "Secret Protest" at the Calais Jungle camp', *Creative Review*, 19 September 2015, available at www.creativereview.co.uk/dougal-wilson-reports-on-secret-cinemas-secret-protest-at-the-calais-jungle-camp/.
Wreyford, Natalie, David O'Brien and Tamsyn Dent, *Creative majority: an APPG for Creative Diversity report on 'What Works' to support, encourage and improve diversity, equity and inclusion in the creative sector*, report for the All-Party Parliamentary Group for Creative Diversity (London: The Stationery Office, 2021).
Wreyford, Natalie, Helen W. Kennedy, Jack Newsinger and Rowan Aust, *Locked down and locked out: the impact of the COVID-19 pandemic on mothers working in the UK television industry* (Nottingham: University of Nottingham, 2021).

Wright, Steve, 'Secret Cinema *Star Wars: The Empire Strikes Back* review', *SciFi Now*, 6 July 2015, available at www.scifinow.co.uk/blog/secret-cinema-star-wars-the-empire-strikes-back-review/.

Yossman, K.J., 'As Secret Cinema launches crowdfunding initiative, is its business model working?' *Variety*, 7 June 2021, available at https://variety.com/2021/tv/news/secret-cinema-crowdfunding-business-model-1234987811/.

Zika, Joel, 'Dark rides and the evolution of immersive media', *Journal of Themed Experience and Attractions Studies* (2018) 1(1), 54.

Index

action vehicles 15, 28, 30, 33, 34, 48, 53, 62, 82, 85, 86, 162
   definition 58 n.26
activism 14, 74, 91, 95, 102, 106, 128, 174
   cultural 104
   immersive 13, 14–15, 9–129
   youth 119
   see also brand activism, audience as activists
activist entrepreneurship 105
advertising 3, 6, 39, 123, 125–126, 147
   agencies 6, 7, 47, 137
aerial
   performance 36, 62, 65, 77, 85, 117, 158, 161
      Brazil 65
   stunts 82, 86, 88, 126, 162
aerialist 65, 117, 149
Alexander, Max 17, 21 n.34, 128, 135, 144, 210–211, 218, 224
Alexandra Palace 39, 98, 175
Alien 19, n.3, 33, 34–35, 41, 50, 52
All Tomorrow's Parties 32
Alternate Reality Games (ARGs) 9, 10, 14, 51, 62, 110, 122
Amy 75
Anvil! The Story of Anvil 30, 35
Arcane: Enter the Undercity 214, 217
Arkham Asylum 214
art
   alternative practice 9
   department 139
   director 153, 155

Arts Council England (ACE) 17
   pandemic cultural recovery programme 17, 21 n.36, 209–210
Asian Dub Foundation (ADF) 28, 45, 48
audience 16, 172–204
   as activists 96, 106, 114–117, 119, 172, 211
   as extras 40
   control 30, 39, 150–151
      house rules 71
   costuming 33–34
   experiential journey 62
   generated content 148
   instructions 37, 67, 76, 85
   flow 33, 100
   labour 198–199
   missions 50, 111, 148, 150, 166, 183, 184, 186, 191, 192, 197
   participation, embodied 7
   reactions 32
   transportation (in-vehicle) 41, 48
   simulated 76
Augmented Reality (AR) 3, 8

Back to the Future (BttF) 14, 72, 73, 74, 78–79, 80–89, 90, 96, 102, 113, 175, 176, 179, 182, 183, 192, 200, 201
ballyhoo 7
Battle of Algiers, The 44–45, 80, 105, 119
Big Lebowski, The 24
Black Cat, White Cat 28

Blade Runner 19 n.3, 36–37, 38, 52, 76, 80, 95, 120, 121–127, 143, 179, 184, 191, 201, 217
Blow Up 38
Blue Velvet 38
Boomtown 9
box office
  success 1, 50, 91
  takings 1, 17, 75, 91, 97, 106, 108, 114, 115, 121, 127, 134, 147
brand
  activations 6, 42, 96
    experience led 6
  activism 15, 96, 113
  alignment 29
  development 12, 119
  embedded branding 15, 33, 39, 40, 41–42, 52, 75, 82, 91, 96, 110, 118, 120, 123–126
    in set design 125
  partnerships 30, 47
  political activism 105
  screen installation 35
  vision 13
  work-for-hire 125
Brazil 14, 62, 63–66, 67, 71, 80, 83, 175
Bridgerton 211–212, 216, 224
Brief Encounter 47
Bugsy Malone 19 n.3, 28, 34, 35–36, 37, 50, 72, 73, 85, 175

cabaret 9, 26, 54
  dark 23, 24–25
cancellations 65, 74, 82, 83, 84
Casablanca 54, 61
Casino Royale 1, 15, 109, 134, 135, 143, 144, 147, 148, 149–150, 155–157, 162, 166–167, 179, 180, 182, 184, 191–192, 193–194, 197, 206, 207
  Shanghai 166–167
Chamber of Horrors 10
Chameleon Collective 27, 28
charities 32, 38, 74, 75, 98, 103, 106, 113, 115

cinema
  early history 7
  early pleasures 8
  exhibition 7, 8, 12, 24, 225
  3D 51
cinephilia 8, 26, 34, 85, 172
cosplay 16, 176–183, 188
  capturing 181–183
costume
  audience in 41
  department 139, 151–152
  design 109
    immersive environments 151
  designer 81, 152
  instructions 29, 30, 31, 40, 47, 54, 67, 68–69, 71, 74, 77, 79, 81, 127
    gendered 77
  kits 108, 109
  periodicity 200
  visual storytelling 200
COVID-19
  during 206–210
  impacts of 4, 114, 205, 216
  prior to 17
credit listings 17, 26, 72, 141
crowdfunding 17, 210–211
cultural capital 188
cultural entrepreneurship 110
Crystal Maze, The 4, 19 n.12
  Live game 4, 10, 19 n.11

dance-along 85, 89
Dead Poet's Society 74
Dirty Dancing 18, n.1, 18 n3, 63, 68, 114, 117, 127, 184, 195, 201, 208, 222
Disney 1, 2, 101, 223
  Land 205
  partnership 206, 225
Diva 43
DJ Yoda 2, 98
documentary films 31–32, 35, 75
Dreams Money Can Buy 24
Dr Strangelove or: How I Learned to Stop Worrying and Love the Bomb 95, 106–108, 110, 119, 120
Dr Who Time Fracture 12, 212, 214, 221

early adopters 16, 174–175
Eclectic Method 25
email instructions 30, 31, 40, 44, 70, 71, 107, 118, 148
Empire Strikes Back, The 95, 97–103, 106, 108, 110, 111, 113–114, 120, 143, 175, 216, 223
Equity 19 n.14, 141, 148
Eraserhead 27–28
Escape Rooms 4, 10
event-led distribution 26, 28, 30, 222
experience
  communities 16, 32, 172–204
  design 12, 15, 26, 32, 37, 40, 41, 88, 149
    principles 14, 61
  economy 2, 4, 19 n4
experiential 6, 20 n.15
  aesthetics 61
  dining sector 36 (*see also* food themed providers)
  events 6

Facebook 11, 37, 42, 43, 44, 45, 46, 50, 70, 80, 175, 183, 185, 188, 189, 193, 197, 211
fairground
  and Circus Archive project 20 n.17
  attractions 7, 8
  moving pictures at 7
fans 11, 78, 122, 136, 154
  established fan communities 176–185
  fantrepreneurship 195
  practices 177 (*see also* cosplay)
  Secret Cinema 72
  superfan communities 185–197 (*see also* PPSC)
fan studies 11
festivals 6, 8–9, 11, 13, 22, 23–26, 33, 56, 61, 214
  infrastructure 12, 15
  music 8, 11, 27–28, 29
film industry 15, 91, 140
film promotion 29, 31
  re-release 29, 30
film set 107
  aesthetic 84
  designers 140

flash mobs 14, 42, 50–51, 61, 81–82, 99, 109, 127, 175
  definition 59 n.45
food 4
  catering 12, 139
  curated 34, 41
  fine dining 55, 67
  menu 36
  prohibition 91
  themed 10, 39, 84, 91, 122, 123
    providers 4, 36 (*see also* immersive dining)
food, beverage and merchandise 155
  department 139
Footloose 92 n. 11
Front of house 16
  department 139, 162–164
Funny Face 27
Future Cinema (FC) 11, 13, 17, 22, 23, 24, 25, 26, 27, 28, 30, 32, 38, 41, 45, 48, 50, 52, 54, 68, 69, 173
Future Shorts (Ltd.) 11, 17, 22, 24

game/s 4
  aesthetics 11
  -based immersive experiences 214
  design 217, 218
    spatialised 15, 156
  influence of 62, 65, 184, 206
  mechanics 11, 108, 111, 156, 166
    currency exchange 51
    easter egg 126, 154
      definition 133 n.79
  studies 11
gamification 217
gangs 32, 77
  allocation to 33, 45, 67
gentrification 81
Ghostbusters 18, 30, 47, 61, 63, 68–69, 72, 73, 141, 207, 215–217, 219
  The Gates of Gozer 215
Glastonbury 8, 9, 23
Global Performance Director 16, 116, 156, 163, 207
Grand Budapest Hotel 14, 75–77
Grease 52

Great Dictator, The 74–75
Great Gatsby, The 4, 6

Hale's Tours 8, 20 n.21
Handmaiden, The 95, 118, 179–180
Harry Potter walk-through exhibition 10
health & safety
    department 139, 164
hero moment 44, 45, 47, 65, 85, 91 n.8, 126, 146, 150, 158, 162

I, Daniel Blake 118
If... 27, 35, 96
IMAX 8, 20 n. 21, 50
immersive 4, 6
  dining 4, 9
  experiences 6
    performance practice 221
  rhetoric of 43
  theatre 8, 214
Immerse UK 2, 3, 18 n.2, 19 n.7
Immersive Entertainment Network 221
immersive experience production model 137, 172
Immersive Gatsby 3, 4, 6, 12, 212
Immersive experience industry
  ecosystem 8, 205
    model (2019) 4, 5, 15
    model (2021) 212
  history 6–8
Imposter, The 31
Instagram 70, 80, 211
intellectual property (IP) 1, 16, 70, 76, 82
  owners 82, 138, 142–143
  negotiations 142–144
  rights 142
  tangential 82
in-world
  communications platform 80–81
  identities (IDs) 29, 43, 180, 121–122, 184, 187, 192
    assignation 40, 46, 49, 50, 54, 55, 63, 67, 68, 71, 77, 85, 126, 132, 147, 148, 177, 178, 179, 180
    cards 44, 67, 71, 108, 157, 180, 184

groupings 32, 71, 77, 85, 150
  (*see also* gangs, allocation to)
papers 39, 54, 55, 106
profiles 54, 115, 163
questionnaires 50, 64, 71, 126, 177, 179
microsites 11, 14, 42, 52, 54, 55, 61, 63, 64, 65, 67, 68, 69, 70–71, 72, 75, 76, 79, 80, 97, 102, 106, 108, 148, 164, 216
  access challenges 92 n. 18
  hidden URL links 70, 73, 216
news channels 36, 47, 71, 80, 102, 110, 112
  radio station 44, 80, 89, 90
  reporter 35, 36, 184
  stories 80, 124, 148
newspapers 39, 41, 46, 71–72, 73, 78

Kill Bill: Vol. I 25

La Haine 28, 48
Latitude festival 23, 28
Lawrence of Arabia 39, 40, 72, 140, 175
Les Enfants Terribles 3, 8, 214
license applications 65, 105
Light Surgeons 24
lighting 72, 84, 145
  automation 86, 100, 112, 157, 158
  cues 101, 158, 159, 160
  department 139, 157, 158, 214
  effects 33, 62, 85, 157, 162
  equipment 90, 100
  design 7, 12, 101, 102, 136, 152
  designer(s) 15, 57 n.15, 76, 101, 157, 158, 208
  stage management of 158, 159
lip syncing 69, 86 (*see also* mirror moments)
live cinema 24, 26, 62, 85, 91 n.1
  events 12
  experience 52, 61
  practitioners 25
  producers 25
  scoring 118

re-scoring 27, 28, 48
  Eraserhead 27
  screen augmentation 34
  sector 28
  VJing 26
liveness 54, 61–62, 80, 110
  simulated 14, 61, 62, 78, 89
lockdown party 206
Lost Boys, The 45
Lost Vagueness 8–9, 23, 24, 26
  documentary 21, n. 26
ludic pleasures 191–193

maps
  meeting points 73
  of site 84
  to venue 71, 73, 77
marketing 2, 6, 7, 12, 14, 42, 45, 47, 50, 61, 70, 81, 91, 125, 137, 144, 145, 157, 182, 183, 197, 200, 201, 216, 225
Marling, Laura 63, 65, 67
massification 16, 108, 136, 167
media partnerships 43
merchandise 12, 79, 91, 97, 98, 148
  accessories 180
  department 151, 163–164
  designer 98, 108
  online stores 79, 127, 147
  studio IP 82
Metropolis 25, 26, 72
  live score 57 n.13
military
  control 44
  experience design 55
  personnel 39
  themes 39, 46, 49
Miller's Crossing 73, 77–78
mirror moments 34, 36, 37, 41, 54, 62, 69, 78, 85, 86–87, 89, 101, 107, 112, 117, 118, 127, 128, 157, 162, 165
  dancing 117
mise-en-scène 26, 27, 76, 84
mobile phones 35, 52
  confiscation of 67, 69, 83–84
Money Heist 214–215
Monopoly Lifesized 12, 212, 222
Motion simulation rides 7, 8

Moulin Rouge! 95, 104, 115–118, 121, 126, 143, 165, 184, 200, 201, 207

narrative
  spatialisation 37, 45, 48, 55, 66, 72
  tracks 55, 64, 68, 126, 136, 146, 148, 149, 154, 156, 163, 184, 188, 192, 201
neo-tribes 32, 77, 174
Netflix 1, 135, 143, 147, 209, 211, 212, 214, 215, 217, 224, 226 n. 19
  Party 226 n.8
Night at the Opera, A 29
Nosferatu 24

One Flew Over the Cuckoo's Nest 39, 76
operations 12, 164–165
  department 139
Other Cinema, The 13, 22, 47, 48, 174

Paranoid Park 24, 26, 27, 28, 33
paratexts 11, 13, 76
participatory
  audience practices 8, 67
  elements 25, 29
  engagement 37
  protest 42
performance
  cast 69
  department 138
  design 12
  direction 12
    global 16
  director 148
  immersive 220
    continuum 220
performers 148–151
  dancers 149
  safeguarding 117, 221
    officer 221
  singers 149
pervasive games 14, 62
play 11, 150, 184, 191–193
pop-up 61
  circus 7
  culture 81
  launch event 98

Index

night club
  Secret Cantina 97
promotional activities 14
screening 104
shop(s) 67, 81, 97, 179
  Hill Valley Stores 80
  Rebel Stores 97
Positive People of Secret Cinema
  (PPSC) 16, 172, 176, 185,
  187–189, 191–197
  badges 195, 196
post-experience
  promotional social media 201
  promotional video 12, 21 n.33, 27,
    29, 30, 31, 32, 33, 35, 43,
    48, 49, 52, 54, 61, 65, 72,
    77–78, 89, 92, 107,
    112–113, 127, 158
post-ticket purchase 70–72, 199–200
Precious 38
pre-narrative
  engagement 12, 14, 44, 45, 50, 54,
    64, 67, 75, 97, 121
  flash mobs 51
  experiences 14, 41, 80
  producer 138, 146, 147–148
  writer(s) 121, 138, 146, 147–148
pre-screening
  narrative 37
  Q&A 32
  show 14
pre-ticket promotion 14, 67, 70
preview events 30
process
  adaptive 166
  automated 166
  immersive 166
  iterative 165
producing 12
production
  design 122, 152–155
    department 139
    spatial 155
  designer 82, 100, 116, 140
  management 138, 146
props
  audience generated 76, 81, 85, 98,
    174, 187
    trading 55, 67, 111
  maker 141

production created 84, 91, 106,
  116, 154, 163, 199
project-based sector 11, 146
projection mapping 7, 69, 76
Prometheus 50–52, 53, 71, 101, 102,
  120, 175
Punchdrunk 3, 4, 8, 9, 151, 183, 212,
  214, 222
  encyclopedia 20 n.24
  Sleep No More 183
pyrotechnics 82

rave culture 22, 107, 206
Red Shoes, The 42–43, 51, 72, 75,
  175
resistance movements
  fictional 42, 43, 47
    Action for Truth (*Stranger
      Things*) 206
    Blackout (*Blade Runner*) 121
    Rebel X (*Empire Strikes Back,
      The*) 98, 102
    Unknown Cultural Movement
      (*Red Shoes, The*) 72
Riggall, Fabien 14–15, 17, 22, 24, 26,
  27, 44, 45, 50, 52, 67, 74,
  83–84, 85, 95, 102,
  103–106, 110–111, 114,
  118–119, 125, 142, 144,
  172–174, 195, 199,
  210–11
RockNRolla 28
Rocky Horror Picture Show, The 20
  n.20, 35
role play 190–191
Romeo + Juliet 17, 95, 115, 127–128,
  141, 175, 177, 182, 184,
  185, 187, 200, 207

sandbox 11, 13, 22–56, 84, 118, 142,
  208
  play 219
Saturday Night Fever 67
scare attractions 10
scenography 8, 72, 78, 102, 153, 190,
  200
Scott, Ridley 51–52
scene re-enactments 28, 29, 37, 49, 54,
  62, 74, 87, 89, 92 n.11,
  100, 111, 187

screenings
  one-off 14, 33
  screen configurations 101, 110, 123
Searching for Sugar Man 31
security 12
  department 139, 164–165
secret
  aesthetic 26
  screening protest 103
secrecy 35
Secret Cinema
  executive team 138
  management 138, 144–145
  Presents... 75
  Tell No One 14, 26, 179
    branding 26
  X 75, 91, 95, 107, 118
    launch 75
  X Presents... Tell No One 92 n.21
Secret Group Ltd. 17
  financial reporting 21 n. 35, 135, 210
  investment in 91, 96, 129, 142
Secret Music 67
Secret Restaurant 49, 55
Secret Screenings 13, 22, 29, 31–32, 32, 48, 92 n.11
Secret Shares 210–211
Secret Sofa 207–208, 216
Secret Swimming 28
Secret Youth 118
SeOne Club 24, 28, 30, 56 n.4
set
  design 33, 39, 42–43, 47, 53, 72, 153–155, 190
  designers 136
  dressing 6, 25, 27, 39
Shawshank Redemption, The 14, 49, 54–55, 61, 65, 67, 71, 72, 73, 76, 96, 149, 207
show caller 160, 161
  book 161
show control 158, 215
Shunt 3, 8, 9
simulacra 84, 91 n.2
sing-along 46, 47, 89, 107
site 72
  construction 12
  development 97

management 12, 138, 145–146
  companies
    Entourage Live 115, 145
    Wonderworks 97, 103, 145
  responsive 97
Social media 11, 35, 39, 70, 80, 97, 103
  accounts 14
  in-world 47
  marketing 42
sound
  composition 12
    soundscape 152
    soundtrack 111, 118, 127
  department 139
  design 12, 158–159
  designer(s) 52, 112
Sounds Like Teen Spirit 31
special effects 12, 33, 62, 85–86, 122, 135, 147, 216
sponsorship 29
  Absolut Vodka 32
  corporate 13
  Nokia 29, 30, 123
  premium brands 75, 117–118
  Stella Artois 25, 29
  Studio Artois Live 25
  Windows Phone 33, 39, 40, 47, 52, 123
stage management 12, 159–162
  department 139, 159
Star Wars Experience: Galaxy's Edge 101, 223
Stranger Things 1, 15, 18 n.3, 134, 135, 143, 147, 148, 149, 154, 158, 161, 162, 166, 177, 179, 182, 184, 188, 192, 197, 201, 206, 209, 210, 224
  drive-into experience 135, 210, 226, n.19
stunts 7, 62, 88, 117
  aerial 85, 86
  directors 149
  doubles 88
  safety 89
sub-cultural 29
  identities 147, 174

theatre 15
  immersive 8
  in-the-round 8
  promenade 8
  professionals 140
  street 8
The Harder They Come 32
themed cocktail bars 4, 10
themed restaurants 10
theme-park
  immersive 223
  influence 62
  sector 15
  tourist picture opportunity 39, 41
Third Man, The 48, 49
ticket
  holders 29, 50
    premium 74
  phased release strategy 78, 79, 98, 99
  pricing 29, 69, 97, 101, 111, 118
    stratification 14, 49, 55, 111, 115, 123, 126, 127, 188
  vendors 93 n. 34
  VIP 55, 110
  website crash 78
Top Gun 45
transmedia storytelling 80
trapeze 43
  artist 36
Troxy 31, 33–34, 38, 47, 50, 63, 67, 68, 69, 74, 92 n.11, 118
tweeting 34, 40, 43
  wall 33, 46, 52
28 Days Later 95, 100, 105, 108, 109, 110, 111–112, 118, 120, 158
20th Century Fox 52
Twitter 11, 33, 44, 46, 70, 80, 188, 211

venue
  repurposed 33
  seating configuration 118
  warehouse 33, 95, 96
Victoria 95, 107–108
video design 12, 52, 53, 106, 122, 156–158
  department 139
  multi-screen 123

Video Effects (VFX) 69
VIP
  experience 110, 126, 148
  hospitality team 139, 163
  tickets 55, 148
Virtual Reality (VR) 3, 7
Voight-Kampff test 38, 126

Warner brothers 10
War of the Worlds Immersive Experience 4
Warriors, The 32
Watchmen 30
website
  design 12, 76
  designer 64–65, 77
  fictional 11, 54, 63
  in-world 14, 42, 54
  Secret Cinema 11, 43
    subscribe 70
  mailing lists 64
Who Framed Roger Rabbit? 61, 69, 73, 87
Wilderness festival 23, 28
Wings of Desire 36
Wolf of Wall Street Immersive Experience 4
worldbuilding 50, 62–63, 68, 71, 76, 77, 78–81, 91, 95–96, 109, 111, 120–122, 125, 149
  extra-dimensional 63, 71–72, 80, 109
  inter-dimensional 63, 78
  intra-dimensional 63, 78, 79
  multi-dimensional 63, 64, 77
  retroactive 121, 123, 217
  trans-dimensional 62, 68
  fictional organisations
    Brave New Ventures (*Prometheus*) 50, 71
    Department of Cultural Surveillance (D.O.C.S) (*Dr. Strangelove*) 106
    Earth Cargo Airlines (*The Empire Strike Back*) 120
    NSH (*28 Days Later*) 110
    Utopia Skyways (*Blade Runner*) 80
    logos 110, 120

EU authorised representative for GPSR:
Easy Access System Europe, Mustamäe tee 50,
10621 Tallinn, Estonia
gpsr.requests@easproject.com

www.ingramcontent.com/pod-product-compliance
Lightning Source LLC
Chambersburg PA
CBHW051605230426
43668CB00013B/1983